CHOPIN
AND
BEYOND

CHOPIN
AND
BEYOND

My Extraordinary Life in
Music and the Paranormal

BYRON JANIS
WITH
MARIA COOPER JANIS

WILEY
John Wiley & Sons, Inc.

Published by John Wiley & Sons, Inc., Hoboken, New Jersey
Published simultaneously in Canada

Photo credits: Pages ii, 225, photos by David Douglas Duncan; page 12, photo by Pierre Boulet/Life; pages 109, 110 (chap. 11), photos by Peter Gravina. All other photos are from the author's collection.

Library of Congress Cataloging-in-Publication Data:

Janis, Byron.
    Chopin and beyond : my extraordinary life in music and the paranormal / Byron Janis with Maria Cooper Janis.
        p.   cm.
    Includes bibliographical references and index.
    ISBN 978-0-470-60444-1 (cloth : alk. paper); ISBN 978-0-470-77058-0 (ebk);
    ISBN 978-0-470-87232-1 (ebk); 978-0-470-87233-8 (ebk)
        1. Janis, Byron.   2. Pianists—Biography.   3. Parapsychology—Biography.
I. Janis, Maria Cooper.   II. Title.
ML417.J34A3 2010
786.2092—dc22
[B]

                                                                    2010010788
Printed in the United States of America
10 9 8 7 6 5 4 3 2 1

To Maria
Who showed me the love I knew existed but
never thought I'd find.

Read not to contradict and confuse, nor to believe and to take for granted, but to weigh and consider.
—SIR FRANCIS BACON

Contents

Foreword
by Maria Cooper Janis

For forty-three years I've lived with, traveled with, laughed and cried with, and, most of all, loved an amazing man. It has been and continues to be an incredible, fantastic adventure: every day completely unpredictable, never knowing what the next five minutes will bring.

I have often been asked what it is like to have both a famous father and a famous husband. In a way, one prepared me for the other. It's kind of like being in the middle of a hero sandwich because both these men are giants in their own field.

This is not a book about Gary Cooper, my father, although every day I carry much of him with me, along with the lessons I learned from him about living with an artist. He has helped me to understand and feel the world of creativity—its demands and the price it asks of those who travel on that road and of those who travel with them. Byron's own voyage has taken him to both familiar and strange shores. "Do you dare to travel with me?" he seemed to ask of me, as I listened and gave him my ears and my heart for a journey of the soul.

Touring with a concert pianist is an unusual way of life that is never boring. It gives the gifts of beauty, new places, and new cultures. And always there is the common language of music bringing strangers together. Orchestra rehearsals have a drama all their own for me, as I am a painter. I had a rehearsal hall full of captive subjects to draw and music to take me away to wonderful worlds.

Byron's whole life has been music from the age of three. He was fascinated by sounds as his young fingers explored the piano keys. By four, he had discovered those sounds could become music, and he was off and running. He will tell you about those highly unusual childhood years in the chapters to come. Fame and glamour arrived while he was still young; Byron navigated the transition from child prodigy to great artist with a humility and grace that is rare.

Later he discovered another gift within himself besides music. It would expand his horizons and in a very real way open his perception of reality to encompass issues beyond. How extensive is my repertoire? How big is my career? How much is my fee? He certainly knew how important all those things were, but Byron was, in a way, a kind of amphibian, someone who could live in two worlds at once—our sensory reality as well as the world beyond our five senses. He lives at the

Byron and me walking in the park at Thoiry in the mid-1970s.

interface of mind/matter interactions, where telepathy, psychokinesis, and healing can occur. Extraordinary things happen around Byron, some of which he generates himself.

In 1964, Byron, one of the most romantic young idols of the classical music world, entered my life, and on my mother's honeymoon no less. To quote an old family friend, Ernest Hemingway, "the earth moved." My soul was moved and my life changed totally. We met again three nights later at Byron's rented villa above Villefranche on the French Riviera. What does a young woman do when a shy artist with incredible deep energy burning in his brown eyes looks at her and then goes to his piano on a terrace overlooking the moonlit harbor? That evening, Byron played for his guests, but I felt he was playing only for me. He gave us an encore, a beautiful haunting and romantic song called "Moscow Nights."

Now, I am from Hollywood—Beverly Hills, to be exact—and the first things I learned were the fiction, the folly, and the transience of a reaction like the one I was having. But there it was, and the immenseness of it erased any skepticism that this kind of thing could be real and point toward a future. It was so strong that I did not care if I got hurt. There was an inevitability about this. If the consequences were to be powerful and shattering, that too seemed to be a necessary part of my life from that moment on. In much less time than it takes for me to tell you this, I *knew something*, and it was wonderful. But at the time, Byron was a married man, and I would never walk through that door and break up a family. As I muttered "Oh, damn" under my breath, I rode with the moment and blanked out any hope for a future with Byron. At least I had experienced one real, true, beautiful moment in which all was known, all was said, all was given—and we had only shaken hands.

But who is Byron Janis? With time I would learn about this man who is an artist, a perfectionist, a man impatient with mediocrity, a warrior, and a risk taker—all of these the notes in the music that is his life.

Byron has a modesty and a shyness about himself that almost seals his lips against revealing the physical and mental cost of his musical

and extrasensory gifts. And the cost *has* been extraordinary: the need
to maintain a peak level of physical fitness; to overcome an injury to
his left pinky finger, numb since he was eleven; to endure bungled
bursitis surgery on his right shoulder and creeping insidious arthritis
in both hands, both wrists, and all ten fingers. He has been in an
adrenaline-fueled overdrive for extended periods of time. Think of
the charge to the finish line in the New York Marathon, the final
furlongs at the Kentucky Derby, the last lap of the Indy 500—this was
Byron's daily pace. It had to be. And although he had the counsel of
great rheumatologists and powerful topical treatments to help with
the pain, he never abused alcohol or drugs. He took only prescribed
medicines in spite of their bad side effects. Mind over the supposed
limitations of matter carried him forward.

A person who is suffering often cannot speak of the truth of his
pain, physical or mental, because if he did it would break his heart.
Byron is no exception. He has lost immeasurable amounts of creative
time and has had to severely limit the scope of the music he could
have written due to a disease that is particularly devastating to a concert pianist. But throughout his travails, his unique sense of humor
never abandoned him.

When the botched surgery seemed to eliminate any hope of playing again, severe clinical depression followed, caused by the deep
inner knowledge that his tools, his hands, were less and less obedient
to the drives of his soul. I watched as the burnout came; it was like a
slow-motion train wreck. When his mind alone was no longer able to
drive his body any further, a fatigue of monstrous proportions moved
through him as if he was falling into an ice-filled river, going numb
and slowly sinking, and there was no way to stop it. Even the person
closest to him couldn't haul him to safety. I seriously wondered if
Byron could hold on long enough for the medications to kick in and
turn the depression around.

Days darkened and drifted—the piano held no solace. Endurance
was the only word for the long days and longer nights. The attempts
of close friends to ease his loneliness were as futile as trying to kiss
through the glass window in a penitentiary.

He spiraled down and down. The studio sat silent.

One day, and then another, there would seem to be a few minutes of something lighter on his soul. The opportunity to compose something major arose, and he hesitatingly agreed to try. He would slide onto the piano bench and try a few passages. If his fingers didn't hurt too much, he'd keep on a little bit more.

Then suddenly things changed, and he began to climb out of the deep well . . . slowly.

I remember one particular day. In fact, it was March 24, Byron's seventieth birthday. He went to the piano in the morning and just started playing—scales, passages of music, Chopin, Mozart. Suddenly I heard a melody that was totally new to me. It was a sweet, haunting, lyrical, and happy tune, and I guessed it was a love song. I walked from our kitchen and saw his face—glowing, smiling. His look caught my heart because there was a ray of pure happiness coming from him and spreading through the living room.

His smile and his music blended into one act of joyous creativity. Byron was being touched by the muse—spirit—fire! There it was. A new song. He was composing the score for a musical of *The Hunchback of Notre Dame*. Suddenly, the idea for a new song hit him. It was born from the desire of Quasimodo to feel love. He sings of his unbounded joy in loving.

I felt that this song was a portrait of Byron. He was caught up in the creative act and the joy of loving. After a while he noticed me, looked up, and said, "This is my birthday present to myself!" and he grinned like a sixteen-year-old boy.

It was a birth. It was a rebirth!

Somehow Byron had learned to bless his struggles—and learned to let his struggles bless him. And so he created a new song on his birthday.

He gave birth to himself.

One good moment begot another, and eventually Byron would soar. He was playing again—freedom! He seemed to override pain, and his body somehow broke out of the limits his illness had imposed. He was at home in the universe once again.

If I praise Byron for his courage and perseverance, he brushes it off. One year at the U.S. Open tennis tournament, an announcer said, "The mark of a champion is that they fight back from the tough spots." I grabbed Byron's arm and said, "See?"

He laughed and replied, "Well, I just don't like to be told that it can't be done!"

I believe that music is also Byron's form of prayer. When he's at the piano, it's his personal way of speaking to God.

But even after his rebirth and return to playing, sometimes his body would balk or refuse to comply. Then what? He went into overdrive. Endorphins seemed to kick in, his mind overrode all the limitations his body imposed, and he just did it! For a period of time, Byron could transcend limits, and superhuman strength would flood into him. He let himself "be played."

After the ecstasy, as they say, comes the laundry. The morning after a concert Byron would attempt to pick up a spoon at breakfast, and it would be so painful for him that his thumb and second and third fingers could barely hold on. His swollen and inflamed wrist and upper arms would mock the virtuosity of the night before.

But this superhuman strength was not new.

For nearly all his life, Byron has had to compensate for or overcome something. Since the age of eleven, Byron kept a devastating secret, about which he writes in this book, and determined that nothing would stop him from his love of performing music as long as he could maintain his high standards. Music was his soul, not a ticket to stardom. One night, exhausted after what was a great performance, we sat in a hotel room eating BLT sandwiches when Byron grabbed my hand, his own wrapped in ice to bring the swelling down, and said, "I have been pushing my life, pushing my fate, all these years. I've got to let God work through me now!" Shortly afterward he joined the Arthritis Foundation.

But Byron's music is only one, albeit important, aspect of his life story.

Parallel to music, our lives have been touched by something unfortunately referred to as the "paranormal." (There is nothing "para-" about it). Much research in the scientific community focuses on what is called exceptional human experience (EHE). Many of these experiences can be grouped under the headings "parapsychology" and "extrasensory perception." They include clairvoyance, telepathy, psychokinesis (the ability to move or deform inanimate objects through mental focus alone), and creative inspiration, automatic writing, healing, and remote viewing (extended perception). The umbrella term for all of these phenomena is *paranormal science investigations*. These feelings and phenomena have been reported in all cultures since earliest recorded times.

Byron and I encountered EHEs in our lives even before we met and most dramatically in our ensuing years together. I believe Byron was born with these gifts. What else can one say of a child prodigy whose mind and motor skills at the age of three already functioned in so many ways like those of an adult? Along with the mechanics and techniques of being an artist, by all accounts Byron was developed beyond his years in emotions and intellectual process. "I never was a child," Byron has said. "Well, of course I was—but I wasn't."

I think he has always lived in two worlds. He could ride the winds of music and slip over the barricades that separate how and what we experience here from other, more expanded worlds. His musical challenge—traveling to "strange spaces," as a critic wrote—was to bring back to us earthbound souls the visions and feelings of other dimensions. Judging by the response of his audience, he seems to have achieved that.

Byron and I have found it a real challenge to understand and incorporate many of these phenomena into our everyday lives. But it is a worthy endeavor because we are so enriched by them. When unexplainable things burst in and out of our usual activities, we are constantly reminded that the world *is* full of miracles.

1

CHOPIN WALTZES
THOIRY, BERLIN, YALE

LEFT PARIS WITH MY WIFE, Maria, on a gray October day in
1967 for a visit to the five-hundred-year-old Château de Thoiry
to meet the Viscount Paul de la Panouse. As we drove through the
picturesque French countryside, with its charming villages and
lovely woods, little did I realize that this would be one of the most
important days of my life and that the day's events would command
front-page headlines around the world.

I had been on a concert tour in France for several weeks, and
Maria was traveling with me. One night in Paris, we dined with a
friend of the de la Panouse family, Claudine d'Aigueperse, who told
us that the Viscount Paul was a great admirer of mine and that he
would like us to come out to Thoiry and meet him for lunch or tea.

1

Thoiry, she said, was "a gem of a château," comparable to a Fabergé egg in its beauty and the intricacy and compactness of its design. I said, "Wonderful. I would love that," and arrangements were made.

We drove through Monfort l'Amoury, a little French village that had been the home of the great French composer Maurice Ravel, and then along a small country road that wound through lush meadows and dense woods that gave us a sense of traveling through an enchanted landscape. Quite abruptly, the forest ended, and in a clearing on top of a hill, at the end of a mile-long vista of French gardens and a double alleé of 250-year-old lime trees, the Château de Thoiry burst upon us like a magnificent architectural bouquet.

The Viscount Paul de la Panouse came to greet us as we drove up the gravel roadway to the entrance. We could feel his warmth as he came toward the car to meet us. There was something very special about him. I felt an immediate kinship, and before too long, he became just "Paul."

As we went into the castle, Maria whispered, "Dear God, he looks like you; he could be your younger brother!" Paul was about thirty

Paul de la Panouse and I are standing in front of his family home, the Château de Thoiry, holding the newly discovered Chopin waltz manuscripts.

(I was thirty-nine), and he was slightly shorter than I was, about five foot eight. He had a staccatolike walk, which I gather was the result of a difficult birth, but he handled it with ease even though it was quite a serious impediment. Maria couldn't help commenting again on our resemblance—the same broad cheekbones, broad jaw, strong forehead, and brown eyes. His eyes were remarkable—childlike, seemingly capable of infinite wonder, and yet I saw passion there, too. As I got to know him it became evident that his was one of the brightest minds I had ever come across, an intellect that could speak with great knowledge on many subjects.

During lunch, we asked Paul if he would tell us a little about the history of Thoiry. "With pleasure," he said. He began by explaining his family's background. There are 150 noble families in France, whose noblesse is said to be immemorial because there were very few archives at that period in history, and many of them have since disappeared. The first documents concerning these families appeared between 1000 and 1200 AD, proving that there were already nobles at that time. Among these 150 noble families, the de la Panouse family is dated as the fiftieth-oldest family in France. Interestingly, Paul told us that there are between ten thousand and fifteen thousand families in France who have adopted noble names but who are, in fact, not of the nobility.

He continued, "In 1559, Raoul Moreau gave birth to the château. He was a man of wealth, treasurer of the king of France and also an alchemist. He didn't find the philosopher's stone he was searching for, but he did find the ideal place to conduct his research. He chose this hilltop location because it united the characteristics necessary to harness the forces of 'heaven and earth.' He knew that the telluric forces were magnificent at this point due to the magnetic fault running from the nearby city of Chartres to Amiens, thereby creating the vital ambience needed for his esoteric studies." It was interesting to hear that the great Renaissance architect Philibert de l'Orme used the golden mean, also known as the "divine proportion," to construct this rare, architectural monument that was in perfect harmony with nature's forces and the sun's course. It was apparently perfectly placed in time and space. The château was designed to be a transparent "bridge of light" in whose central arch, the grand vestibule, the sun seems to rise and set following the summer and winter solstices. The architect, by staggering the placement of the windows on either side of the grand salon, gave the room almost twice the amount of light it would normally have had. That the imperfect alignment of the windows was imperceptible was a tribute to the great artistry of de l'Orme.

Strangely enough, the same principle can be applied to music. A phrase must be given the same kind of disciplined freedom so all of its beauty can shine through. We call it *rubato*, which comes from the Italian word *robare,* meaning "to rob." In music, its basic meaning is "to give and take." In other words, if you take a little time here, you must give it back there. How you take it, how you give it back, is the hallmark of a great artist. Again, it should not be perceptible. Done poorly, however, it becomes very obvious when there is more taking than giving, or vice versa.

As we finished lunch, Paul suggested that we take a tour of the château. He asked if we would like to see the archives room. That hardly required a reply! He ushered us into a huge room filled with old trunks scattered willy-nilly around the floor, ancient-looking books piled from floor to ceiling, and bundles of precious historical papers and letters. What beautiful chaos!

We were overcome with emotion at the sight of all these extraordinary documents, the indescribable feeling that we were being shown historical treasures that few had ever seen. Letters from the time of the Crusades, coded messages from one king to another. "Do you think we should behead so-and-so? We must think of the repercussions." There was even a letter on the bounty to be paid for eliminating a certain number of wolves in Paris.

Wandering around in this maze of history, we noticed a beautiful wooden trunk held together with copper nails and covered with boar's skin. The trunk was surely one of the most unusual and eye-catching I had ever seen. "What's inside that?" I asked. Paul replied, "It belonged to my great-great-grandmother Clémence de la Panouse, who was a very beautiful lady, as you can see from her portrait in the foyer." He pointed to a label on the trunk that said "old clothes." Upon opening it, we saw carefully folded layers of lavish dresses and shawls that Clémence had worn. Maria was overwhelmed as she gently lifted each layer, and that's when we noticed the letters.

I asked, "Whose are these?"

Paul examined them and said, "Oh, those were the letters of Eugène Sue." I had known him as a French writer and diplomat and author of the famous book *The Wandering Jew*. I remembered that Sue, besides being an admirer of Paul's great-great-grandmother (from the number of letters, obviously a fervent admirer!), was also a friend of Chopin's.

As we chatted about these letters, I suddenly stopped in midsentence as I noticed the corner of something that looked like some sort of handwritten manuscript. As I carefully lifted it out, I saw that it was two music manuscripts that had been tied together with a slightly frayed, pale blue ribbon. It just took a few seconds to realize what I was holding in front of me. Paul said, "Ah, yes, that's just something

I am holding one of the Chopin manuscripts from the eighteenth-century trunk in which they were found.

Clémence wrote. I was told she was always scribbling down music of one sort or another."

Wide-eyed, I replied, "Oh, no! Paul, these are nothing she scribbled on her own. They are Chopin!"

He looked dumbfounded. "Chopin?"

"Yes! These are two waltzes of Chopin. And I can tell you from just a quick glance that there are differences between these and the published versions."

I was so elated by the discovery that I could hardly contain my excitement. There was no known manuscript of the Waltz in G-flat, op. 70, no. 1—the other was the famous *Grande Valse Brillante,* op. 18—but here they were in front of me. My eyes began to fill with tears of joy. You can imagine what an unforgettable moment this was for me. And that delicate blue ribbon—there was something so intimate about it. I wondered about the hands that had tied it.

I quickly went to the piano with the manuscripts and excitedly pointed out their differences. I had never felt so happy in my life. I have had a lifelong fascination with Chopin. It began when I was a child, eight or nine years old and already performing his music. I asked my mother to please get me any book about Chopin she could find. I wanted to learn everything I could about him and his music, which affected me like no other. But I also felt a strong kinship for him as a person, which deepened as I grew older. His natural, bittersweet and melancholic nature (*zal* is the Polish word for it) was a quality my Polish blood understood very well.

Though we stayed only a few hours at Thoiry that day, it was to become a very special home in France for Maria and me. It was a place where we spent many happy times and many sad ones, when I was battling problems with my hands. During that struggle, it was at Thoiry where I wrote my first piece of music (a French folksong called "I Love the One Who Loves Me"—needless to say I was thrilled when Eddie Marney, who had written many songs for Edith Piaf, wanted to write the lyrics for it).

When we returned to our hotel, I wrote in my journal, "This is a day I shall never forget. I held in my hand two Chopin waltzes that

I am communing with my musical friend at the Château Thoiry in 1968, where Maria and I spent many happy—and sad—times.

had never been seen since he penned them in 1833!" Mentally, I found myself caressing the pages.

The next day we went to Berlin. It would be the first time I had ever played in Germany, though I had been invited more than once. The horrors of the Nazi era haunted me, and emotionally I had not found it possible to perform there before. But twenty-two years had passed, and by 1967, Berlin was inhabited by a new generation not responsible for the devastating crimes that had been committed, and I felt it would be wrong not to go and play for them. I asked that a meeting be arranged with some young professors. I steered our conversation to the war years and asked how their parents reacted to what was going on—people (Jews) disappearing, *Kristallnacht*, and so on. "Oh, they never knew," said some. "What do you mean they never knew?" argued others. "Of course they did." As I had suspected, the scab covering the not-yet-healed wound had been picked open.

Later, we were having tea in our room at the Hotel Kempinski in Berlin when suddenly my right arm began to gesticulate wildly and

uncontrollably. I was amazed at the ferocity of the movements. I tried
to stop them, but I couldn't. It was one of the strangest feelings I've
ever had—nothing like this had ever happened to me before. "What
is this?" I asked Maria. "What the hell is going on?"

Maria, a researcher in parapsychology, didn't seem too rattled by this
manifestation and responded, "Maybe you want to write something."

"I don't know," I replied. All I knew was that my arm was shaking,
and I could not understand what was happening.

She put a pen in my hand and some paper on the table in front
of me. With the same intensity of movement, my hand swung down
to the paper and began to write: "Tell your friend Paul to look again
in the archive room, and he will find something that will identify the
waltzes further."

Period. Full stop. Quiet hand.

"This is incredible," I thought. But Paul was a new friend, and I didn't
know what to do. Should I call him and tell him this? I knew the archive
room was such a mess it could take ages to find anything. And the message had certainly come to me in a strange way (I had no intention of
telling him how). But the experience had been too intense to ignore.

Soon I was on the phone: "Paul, would it be possible for you to look
in your archive room and see if you find anything else to do with those
waltzes? I know it's asking a lot, but somehow I just feel there might
be." There was a short silence, but he didn't question me. He just said,
"Oh. Okay. Okay! I'll do it." I was stunned when he called me back
the very next day and said, "I spent six hours looking, but I have found
something! A folder, with my great-great-grandmother's handwriting
on it: 'Autographe. 2 Valses. Composées et donneés par F. Chopin.
1833.' Translated from the French, it says, 'Autograph. Two waltzes.
Written and given by Chopin, 1833.'" It was hard to believe that he
had discovered this folder so quickly. My message was on target.

For the first time, we discovered that Chopin might have had
a romantic link to Thoiry, a total revelation to Paul. The waltzes
had been a present that Chopin, then twenty-three, had given to
nineteen-year-old Clémence, a girl who loved music. He adored
beautiful young women, and the ever-romantic Frédéric had obviously

been captivated by her beauty. Having little money, Chopin gave her these waltzes much as other admirers would have brought a dozen roses—quite a preferable alternative, I would think!

Chopin never intended to publish these two waltzes, as he had given them as a gift, and he was very much the gentleman. But, in 1835, out of financial desperation, he did publish one of them, the famous E-flat waltz, the *Grande Valse Brillante*. He needed money to make a trip to the Rhine music festival in Germany where some of his works were to be performed, and he probably wanted to show them that he could write a waltz. (Despite Chopin's orders to destroy any of his music that hadn't already been published, some six years after his death his very good friend Jules Fontana ignored his wishes and published the Waltz in G-flat, op. 70, no. 1. His source for the score was not known until after my surprising discovery.)

The only dance music Chopin had known before his visit to Vienna in 1832 was the mazurka, the native Polish dance. He often took melodies from native folk music and turned them into these unique musical gems. From Vienna, he wrote to his family, "They dance a very strange dance here, called a 'waltz.'" The *Grande Valse Brillante* was the first waltz that Chopin ever wrote and one of the few that was meant exclusively for dancing (the English called it *Invitation to the Dance*). He went on to write many other waltzes, some for the heart and some where the feet join in.

When I got back to New York, I called Harold Schoenberg, the chief music critic for the *New York Times*. He was totally fascinated when I showed him a photocopy of the waltzes and said, "This could probably be a front-page news story, but we will have to have the original manuscripts authenticated."

It seemed the only person qualified to authenticate them was François Lesure of the Société Française de Musicologie in Paris. Lesure did indeed confirm that they were in Chopin's hand. His letter of authentication, dated December 11, 1967, states:

The manuscripts of the waltzes Op. 18 and Op. 70, No. 1, which belong to the Count de la Panouse, appeared of extreme interest

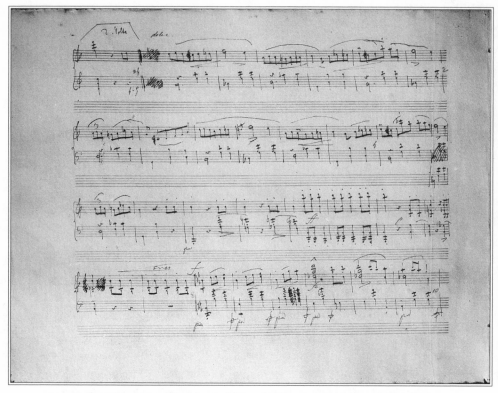

A page from the manuscript for the Valse Brillante *op. 18 that I found at* Thoiry.

to me. In my opinion there is no doubt that two Chopin manuscripts are involved: a comparison with manuscripts that we
have in Paris makes the matter entirely convincing. This discovery will gratify all lovers of Chopin and bring to specialists
new elements of appreciation of his music. As for pianists, it
will enable them to approach the original to greater advantage,
above all the Op. 70, No. 1.

Schoenberg wrote a front-page story for the December 21, 1967,
New York Times that began, "That rarest of all musical items, a hitherto
lost complete manuscript of a major composer, has come to light in
a château in France." The story was picked up in newspapers and

magazines around the world. Walter Cronkite even announced it on the *CBS Evening News*.

I was amused to read in that same issue of the *New York Times*, in the "Man in the News" column: "On stage, Mr. Janis's thin, almost emaciated appearance seems to bring out the protective instinct in the female concertgoer, not unlike Chopin himself. After he plays a Chopin nocturne, one half-expects to see George Sand come out to carry him off to her Mediterranean hideaway."

Two years later, on June 30, 1969, I played the waltzes in public for the first time at a small private recital at Thoiry attended by Mrs. Joseph Kennedy; Ambassador and Mrs. Sargent Shriver; French finance minister Valéry Giscard d'Estaing (who later became prime minister); Mr. and Mrs. Pierre Salinger (press secretary for President Kennedy); the Comte Antoine de la Panouse; the Viscount Paul de la Panouse; my wife, Maria; and my son, Stefan, who was then thirteen. Paul's father, Antoine, mused, "Byron, do you realize that you are the first man to play these versions of the waltzes since Chopin himself?"

But the story of the two waltzes does not end here.

In 1973, Yale University asked me to come to New Haven to discuss teaching a master class. I was already beginning to suffer from the terrible arthritis that at times would affect my performance schedule, and I had always planned to do some teaching. After lunch, Howard Samuels, the head librarian at Yale, asked me if I would like to see their collection of musical manuscripts in Sprague Hall, one of the finest anywhere. Manuscripts have always excited me—to touch the paper on which the great works of music have been written and to feel the close presence of the composer's hand felt to me almost like being there at its creation. That day, I held in my hand the manuscript of Brahms's *Haydn Variations* and some works of Bach, Schumann, and countless others.

To this day, I can't conceive of any rational motive for what I did next, but just as we were leaving the archive room, I stopped and pointed to a folder that was sitting on a high shelf. "What's that?" I asked.

Just prior to the first "official" performance of the waltzes at the Château de Thoiry I am at the piano with Maria, Stefan, and the de la Panouse family and their cheetahs.

"I don't know. Let's see," Samuels replied as he climbed a small ladder to get the folder. "Oh, it seems to be marked 'Chopin.'"

"Oh, great! Let me see it!" Anything to do with Chopin, known or unknown, was especially exciting to me.

Surrounded by five eminent Yale music professors, I sat down at a table and opened the folder. My heart stopped beating. I was speechless.

"What's the matter? You don't look well. Are you all right?"

"But you don't understand," I said. "This is not possible!"

"What's not possible?"

"Nothing, really." I couldn't speak. "I must catch my train. Do you mind taking me to the station?"

Against all logic, in that folder, unbelievably, astonishingly, were the *same two waltzes* that I had found at Thoiry, and they appeared to be in Chopin's hand! The same distinctive bass clef was unmistakingly present here. And I quickly noticed they were both dated 1832. This was one year before Chopin's gift to Clémence and three years before their publication. I also noticed some startling differences from the 1833 versions.

Forgive me, dear reader, if I did not think this was mere coincidence. The odds of my discovering the same two waltzes twice would be astronomical. It seemed I had entered the realm of synchronicity (even beyond!), a word coined by the famous psychiatrist and philosopher Carl Jung to describe "two or more events that are causally unrelated occurring together in a meaningful manner." Synchronicity, unlike coincidence, is not a random event. In a broader sense it is the sign of an underlying connection or interrelationship between all things about which we really have no understanding at the present time. As the years have passed, I have come to see how that deeper meaning is revealing itself in my life.

Overwhelmed, I could only speak in monosyllables to the professor, who valiantly attempted to make conversation on our drive to the train.

Once on board the train, I slowly began to focus on what had happened. Were my eyes and mind deceiving me? At first I said to myself, "Byron, you are dreaming. You are hallucinating." But by the end of the ride, I knew. "No. You actually did see those waltzes." I could hardly wait to tell Maria.

The culmination of the story of the twice-discovered Chopin waltzes came about due to another synchronous event.

I went directly from the train station to the apartment of our close friend Jacques Kaplan, a pioneer in faux fur design and an art gallery owner, on East 71st Street. He was hosting one of his ever-happening open house evenings, at which friends would drop in from every corner of the globe. That night, while I was brimming with the unbelievable events of the day, Jacques introduced me to a friend who had just arrived from Paris who, of all things, turned out to be an independent film and television producer. As Maria and I made a private toast to Chopin, I regaled some of the guests with the seemingly impossible occurrence that had just happened. The producer jumped up, exclaiming, "*Mon Dieu!* This would make a fantastic documentary. Please call me and let's talk about it." Eventually we were able to work out a schedule for filming between my concert engagements. In the summer of 1975, we began shooting the story of Chopin and this extraordinary musical discovery.

The following morning I phoned Howard Samuels at Yale to ask if I could look at the Chopin manuscripts again and arranged to return that very day. The differences between the versions were fascinating: accents were put on different notes, giving certain sections a syncopated rhythm; one had some measures deleted; another section was now marked *dolente*, with pain, and a few octaves were substituted for single notes. What could cause these very same two waltzes to be wedded again in these two unrelated sanctuaries thousands of miles apart? What was the connection? How could Yale have been unaware of the many news reports about the discovery? Why had they made no mention of the fact that they had two other versions of the manuscripts in their own collection that hadn't been catalogued?

When it was published, Chopin had dedicated the E-flat Waltz to Laura Horsford, one of his students, who apparently gave the manuscript to her family. Eventually, a family member and alumnus of Yale gave it to the university on permanent loan.

I called Harold Schoenberg once again at the *New York Times*.

"What have you got for me this time?" he quipped.

"Could you come to the apartment? I found something that might interest you."

I showed him a copy of the Yale waltzes. He looked at me for a long time in utter disbelief, then said, "I am not even going to tell the editor about this. He simply won't believe it!" A short paragraph appeared in the *Times* the next day titled: "Janis finds two more Chopin manuscripts." But throughout the music world, there were major headlines announcing this "coincidence."

2

BEGINNINGS

I T WAS A NINE-MONTH BATTLE to get born, but I was not to be denied. My mother apparently had had an extremely difficult first pregnancy, and she claimed she wanted "no more children!" She evidently had tried a variety of harmless means to stop my "progress," but I proved to be too formidable an adversary. Nothing was going to thwart my mission. I was so grateful that she didn't make me aware of these attempts until many years had passed. Otherwise, some Freudian psychiatrist would undoubtedly have had one mightily paranoid patient on his hands.

I burst forth at 6 p.m. on the twenty-fourth of March 1928 with a full head of hair. On first seeing me my aunt Mary exclaimed, "Oh, Hattie, he looks just like Chopin!" That was not the last time in my life I would hear that remark. My Polish blood must have been showing. My father was Polish and my mother Russian but of Polish ancestry.

Being born into a family of such mixed Slavic heritage is to be launched onto a high sea of emotions and drama. Copious weeping was one of my mother's specialties. She cried when the news was good, and she cried when it was bad. It was impossible for me to gauge during these lachrymose outbursts whether my mother was sad or happy. I just had to guess.

Clearly my mother loved music. After a day of hard work, she'd pay fifty cents to stand in the uppermost balcony of the theater to hear the two greatest singers of the time, Fyodor Chaliapin and Enrico Caruso. Her greatest luxury up to that time had been the purchase of a musical instrument even though she herself could not play. Even at a time when it was difficult to put food on the table, she let it be known to my father, who benevolently acquiesced, that she intended to live in a home where at least her children might learn to play the piano, an instrument she had always loved. As a young girl, whenever she had heard someone at the piano, she'd sneak away from her chores and listen through the open window, transfixed.

Until the Depression came along, my father was part owner of a chain of Army-Navy stores that provided us with a healthy enough income. When the business partnership dissolved, we moved from McKeesport, Pennsylvania, the town of my birth, to Pittsburgh, where the sole surviving store was located.

After a few toddler years in the Iron City, at age four I was enrolled in a prekindergarten class at the nearby Colfax School. I had not one but two teachers: Miss Sweetring, who informed the class upon our first meeting that we would never forget her name (and I never have), and Miss McSweeney. After Christmas we were asked to bring our favorite new toy to school. I chose the xylophone my uncle Benny, my mother's brother, had given me. As Miss McSweeney sat at the piano playing children's dance music, I began to play my xylophone and, without thinking, imitated exactly the melody she was playing. "Why don't you try that on the piano, Byron?" she suggested, then lifted me onto the piano stool. I quickly showed that I could. I remember thinking, "Gosh, this is easy."

In my prekindergarten class at Colfax School; I am at the back on the left with the bangs, just about in front of the first piano I ever played.

I can still see Miss McSweeney pinning a mysterious note for my parents to my little jumpsuit and recall thinking, "Uh-oh, I must have done something wrong." I was convinced I was in trouble when both teachers appeared at my house two days later. My mother asked that I leave the room, but I managed to listen through a crack in the kitchen door. "Your son possesses an unusual musical gift," they said. "Byron has an incredible ear, and since you have a piano in your home, we suggest that he should begin taking piano lessons." Whew! Was I relieved and happy—no punishment *and* I would get to take piano lessons. Piano lessons would have been punishment for most four-year-olds, but not for me.

That her youngest child was old enough to begin piano lessons was a dream come true for my mother. I never needed to be told to practice—music came naturally to me. Uneducated in any formal sense, my mother would have been lost in a music appreciation course and probably bored. But even at this young age I was beginning to understand that knowledge and power are not transmitted solely through sequences of logical cause and effect. My mother was rather a distant maternal figure in many traditional respects, but in teaching me to feel deeply and grasp for the essence of things, she conveyed one of the greatest gifts anyone can ever give another.

I was already an avid fan of baseball and of my beloved Pittsburgh Pirates, and I played ball every chance I got. I was playing catch with my next-door neighbor Edgar on the day my new piano teacher was to arrive. A Mr. Abraham Litow, of Russian descent and the Leningrad Conservatory, had been recommended to my parents. While Edgar and I played, I kept shooting nervous glances down the street. Finally, I spotted a tall man walking briskly and stiffly in our direction. He was nattily dressed in a dark gray suit and vest, and as he came closer I thought he looked kind of strange. I distinctly remember hoping that this was not Mr. Litow.

When the man turned up our walkway, as I somehow divined he must, I ripped off my glove, shouted a good-bye to Edgar, and quickly entered the house through the back kitchen door. My mother answered the doorbell, and I heard him announce in a thick Russian accent, "I am Abraham Litow, Byron's piano teacher." Mother took his coat as she welcomed him, and I stayed in the kitchen. "Nu, where's Byron?"

And that was the first of hundreds of "nu's" I would hear in the next three years. Every sentence seemed to begin with a "nu." I apprehensively came out to meet him. He looked quite foreboding with a very stern, almost mean, expression on his face. He had a large protruding forehead with a receding gray hairline, a rather large nose, tight thin lips, and a noticeable cleft chin. Yet on the rare occasions when I saw him laugh, he looked almost likable.

Meticulously, he set down his briefcase and withdrew some sheets of paper. "This is music of Mozart, Bach, and Schubert," he said. I wondered why they were handwritten rather than the black and white notes I had seen printed in my schoolteacher's music. Mr. Litow then said, "This is the Litow Method of teaching." He had substituted letters of the alphabet in place of notes. Although it was actually kind of exciting to be learning music written in a special language invented by my own teacher, I remember being even happier when the Litow Method was finally dispensed with and I learned to read notes on the music staff like everybody else.

Although Mr. Litow was my first piano teacher, other things about his teaching technique seemed strange. When he placed a glass of water on top of my hand, I thought it was a funny game to help me reduce hand movement in the playing of scales. I quickly found out it wasn't when I spilled some water and was soundly rebuked. I guess it wasn't a game! Soon thereafter, the punctual knock on the door and the ceremonial ushering in of my teacher by my mother (who, by strict request, would then disappear into the kitchen) would begin a lesson in which fear threatened to rob me of the pure fun and joy I had theretofore experienced at the keyboard.

I remember one day in particular when I took out my copy of Bach's "Solfegietto" and waited while Mr. Litow closed the door to the dining room, placed his apple on the table, removed his gloves, coat, and hat, and set his briefcase beside his chair.

"Nu-ah-um, have you practiced well?"

"Yes, sir," I quickly replied.

As I began to play, I watched out of the corner of my eye as Mr. Litow removed a wooden ruler from his briefcase and held it loosely as he listened. I considered two possibilities. One, he was going to measure the span of my hand as my fingers stretched over the keyboard. Two, he intended to conduct with the ruler as a baton. Of course, as I pondered all this, my focus shifted away from the music and I hit . . . a wrong note.

Bam!

That's when I discovered the third possibility. He'd walloped my straying hand with the ruler, slamming it down hard between the wrist and the knuckles. As my hand throbbed with pain, I sat quietly for a moment, and then an uncontrollable shudder shook my whole body. Silently, I repeated the passage, correctly this time, only the joy I usually felt had been entirely crushed. Emotionally, I was as numb as the back of my hand. I was shocked and deeply confused by this punishment. Of course, between that and the mounting fear of what might happen next, the inevitable happened.

Bam!

Down came the ruler again, accompanied by the admonition, "Wrong note!" My still-tender hand stung even more this second time. But, filled with a sudden dread, I bit my tongue, determined to hold back the slightest hint of any reaction. Not a whimper would ever escape to attest to my humiliation.

Ironically, what was also hurting me was the sudden realization of my own harassment of my sister with those identical words. Thelma, three years older than I, had started taking piano lessons when I was only three. I had taken a strong interest in her instruction, and it was jarring to me whenever she struck a wrong note. When she was practicing, I listened in from the top of the stairs and would shout down, "Wrong note!" From the relative safety of the second floor, I could enjoy my superiority. Now I comprehended the injury I'd

I am at the grand old age of four, just about when
I began my piano lessons with Abraham Litow.

been doing my poor sister. Mr. Litow had indeed imparted an important lesson to me that day, just not the one he had in mind.

All I remember of the rest of that lesson is Mr. Litow's command,
"You must work harder!" I nodded, still silent, before following him
dutifully into the kitchen, where my mother was preparing dinner.
I hid my still aching hand in my pocket, embarrassed at how red
it was.

"Tell me, Mrs. Yanks," he sweetly inquired, "do you have an apple?
The one I purchased seems to be not good." (My father's name was
changed to Yanks when he came to this country.)

"Of course, Mr. Litow," my mother replied. She took an apple
from the refrigerator, washed and dried it, and handed it to him,
saying, "How did the lesson go today?"

"Good, good," he answered. "The boy is learning quickly. Good,
good."

He seemed pleased with his new apple, then made his smiling
good-byes and was off. I remember wishing the apple would turn
rotten in his hand and give him a bellyache.

These were the days when corporal punishment was as much a part
of American education as blackboard and chalk. One day when my
mother witnessed the ruler's whip, she very indignantly intervened,
demanding, "What's the meaning of treating my Byron this way?"

Mr. Litow explained very sweetly, "Oh, Mrs. Yanks, your Byron is
benefiting from the very same exclusive treatment I was given in
Russia at the Leningrad Conservatory. Do you wish me to baby him,
Mrs. Yanks? Do you wish your son to play wrong notes?"

My mother grudgingly conceded that if it was good enough for
the Leningrad Conservatory, it was probably all right for Tillbury
Street.

As I tell the story today, Mr. Litow does come off as a bit of a mon-
ster, but that conclusion would be unfair. At the time I was certainly
furious with him, but I also knew, I could hear for myself, that I was
improving. I played fewer and fewer wrong notes. And as time went
on, the ruler was kept where it belonged: in Mr. Litow's briefcase. The
Siege of Leningrad had ended.

I remember this moment, dressed up to play for friends and neighbors at home on Tillbury Street in Pittsburgh when I was six.

After about six months of lessons, I had my very first public performance. I was five years old, and one of Mr. Litow's older students became ill and could not fulfill a radio appearance. As I'd been practicing Bach's "Solfegietto," it was decided that that was what I'd play, live on radio station WJAS in Pittsburgh.

I wasn't at all nervous. I loved the sensation of being heard by others. It felt like the most natural event. It was exciting and great fun.

Soon thereafter, Mr. Litow began teaching me several four-hand pieces. What I didn't realize at the time was that my teacher was preparing me to play with him. Once the new pieces were mastered, we played Schubert, Beethoven, and Mozart in churches, synagogues, clubs, and private homes, and on several radio broadcasts. I had not yet turned six. His reputation as a teacher was naturally enhanced by our success. At each of these functions, we'd be billed or introduced as: "Byron Yanks, boy prodigy, and his teacher, Abraham Litow." Certainly, you might think that he was using me to attract students. True, perhaps, but even so I felt I benefited more.

One day he did try to repay my hard work by taking me to a Pirates game. I was so overjoyed at the prospect of seeing my heroes in person at Forbes Field that I could hardly sleep the night before.

This was not just any baseball game. It was a late game in the pennant race between the Pirates and the Chicago Cubs to determine which club would go to the World Series. The stadium was filled to capacity and the air was electric with anticipation and cheers. All of which, I soon realized, was totally lost on Mr. Litow. He had about as much interest in American baseball as I had in knitting.

Unfortunately, his disinterest was to prove my undoing. In the bottom of the sixth Pittsburgh was down a run and the entire stadium was as taut as a steel spring—every spectator on the edge of his seat. Well, everyone except for my piano teacher, who picked that precise moment to stand up and announce, "Nu-ah-um, that's enough. We will go home now."

What? Home? Now? Whack me with two rulers, place any number of glasses of water on my hand, do anything to me, but not that! He had to drag me away, nearly choking with anger. I sulked all the way home and tore out of his car to reach the radio as fast as I could. To my horror the Pirates went on to lose the game. If only I had been there to try to cheer them on!

I had other enjoyable musical experiences that did not include playing with my teacher. When I was six, I played the role of Mozart in the school pageant. My mother used her expert sewing skills to make me a costume with a lace jabot that really helped me look the part. I remember thinking that acting was almost as much fun as playing the piano. When I was seven, I played for the great pianist Walter Gieseking, who was performing in Pittsburgh at the Syria Mosque. After his rehearsal, I was taken to play for him. In a newspaper interview he said, "I played no better at that age than young Byron Yanks does." It was high praise indeed. Gieseking had been an extraordinary prodigy. I wish I hadn't found out later that he had been a Nazi.

When I turned eight, Mr. Litow announced to my mother that he had nothing left to teach me and boldly went a step further.

He telephoned one of the greatest pianists of the day, Josef Lhévinne, whom he did not know, but they had Russia and Russian in common, and that seemed to do the trick. Both men had studied at Russian conservatories, Litow in Leningrad and Lhévinne in Moscow. He and his wife, Rosina, a superb pianist and teacher in her own right, agreed to hear me play in New York.

I have always thought that one of the reasons my father immediately agreed to this proposition was that he was going to be able to drive us to New York City. My father loved me. He loved my mother. He loved my sister. But he was crazy about automobiles, and he loved nothing so much as taking his family out in his car for a spin.

Driving with my father was not, however, one of life's more tranquil experiences. He was very short but also very proud. If only he'd used a seat cushion, one would have at least gotten the impression that he could see all of the road. On one of our spins, my mother, my sister, and I were in the backseat, to better avoid my father's irritating cigarette smoke. He was a chain-smoker, and on this drive he ran out of cigarettes. Locating a little shop at the top of one of Pittsburgh's many steep hills, he parked in front of the store. But in his haste, he failed to completely engage the emergency brake, and he neglected to turn the wheels into the curb. While he was inside the store, the car slowly started to roll backward—with his entire family in the backseat. My mother started to scream as the car picked up terrifying speed. Thelma and I were holding onto her for dear life. "We're going to die! We're going to die!" my mother wailed. People on the sidewalks started pointing and shouting because at the bottom of that hill was a sheer cliff, and we were headed straight for it. Sudden death seemed certain.

Alerted by all the commotion, my father dashed out of the store and, in an act of adrenal desperation, began running after his retreating automobile and family. Of course it was futile. And then something remarkable happened. Near the bottom of the hill, just before the car reached the cliff's edge, some bales of industrial wire—God only knows where they came from or what they were doing there—became entangled in our car's rear axle, forcing the whole car to lurch suddenly sideways and come to a complete halt. I remember an immediate silence followed by an outburst of uncontrollable tears of relief and my mother repeatedly shouting, "Sam!" as she watched my father running hysterically down the hill. People, totally amazed, began surrounding us, shouting, "It's a miracle! It's a miracle!" It made one big impression on this little boy, I can assure you.

My father loved driving at night even more than during the day. On our pilgrimage to New York for my audition, he strung up a hammock in the backseat so I could sleep. With Mother and Thelma in the car, there wasn't room for Mr. Litow, so he drove himself. When we pulled up at the Kew Gardens, Queens, home of Josef and Rosina Lhévinne, we must have looked like a small band of refugees piling out of the car, bedraggled and tired (except for me—that hammock sure helped).

"Mrs. Lhévinne will be with you in a moment," the woman who answered the door said, then ushered us into an enormous room that housed two grand pianos.

And then, there she was—Rosina Lhévinne. She was of medium height with piercing yet kind eyes that seemed to be sizing us all up. In her rather heavy Russian accent she asked each of us, "How do you do?" I felt a warmth about her and liked her from the start. A minute later, her husband came in. He was very tall and had very blue, very pensive eyes.

"Josef, this is Byron," Rosina said. Those blue eyes of his smiled at me as he patted my head.

Mr. and Mrs. Lhévinne gently inquired about my school, my friends, my hobbies, and my favorite subjects, doing their best to put this very shy young boy at ease and encourage him at what might prove a turning point in his life. My life!

I was directed to sit at one of the grand pianos. Mr. Litow deposited himself at the other one. The work he'd prepared me to audition with was Beethoven's "First Piano Concerto" and he began to play the long orchestral opening part. He must have been practicing it for weeks for the chance to be heard by the great Josef Lhévinne. But just as he began, Mr. Lhévinne interrupted him to say, "Never mind, Mr. Litow. We don't need to hear that. Let's just start where Byron comes in."

*I am eight years old, arriving in New York with my mother, father, and sister
and my first piano teacher, Abraham Litow, to audition for Josef and Rosina
Lhévinne.*

Poor Mr. Litow. He seemed crushed. "How hard he must have
worked on that section," I thought, "and not to be able to play it
in front of one of the greatest pianists of the time." I will never
forget the look on his face. I was upset as well. Even at that age,
I was extremely sensitive to other people's feelings. I tried to put it
out of my mind as I started playing, and the music took over. Just
as we started, however, I had to stop because, though I stretched
and stretched, my eight-year-old legs were too short to reach the
pedals.

We tried to attach what my sister called the "pedal controller" that
Mr. Litow had built to allow me to reach the pedals, but it wouldn't
fit on the pedals of the Lhévinnes' piano. My father offered to lie
on his back under the piano and hold down the pedal controller,
which he did the entire time I played.

I played the first movement of the concerto all the way through, and
when I finished, I turned and saw that the Lhévinnes were smiling.

"Very good!" they called out before conferring with each other animatedly in Russian. Then Mrs. Lhévinne asked me to move to the other side of the room, far away from the piano, while she sat and played various individual notes. She asked if I could guess which notes she was playing. I was correct each time, no matter how many notes she tested me on.

"Byron," she said, smiling, "you have perfect pitch." Meaning that I could instinctively identify every note just by the sound. This is a rather useful gift in various ways, particularly if you are wondering which note to strike next. You will hear it in your head first, and your fingers will know where to go.

At the end of the audition, the Lhévinnes spoke to Mr. Litow and my parents. As it was a very large room I could not hear the discussions that were taking place, but from their facial expressions, I felt it had gone well. As we left, a very warm smile from Mrs. Lhévinne and a very faint smile from Mr. Lhévinne with another pat on the head bade us good-bye. Walking to the car, my mother said, "Byron, they want you to come to New York to study with them." I started jumping up and down and couldn't stop. "They think you are very talented and feel you are ready for more advanced study. They would like to take you as a pupil in six months' time," my mother continued. I was so excited that I would be studying with Josef Lhévinne and his wife in New York. What a tremendous honor. I had heard he was one pretty great pianist. What a gift Mr. Litow had given me! But I knew one thing moving to New York wouldn't change: I would still be rooting for my beloved Pittsburgh Pirates.

In the six months before I moved to New York, Mr. Litow gave me the greatest gift of all: he introduced me to Chopin with the Waltz in B Minor. As I studied it, something inside me shifted. I immediately felt so close to the feelings that lay beneath that beautiful, plaintive theme, a simplicity that seemed to go straight from Chopin's heart and soul into mine. I shuddered with all the emotion I was feeling; I couldn't hold back my eight-year-old tears. It was to be the beginning of a lifelong love for the man and his music that would bring many magical events into my life—as well as moments that would defy explanation.

I couldn't wait until the time came to go to New York. Little, however, did I realize what family suffering would attend our pilgrimage. Or the degree to which I'd hold myself responsible for the ensuing sorrow. All I could think of at the time was the adventure ahead.

But there was a firestorm of objections to our move from my mother's family. One of my uncles went so far as to take me to play for Selmar Jansen, a well-known and respected piano teacher at Carnegie-Mellon in Pittsburgh. Jansen offered to give me a scholarship.

My mother's family argued that it was absolutely ridiculous to break up our family as Jansen was such a wonderful, local teacher. But Mother was adamant. She felt I must move to New York to take full advantage of studying with the Lhévinnes despite the fact that Dad couldn't leave his only solvent store.

Squirrel Hill Boy, 7, Who Can't Reach Pedals, Is Praised by Master Pianists

Lhevinne Gives Byron Yanks Audition, See Bright Career for Youth

The key to the future of a 7-year-old Squirrel Hill boy today seemed definitely to be an ivory one.

For Byron Yanks, 7, of 2333 Tilbury Ave., has just returned from New York where he had a successful piano audition with Joseph Lhevinne, concert pianist.

He played symphonies and sonatas which won praise from the musician and the promise that a real career awaited him.

But while there's nothing wrong with the capable hands of the prodigy, when it comes to playing Bach and Beethoven, his feet aren't quite up to his musical career yet.

Special Pedal Arrangement

That is why the youngster must have a special pedal arrangement on the piano when he plays.

And this pedal-box went right along with him when he had his New York audition.

Byron has been studying only a year and a half. And yet—well, there's the Mozart Fantasia, Haydn Sonatas, Beethoven's Fifth Symphony, right down to his finger tips.

Byron, in pre-school days, used to listen to his sister Thelma as she went through perfunctory scales. When he went to kindergarten, he surprised his teacher by his ability to pick out folk songs on the keys.

Began When Five

Before his sixth birthday, he was enrolled as a pupil of Abraham Litow. His teacher put him in the

My mother kept this press story, written after I returned from auditioning for the Lhévinnes, who touted me as a child prodigy.

It was around this time that my mother began to issue certain impassioned pronouncements, such as, "I have to think differently of Byron. He's not my child. He belongs to the world." As you can see, my mother was not lacking in Slavic drama. I did overhear many furious arguments between her and my uncles. One uncle went so far as to write directly to Mr. Lhévinne, arguing that a child should not be the cause of his parents separating. The Lhévinnes politely wrote back, "Investing in Byron is just like investing in diamonds."

It was my father, naturally, who had the final word on the matter. He simply turned to his wife and said, "Hattie, if that's what you think should be done, do it." Even today I find it hard to comprehend such selflessness.

I don't remember saying good-bye to my father at the train station. I don't recall if my mother or father cried, or if Thelma did; I don't remember anything of what must have been a very difficult parting, splitting our family in two, and all because of me. I guess I didn't want to.

Of course, the Depression was all around us. Because I felt responsible for my family's agonies, I tried to help by saving what little money I could. It only cost a dime to see a movie then, but I rarely went. However, Thelma and I did see *Ninotchka* with Greta Garbo and loved it so much that we went again. I'd order lettuce and tomato sandwiches with mayo on rye at the local diner because that was the cheapest thing on the menu. All these years later, I must confess, that combination still sounds good to me.

I was also becoming aware that I had a special talent, a gift even. I remember thinking, "If the Lhévinnes and all these other great people think I have it, I guess I do." I was determined to do everything in my power to become a success. This depth of faith and my determination to make things come out right are qualities for which I am very grateful and that have served me extraordinarily well throughout my life and career.

My dad lived in constant fear of not being able to support two households. He became obsessed with spending as little money on

CARNEGIE MUSIC HALL

PITTSBURGH

Friday Evening, October 15, 1937

B Y R O N   Y A N K S

Nine-Year-Old Pittsburgh Pianist

May Beegle, Pittsburgh Representative

This is a program from a concert I gave in Pittsburgh when I was nine, just before I went to New York to study with the Lhévinnes.

himself as possible. He sold our house and moved into a small room in the house of a family in Pittsburgh. Most of the time, six and sometimes seven days a week, twelve hours a day, he could be found working in what had become his sporting goods store. If I was the clear winner in our extraordinary new life in New York, my father was the clear loser. My mother, Thelma, and I had one another. But for my father, there was no one. He lost us all. But why did my mother have to read me those heartbreaking letters he sent telling her how miserable he was and how he would sometimes just have milk and crackers for dinner? Did she not realize how terribly guilty it made me feel? All I could do was say, "Don't worry, Mother, I will succeed, I will succeed."

Despite all the changes and sacrifices we faced in New York, eventually a kind of normalcy did take hold. Thelma and I made new friends, and she liked her new school. Her only complaint was that we all slept in the same room. The lack of privacy must have been difficult for her, just entering young womanhood.

What did my mother have? She had me and began to live totally through me. I became, in essence, the man of the family. It was a major burden for a small boy. I'd try everything to make my mother smile, to get her out of her frequent sulks. Sometimes she'd smile when I would play the piano. I also learned I could make up silly little rhymes that would eventually break her up into reluctant laughter.

Piano lessons with the Lhévinnes were a great adventure. Mr. Lhévinne was a connoisseur's pianist—control, double thirds, double sixths, octaves—of an extraordinary caliber almost unequaled by any other twentieth-century pianist. He was less charismatic than some of the other great pianists of the day due to the fact that his temperament, his emotional palette, was of a much less dramatic nature.

The Lhévinnes were great teachers as well as performers, though they frequently disagreed on how to teach someone as young as I was. I studied with each of them on alternate weeks. They would argue in Russian: "Teach him this way," "Don't tell him that way," "Why are you telling him that? He has a different hand than yours."

(Occasionally, English would emerge.) A debate in Russian would continue for some minutes, with me sitting there all the while, unaware of what was being said. However, I didn't need to understand Russian to know I was in the middle of two warring parties.

Inadvertently, the Lhévinnes impressed upon me one of the greatest lessons of all—that there's more than one viable way to approach something. I observed early on that great experts will often disagree, which was a very liberating lesson in flexibility—how important that was in stopping me from idolizing and imitating others.

The Lhévinnes had very individual teaching styles, and it was much more difficult for Mr. Lhévinne, for example, to communicate with me verbally, in part because of the language barrier but also because I was only nine. But that barrier was sometimes the source of his best lessons.

Once, while I was learning a piece titled "Run, Run," from *Scenes from Childhood* by a Brazilian composer named Octavio Pinto, he took my hands off the keys, got down on all fours on the floor, and crawled around the room very quickly. When he stood up, he placed my hands back on the keyboard and, with a nod of his head, directed me to proceed. He was showing me how to *feel* the way the piece should be played. I was, of course, very amused to see the great Mr. Lhévinne on the floor, but beyond that, I was learning that having humor and being playful were not only acceptable but encouraged.

Both Lhévinnes seemed forever to be teaching me scales. "A beautiful building needs a foundation," Mrs. Lhévinne would stress repeatedly as I worked again and again at those damnable scales. One afternoon, I was studying with Mr. Lhévinne, and my scales were not up to snuff. He stopped me and motioned to look at him. He rose from his chair and took a few even steps. Then he broke into a running pace, taking a few exaggerated steps, before returning to walking in even steps until he once again hurried his pace. When I returned to the keys, I understood that my scales needed to be played more evenly. Once again I was delighted to see Mr. Lhévinne, the ultimate authority figure in my musical life, behaving like a little boy, but his message got through.

Mrs. Lhévinne generally taught me the more technical aspects of playing and how to sit so my body was always centered, like a fulcrum, as my arms moved right or left as required by the passage I was playing.

I couldn't help noticing how different the Lhévinnes looked from one day to the next. I couldn't figure it out until one day I realized it was their hair. His seemed a little lopsided, and hers was positioned askew from the way she usually wore it. Their heads looked tilted! They had no idea their wigs were migrating about their scalps, or so it seemed, not even when they looked directly at each other. Now that's the sign of putting priorities where they should be! Even here I learned an invaluable lesson about concentration.

I was told that Rachmaninoff once said to Lhévinne, "I want to play something for you, but I don't want to hear your opinion. I just want to play it for you." He wanted an audience, not a critic. The feeling of performance occurs whether you're playing for one person or for three thousand. You can't perform for yourself, and this served him as a good test run.

The Lhévinnes' heavy travel schedule meant I also studied with one of their assistants, Dorothea Anderson LaFollette, who was also teaching my schoolmate at Columbia Grammar School, William Kapell, six years my senior. School adjourns for the summer, but music lessons never do. Willie and I followed our teachers up to Camden, Maine, where the Lhévinnes kept a home near the ocean. My mother, Thelma, and I lodged at a boardinghouse run by a Mrs. Ware. It was only a short hop to the Lhévinnes' compound, where Willie and I would go for lessons, and all of us enjoyed their beach parties and cookouts.

Willie's mother left after getting him as settled as he was ever going to get. But when he was left virtually on his own, at age fourteen, all hell broke loose. It began with small pranks, like hiding somebody's stamp collection or taking the cream off the top of the milk bottles, but soon his demonic teenage hormones took over.

One day, Willie took my hand as if to shake it, in uncharacteristic friendship, and then proceeded to squeeze it in a viselike grip, as hard as he could. I cried out in pain. I was much too small to fight back.

I'm afraid Willie's jealous attack was the price I paid for being the Lhévinnes' favorite. No doubt his aim was to sideline me for that summer. It seemed Willie didn't think there was room in Camden, Maine, for two young prodigies. Eventually, he learned that mastery was the best edge a musician could give himself, and William Kapell did indeed become one of America's greatest pianists.

One of my favorite memories of my progress at this age took place later that fall at the Kew Gardens home of the Lhévinnes. I was playing the first movement of the Chopin E Minor Concerto while Mrs. Lhévinne played the orchestral part on the second piano. Mr. Lhévinne was upstairs.

"Rosina," he called down, "how did you play so well? You have not practiced that concerto in a long time." A moment later he came into the room.

"Josef, Josef," she replied. "That was Byron."

He looked stunned but said nothing.

Mrs. Lhévinne said, "Well, Byron, you see how well you played." And she bent down and kissed my cheek.

One day Mrs. LaFollette announced to my mother that she wanted to teach me without added lessons from the Lhévinnes. That didn't sit too well with my mother, nor did it with the Lhévinnes. I had had my last lesson with Mrs. LaFollette! They then asked Adele Marcus, another of their associates and a marvelous pianist herself, to consider teaching me as their travel load increased. At my audition, I played one of Mendelssohn's "Songs Without Words" for her. For some reason, she sat down and played it for me and then asked me to play it for her again. She stopped me halfway through to say she'd accept me as a pupil. She certainly seemed much warmer than Mrs. LaFollette, and much prettier, too.

Adele Marcus had a wide acquaintance in the musical world, and when I first started studying with her she quickly introduced me to people who changed my life. Most significant, she arranged for Samuel Chotzinoff to hear me play.

Mr. Chotzinoff was a well-known accompanist and music critic, as well as the music director of NBC. He was married to Pauline

Heifetz, the sister of the incomparable violinist Jascha Heifetz, and he was the one who brought Arturo Toscanini, the great conductor, to the United States at the request of "the General," David Sarnoff, who formed the NBC Symphony for him. Sarnoff was the head of not only NBC but also of RCA and probably the most powerful person in the media world of that era.

Samuel Chotzinoff seemed impressed by my talent, and it was the start of a lifelong relationship in which he played the role of my musical mentor. In fact, in my own father's absence, Mr. Chotzinoff became a much-needed surrogate father to me, and eventually I began to call him "Chotzi." He immediately set in motion several things that made life much more pleasant for me and my family. First, he secured a scholarship for me at Columbia Grammar School, one of the best private schools in New York. By this time, Mother, Thelma, and I had moved into our new, larger apartment on the Upper West Side of Manhattan—though it still possessed only one bedroom. General Sarnoff gave me a gift of my first baby grand piano. How wonderful it was to play on that piano instead of on my little rented upright.

When I was ten, Chotzi arranged for me to play on *The Magic Key*, a radio show hosted by the famous theater critic Alexander Woollcott—later immortalized by Kaufman and Hart as the "Man Who Came to Dinner." Milton Cross, who was the host and announcer for the Toscanini NBC Symphony broadcast, was also the show's announcer. This was *the* Sunday afternoon variety program. It's also when my name changed. Chotzi and Mr. Cross suggested we switch it from Yanks to Jannes (pronounced "Yan-nes") for my appearance on the show. So Byron Jannes I became.

Soon after, Chotzi arranged for me to play for Mr. and Mrs. William Rosenwald, the son of the founder of Sears, Roebuck, at a party at the Rosenwalds' apartment in the Waldorf Towers. I played a short program of Mozart and Chopin. I was thrilled to meet Walter Damrosch and Leopold Stokowski, and I remember that I was particularly thrilled to meet Judge Samuel Rosenman, who was a speechwriter for President Roosevelt. After that evening, the Rosenwalds took an active interest in my future and started helping me financially.

I took lessons at Mr. Chotzinoff's Chatham Square Music School on the Lower East Side, where I studied counterpoint and composition with the noted American composer Roger Sessions. I took piano lessons with Miss Marcus at her studio under the school's auspices.

I did have a regular life as well, though all my music study made it difficult for me to feel like just one of the kids. I was the victim of more than one schoolyard bully, and it was hard to fight back because of the possibly of injuring my hands. One day, I was unable to dodge an encounter, and the bully and I ended up squaring off in the playground. I punched him out, much to my schoolmates' amazement (and mine). That was the end of my being taunted, at that school at least.

Growing pains and childhood details aside, my very unusual life was moving along at quite a wonderful pace with the excitement and beauty of making music; my days as an eleven-year-old were filled with schoolwork, fascinating grown-ups, funny games with the Heifetz family, and, most of all, practice, practice, practice. I loved it all.

One of life's great moments for me was the time I finally managed to show up for a softball game with my classmates. Since I was that "sissy piano kid," of course I was picked last when we were choosing sides. I came up to the plate for my first time at bat and, on the very first pitch, ripped a solid double to left field. Not even a wonderful performance of a difficult Chopin étude could have made me happier. The roar of my teammates was an unexpected dividend, and I quickly went from being a "piano sissy" to being a hero.

Life was going along quite idyllically, and my diary offers a little humor and a poignant window into what transpired next. The entry for January 24, 1940, says:

Thelma went to "Gone With the Wind." She came out an old lady, it took so long.

Later that week, another entry indicates the development of my young career:

Tuesday, January 30, 1940
Marvelous news!! Mr. Chotzinoff arranged a radio broadcast
for fifteen minutes all by myself. Isn't that marvelous? I went
to Miss Marcus' house to think up a program.

A few days later, I recorded in my diary, in the understated manner that children have when they deal with totally overwhelming things, a nightmarish event that continues to affect my life to this day.

Sunday, February 4, 1940
Something terrible happened. I cut my fifth finger pretty badly.
The doctor took me to the hospital. Boy, what a day I had.
Gee, I felt awful. It hurt so much before they operated and
I lost so much blood. But everything is alright.

It happened when I was practicing one Sunday for a radio recital I was to give the following week, when Thelma began teasing and taunting me until I finally reached my boiling point. She ran out of the room with me in hot pursuit through the living room, which was separated from the kitchen/dining alcove by a French door—a door with many panes of glass. She slammed the door and it almost shut, but as I reached out to keep it open, my hand went crashing through one of the panes, shattering the glass. I quickly withdrew it and felt an excruciating pain. Blood sluiced all around me. I looked down and saw my little finger dangling from my left hand. I could see the bone underneath the skin that was hanging down—it was horrible, and blood kept coming. I remember crying with pain and becoming quite hysterical. The frightening sight of it all made me violently sick. My mother tried to comfort me and got a towel, which she wrapped around my finger like a tourniquet to stem the flow of blood. I remember she was trying quite unsuccessfully to stay calm.

In 1945, I am with my twenty-year-old sister, Thelma. I am seventeen, six years after the horrible accident.

As it was a Sunday, there was no surgeon on duty at the nearest hospital. Mother called Dr. Greenberg, our family doctor, who rushed to meet us at the hospital. My uncle drove us—all the while my mother changing towels that she had brought with her to keep my finger tightly wrapped. I was crying, and my mother finally lost all her composure and started crying as well.

I remember a nurse wheeling me on a gurney down the corridor, and watching the elevator floor indicator slowly descending. It seemed forever. "Why is it taking so long? Please, make the elevator come! It hurts!" I began to sing in a high-pitched, terrified voice, "Di, di-da, da, da-di, da, da . . ." from one of the pieces I was supposed to play on the radio the following week. The nurse looked at me strangely as

I tried to sing until the elevator arrived. At that moment, I wondered if I would ever play again.

I was quickly rolled into the operating room and the ether mask was put over my face. I smelled a horrible odor and slowly, ever so slowly, seemed to be descending into a large black hole. I felt dizzy and desperately wanted to hold onto something, but there was nothing to hold onto. Then, suddenly, I was awake, and I thought the operation was all over. But because I had just eaten lunch I had just thrown up, and I had to go through the terrible process of the ether mask again.

I began to regain consciousness when I was back in my hospital room and became aware of two doctors quietly conferring. But they filled my head with a sound of doom: "If an infection sets in, we will just have to take that finger off." Oh my God, no, no, that can't happen—that *will* not happen. I did not want to stay awake, and I didn't.

I knew the accident was very serious, but I refused to believe that I would never play again. To this day, I still can't feel that little finger. It is totally numb, as both the tendon and the nerve were cut as I tore my hand out of that pane of glass. What's more, the joint won't bend. Since the accident, I had control of only nine fingers. At the time, just about everyone gave up on me, including Mr. Chotzinoff. "Well, what a shame. Big talent, but it's over." My father's comment was, "Hattie, nice job you're doing up there!"

Fortunately, Adele Marcus still believed in me and kept working with me. My diary shows the progression of events after the surgery.

Monday, February 5

I came home from the hospital. Thank heavens. I didn't like the hospital so much. Thelma didn't go to school. In the evening, Miss Marcus and her cousins came over.

Tuesday, February 6

Didn't go to school because of hand. Doctor was here and said everything was alright. I saw in the paper my name for the broadcast. Paul and David came up and played a little.

Wednesday, February 7

Got up feeling fine. Felt fine all day. Heard the broadcast which I was supposed to play on. Some other young boy played. It wasn't so hot.

Saturday, February 10

I didn't go to Chatham School because I had to go to the doctor. He put a stick on the back of my hand, so my finger shouldn't heal curved. He said nothing is touched and is healing very good.

When the doctor finally took out the stitches, it hurt horribly, but I thought, "It's over now. I'll be practicing soon." It was as if I thought the finger had simply regenerated itself. In my mind it already had. So much fear was pulsating around me, I simply could not afford to be the source of any such thoughts myself.

Thursday, February 29

I had a lesson this morning. It was pretty good for the first lesson. I listened to "Baby Snooks."

Saturday, March 2

Went to the doctor. He said everything is okay. He said that we should try to get a heat lamp from a friend or buy one. Violetta loaned me hers.

Sunday, March 3

Rainy day. I practiced good today. Thelma, Mother and I went to see *Ninotchka*. I baked my finger this morning and evening.

So I was back at it within a month's time. And barely two months after the accident, I was performing on the radio again. What a great feeling to prove wrong everybody who had given up on me.

Wednesday, April 10

My broadcast! It was swell. Wasn't nervous at all. Mr. Chotzinoff told me to study up a first movement of a concerto and I would play with Leopold Spitalny. Boy, was I happy.

I realize now there must have been many others who assumed my career as a pianist was now as dead as the nerve in my little finger.

But my career was not over. All my powerful new friends in high places knew that I had talent. What they did not yet realize was how determined I was. Or how little I comprehended the full consequences of the injury.

Three weeks after the accident I returned to Miss Marcus for that first lesson. I had to bend the top joint of the injured finger with my other hand simply to move it. I could not hide my terror when my fingers touched the keys for the first time and a current of pain ran up and down my arm. I could not hide from Miss Marcus how much it hurt just to put my finger down on a piano key. But my passion and perseverance were evident even at that age, and Miss Marcus believed in me and stood by me. Sometimes all you need is just one person to believe in you and you feel that you can do anything—but only as long as *you* believe in yourself.

As my finger healed, I worked on Clementi's "Gradus ad Parnassum," which had some very unusual fingerings as well as exercises for double thirds and double sixths and pieces by Beethoven's pupil Czerny.

"Just do the best you can," Miss Marcus consoled me. "There are many people with bad shoulders who play the violin until they're eighty-three. You're going to play the piano, and you're going to play a lot of piano." Deep down, I knew she was right; I had never thought otherwise.

Barely two months after the accident, I was playing on the radio again, but there was a difference. For the first time in my young life I began to have nerves about performing, because my little finger was less than reliable. I found one way for me to be more certain that it would grasp the right note was to tighten my hand, which gave me more control. Most important, I learned to use my eyes in a new way. Instead of focusing them on the keys directly in front of me, I would slightly raise them so I could use my peripheral vision and see both hands and the entire keyboard at the same time. This gave me the added security that I could guide my little finger to the note I wanted. That's been the procedure I've had to follow ever since.

In the meantime, matters were not going all that well on the home front. One sorry example should suffice.

Delphine Dodge Godde, the Dodge automobile heiress, who was a student of Adele Marcus's, invited me up to Rye, New York, to play for her. I had never seen an estate like that before. Mother wasn't asked to go, which deeply upset her. The results were evident when I got home. Mother opened the door for me and then headed straight to the kitchen. Barely speaking to me, she set to scrubbing the floor with a vengeance—down on her hands and knees, as if her only function in life was to be a charwoman.

She could only have been doing this to upset me, and she succeeded. I was furious. I felt such resentment and disgust. I thought, "How dare you do this to me!" and I started yelling at her. What saved my life, really, at hard times such as these, is that I fought hard; I didn't just accept the shackles of her martyrdom. Too much of the time my mother made me feel as though I had to act the parent, the husband, the everything. It seemed I was never allowed to feel entitled to any happiness that did not include her. But I understood that her position of having to live without my father was very difficult for her to endure.

Nevertheless, I had a difficult time letting go of scenes like this, which were all too frequent, and it was not easy for Thelma, either. She rightfully felt I was getting all the attention. At nine years old, for me music now took on an added role. It also became a refuge for me, a place where I could shut out all my life's conflicts.

Some of Thelma's jealousy was directed at our mother. Their fights would occasionally become physical, and it was terrifying for me to have to intervene. The one big mistake I made was always to take my mother's side. But either way, I felt horribly trapped, locked in an intolerable situation with no one to turn to.

But Chotzi gave me artistic attention, and his support was so important for me. He took me to one of the last concerts by the pianist Paderewski, who was well into his eighties. Afterward, Chotzi said,

"Now you know how not to play." He later took me to a rehearsal of Toscanini and Horowitz and said, "Now you know how to play." My heart leapt as I heard all that thunder and beauty coming from the piano. How inspired I was. I went home and practiced harder than ever and dreamed of one day playing like that.

3

DEEP IN THE
HEART OF TEXAS

I HAVE ALWAYS FELT ESPECIALLY LUCKY in one regard that has bedeviled so many others. Ever since I was four, I have known who I was. I never questioned it. I never searched for myself like so many, with their backpacks, gurus, and psychoanalysts. I found my identity in eighty-eight keys. Fifty-two white, thirty-six black. My life has always been clear and filled with purpose, free of the mazes others are often lost in, but I struggled in other ways.

I was thirteen and had been working hard and developing a new repertoire: Beethoven, Mozart, and most of all Chopin. I remembered reading a book that spoke of his strong belief in other worlds, and I felt something resonate within me. Chopin and the German poet Heinrich

Heine shared a passionate belief that there were other worlds. Chopin referred to this other realm as *là-bas*, the French term for "over there." Heine asked Chopin if the flowers burned with more intensity of color there than they did here. And if, in the moonlight, the trees still sang with such harmony. That feeling seemed to open up a new place inside me, or perhaps it identified an uncharted landscape I had yet to explore. I was happy reading that I was not alone in my thoughts. I remember looking up at the night sky and the stars that summer in Maine. With no city lights to contaminate the dark, I realized for the first time how many there were. Mr. Lhévinne was a devoted lover of astronomy and kept a telescope in the library. He actually discovered an asteroid that was named after him. I remember with a tingling feeling the excitement of looking through that telescope and being told I was seeing millions of years back in time.

In those days, my portal to other worlds was the bathroom of our New York apartment. My two friends from downstairs, Paul and David, and I would flush the toilet and imagine we were traveling in some kind of space vehicle that would take us to a mysterious and unknown place. Being an Aries, I always managed to make myself captain.

One night before I went to sleep, I suddenly heard a powerful voice inside me proclaim, "I want more than music." The next day I thought about that and realized it was not just a passing thought. I still felt exactly the same way, even more so. But I was very puzzled—music was the core of my life and meant everything to me. It didn't make sense, but I couldn't shake off the compelling feeling that I was laying down a parallel track that was to be with me for the rest of my life.

There were mysteries in the universe I felt I had to know more about and, through music, some new doors seemed to be opening. I did not question my feelings. I realized that music had given me the key to those doors and had led me to them. Later when I was sixteen and I felt I'd played particularly well, I started taking an extra bow onstage—my private acknowledgment to the unknown who had been my cocreator that night.

But at that time, with school, music, girls, lust, and love all vying for my attention, I at times forgot that little voice that kept insistently murmuring, "I want more than music." But it has never abandoned me for long.

Once again fate would boot me out of the pan into the fire, and the next moment it would pick me up and cool me off. Just when I thought I couldn't stand my home situation one minute longer, another life-changing series of events unfolded.

Three months after the accident, Adele Marcus married Fritz Kitzinger, a talented conductor and pianist who accompanied singers such as Ezio Pinza and Grace Moore. Mr. K took a position with the Hockaday School, a prominent girls' institution in Dallas, and moved down there while his new wife kept teaching in New York. The extraordinary events happened just as I turned thirteen.

First, Miss Marcus received an SOS message from her husband that he needed assistance in Dallas. He had more work than he could handle by himself. Second, in Pittsburgh, my father's secretary embezzled every cent he had. My father ended up in the hospital, and my mother had to go back to Pittsburgh to take care of him.

Suddenly, I had neither a mother nor a teacher. What was to become of me? I was only thirteen. I couldn't venture out on my own. Fortunately, Chotzi instantly intervened. He called Miss Marcus and said, "That boy is doing uncannily well. Can't you take him with you?" Then he called my mother to say, "Byron ought to be in Texas with his teacher."

Meanwhile, Jan Peerce, the famous tenor, happened to be dining with Miss Marcus that very evening, and he said, "I know this lovely couple there, Sam and Ethel Tallal. Big house, kids are off and out on their own." Mr. Peerce got in touch with his friends in Dallas, and the Tallals readily agreed to welcome me into their home. Within a matter of hours, my future was decided.

I would come to understand that this amazing conjunction of events—these synchronicities—of many disparate things happening together had profound consequences for my future.

My father wouldn't allow me to travel alone on the train, so Chotzi arranged for Miss Marcus and me to make the trip together. When I said good-bye to my sobbing mother at Penn Station, I didn't let her see that deep down I felt a sense of relief that I would be free of all those problems at home. At least I wouldn't be around. It was an incredible, unbelievable blessing for me to be able to escape just then to Dallas.

Now at thirteen, I was completely on my own for the first time in my life, at least in terms of immediate family. I was truly happy. And the Tallals were wonderful. Their house was wonderful. My new room was wonderful. They had two married daughters and a son who was off in the air corps. It was his room that I inherited. That first night I cried my eyes out missing my parents, my friends, and everything I had known. But by the next morning, everything had changed; my sadness had turned into excitement about the adventure ahead.

I have always been quick to adapt to changing situations, but never at the cost of compromising my integrity. And wherever I went, my music was always with me. In Dallas, I was there to become a professional pianist, and I found myself not missing any part of my former life.

In fact, I quickly gained a new friend—the Tallals' dachshund, Boobie, adopted me and slept every night at the foot of my bed. Unfortunately, he snored so loudly that it sometimes kept me awake, but I didn't mind. I loved him. I'd never had any kind of pet before.

The public school I attended was a breeze after Columbia Grammar, though I did occasionally get into arguments with my history teacher over the Civil War. To her, I was a damn Yankee. Perhaps changing my name from Yanks was an even smarter move than I'd thought at the time. On the school bus one day I again ran afoul of yet another bully, who was in the same history class as I was and seemed to share our teacher's "damn Yankee" attitude. He was obviously on his way to a physical confrontation with me. By now I had developed very strong hands, and I just gripped his hand and squeezed until he cried "uncle." Perhaps Willie Kapell had taught me a valuable life lesson after all.

I had to admire both of my parents, who set such an inspiring example of perseverance for me through the very hard times they had to face. After my father recovered mentally and physically from his secretary's crippling betrayal, he and my mother started all over

I am with my father, Samuel Yanks, at his store in 1969 (left), and my mother, Hattie, in 1980 (right).

again. My mother found a job pressing shirts, and my father did whatever menial work he could find in those still-difficult financial times. Mother turned out to be quite a good businesswoman, something she'd never really tried before. Slowly, with her help, my dad eventually rebuilt his business.

Adele Marcus and her husband had rented a house not far from the Tallals'. I could walk there in twenty minutes. I not only enjoyed talking with Fritz, I also enjoyed making music with him. He organized and conducted a group of Dallas string players called the Sixteen, and I made my first orchestral appearance as soloist playing a Bach concerto.

In answer to my report on our performance, Chotzi wrote:

I was very glad to get your letter and later your picture and press notices. What pleased me very much was the account of your playing the Bach D Minor Concerto with Mr. Kitzinger. These are the kind of press notices I would wish you always to get because they stress your musicianship, which is vastly more important than anything else. Musicianship, of course, stems from yourself, but I hope you realize as much as I do how responsible Miss Marcus was for the development of your native talent.

Just a few months into my stay in Dallas, Mr. Tallal died suddenly of a heart attack. Once again I was the lone man of the house. I could feel another upheaval about to topple my young life. But nothing could have been further from the truth. Mrs. Tallal seemed comforted by my presence. She and I would sit together many evenings playing cards. Even though she occasionally cheated a little, I didn't mind, and the games were fun.

I formed a great friendship with Joe (whose last name I never knew), who worked for the Tallals. He was the strong workhorse of that house, and he always talked good "horse sense." Though Joe, who was black, was treated comparatively well by the Tallals, I felt there were certain boundaries not to be crossed by anyone in the house when it came to dealing with him.

But those boundaries were an enigma to me, and I'm afraid I crossed them frequently. Joe was a strong, bighearted man with an enormous laugh that was hard to resist. He lived above the Tallals' garage, and we'd often sit together and do a lot of storytelling and laughing. He was one of my favorite people in Dallas.

We shared some unusual experiences, such as the time we witnessed an amazing display of multicolored lights in the Texas sky one evening. Another night we spotted some very strange maneuvers performed by a large pie-shaped object. It streaked across the sky, came to an abrupt stop, and veered off in a sharp, angular direction. Joe and I kept both of these incidents to ourselves. It was transgression enough simply to be hanging around with a black man, much less spotting what looked like UFOs with him. The night skies were gorgeous, with limitless horizons. More than once Joe and I observed something, not meteors, flashing across our line of vision. It would then hover and, like a puppy bolting out a door, simply vanish.

The boundaries got a lot larger outside the Tallal home. I recall my horror the first time I saw the signs reading "Colored" and "White" on public restrooms and sitting in segregated restaurants and riding on buses where the black people were crowded in the rear while seats went unoccupied up front. I was shocked by these indignities, which filled me with anger and disbelief.

It was Joe who drove the Tallals' car, and in time he put me behind the wheel. I couldn't have had a better teacher. In those days you could get a learner's permit at fourteen in Texas, and soon I was given a car to drive, a little Chevrolet. I told Chotzi about my driving lessons, which spurred another of the fatherly letters that regularly came from him.

> I think it fine that you engage in all the ordinary pursuits of a normal American boy, but I am a little biased in favor of the more intellectual side of your life. It's nice to be able to drive a car but it is a little more difficult to play the Rachmaninoff Concerto.
>
> I went down to your old school last Sunday and found your picture still prominently displayed under glass in Miss Bergman's room. When you are a celebrated virtuoso it is not difficult to have your picture displayed, but when it is framed and hung while you are yet a modest and hopeful student it means that you are really liked for yourself. This is even more important than being liked for your playing.
>
> We hope you will come and spend some time with us in Ridgefield in the summer.

At about this time, my name was changed again (I hoped for the last time) thanks to John Rosenfeld, who wrote for the *Dallas Morning News*. He was the most important music critic in the Southwest. He'd become a friend and a champion of mine, and one day he said, "Why are you calling yourself 'Jannes'? Everybody calls you 'Janis' anyway. Why not simply change it to J–A–N–I–S?"

It made sense. "Okay," I said. And that was that.

When I was fifteen, still in Dallas studying with Adele Marcus, Chotzi telephoned her to say, "I've arranged for Byron to play with the NBC Symphony, under Dr. Frank Black." This was the legendary NBC Symphony, Toscanini's orchestra, which was heard on the radio all over the country. A national debut! Can you imagine how excited I was? It was decided that I'd fly to New York and stay with the Chotzinoffs and that I would play Rachmaninoff's Second Piano Concerto. When we arrived at the famous Studio 8-H, where these concerts were always held, I needed to use the men's room. We didn't have far to go, as Chotzi's office was downstairs in the same building. When he took his keys out, I noticed his hands were trembling. I thought, "Wow, he's really nervous!"

I remember having some nerves of my own. But when I walked out onstage, they vanished, I was comfortable and at ease. It felt fantastic to play with that orchestra, and from what I hear I played pretty well for a fifteen-year-old. Toscanini was listening to the broadcast and asked that I be engaged to play again the following year.

Chotzi was married to Pauline Heifetz, the sister of Jascha Heifetz. They lived in a white stone house on West 85th Street, which they shared with Pauline's parents, who occupied the top two floors. In fact, just before I left for the concert, Papa Heifetz heard me practicing and came downstairs. He took one look at me and said, "My dear Janis [he always called me "My dear Janis"], your shoes are not shiny enough." I said, "Oh. I'll take care of that." But before I could move, he reached under the piano, grabbed my shoes, and disappeared into the kitchen. I continued practicing, and before I reached the third movement, he reappeared with the shiniest pair of shoes I had ever seen. Papa Heifetz actually shined my shoes. That was hard to explain, but so was Papa Heifetz.

As at ease as I say I was, I was not, like many performers, without my superstitions. I always played middle C on the piano before a concert to ensure a "well-balanced" performance. I also carried a battery during each performance for extra energy: "Byrite—guaranteed to give satisfaction."

Silly, you say? Perhaps. But something was helping me when years later I was giving a performance of Rachmaninoff's Fourth Piano Concerto in Flagstaff, Arizona. Suddenly, during the first of the three movements—*zing!*—one of the black keys flew off the piano and landed in the front row of the audience. Even worse, it was my very first public performance of this work. When I glanced over at the missing key, all I could see was a jagged sandpapery surface. I wasn't even sure it was safe to touch. Or whether it would still produce a sound. I had to make a split-second decision to continue playing or call off the concert. I knew there was no piano technician on hand to repair the key, so I decided to go for it. That key was very rough and unpleasant to the touch, and my finger had to adjust to a black note that was no longer there. In its place was a piece of wood that was three quarters of an inch lower than it should have been. What a challenge, but I was happy to have avoided a potential disaster. The audience enthusiastically applauded my hard-won victory, and someone in the first row went home that night with a very unusual souvenir.

On I went from Flagstaff to Miami for a recital and, thank goodness, another piano. Suddenly, in the second movement of the Chopin *Funeral March Sonata*—*zing*. Off flew another black key! I was dumbfounded—again? Talk about synchronicity. Out of the corner of my eye I saw the wayward black key resting comfortably on the stage some four feet away. I began to think I should be carrying a tube of glue with me as well as my Byrite!

My very next concert was at the University of Maryland. You're not going to believe this—I didn't either. It happened again. *Zing!* Another black key gone. Was this never going to stop? But third time lucky. That proved to be the end of the saga of the black keys. It has never happened to me again (so far).

But back to some earlier synchronicity that changed my life. On February 20, 1944, when I was sixteen, I played a concert with the Pittsburgh Symphony Orchestra in my old hometown. The conductor was Lorin Maazel, who was all of fourteen years old at the time. But here's the synchronous part. The great pianist Vladimir Horowitz just happened to have played a recital in Pittsburgh the night before and was to leave the next evening. That Sunday afternoon, the manager of the orchestra called and invited him to attend my matinee concert. Before I went on, I was told he was there. I was not nervous but excited; I simply wanted to play the best I could for this great pianist whose playing I revered.

I was thrilled when afterward he came backstage to see me.

"Good," he said. "I liked very much the performance. When are you going to be in New York?"

"Well, I'm in Texas now, but I'm going to be in New York in three months."

You can tell how young I was at the time by my astonishing honesty. Any shrewd adult performer would have said he was planning to be in New York the next morning. Luckily, my naïveté didn't hurt me.

"Please call me when you're in New York," Horowitz said. "I would like to hear you play some more."

In 1944, when I (right) was sixteen and Lorin Maazel was fourteen, he and I performed together with the Pittsburgh Symphony.

So what I said to Mr. Horowitz was, "All right. I'd be very happy to." I still can't believe the casualness of my reply. I had recently heard a recording of Horowitz playing the Second Brahms Concerto with Toscanini conducting the NBC Symphony. It was one of the greatest performances I'd ever heard, and I had thought, "If only I could meet him one day and just talk to him." And when I finally did get a chance to speak with him all I said was, "All right. I'd be very happy to." The reserved part of my nature showed itself at the strangest times.

A few months later, I did arrive in New York, and I, of course, phoned him immediately.

But before I left Dallas, one other rather significant rite of initiation took place.

My new Texas high school was a change from Columbia Grammar in more ways than one. It was a rather rip-roaring place, with hotrodders and fancy cars, and of course girls, and there were lots of pretty ones. They certainly appeared rather sophisticated and experienced even at age fifteen. I'd later learn that the school pregnancy rate was quite high. Academically, it was a different story; I hardly opened a book and got straight A's. Luckily for me, the school did have a soundproofed music room that I'd sneak off to any time I could get away.

Even as young as five, I had been shy yet flirtatious around members of the opposite sex. I still vividly recall my awareness of the girls and women around me at that age.

One day at school, I was headed for the music room and someone was at the piano playing quite beautifully, soulfully. I peered through the slightly open door with great interest and saw a woman at the piano, completely rapt in playing. She must have sensed my presence, and she turned to face me. I could see her eyes were wet with tears.

Flustered, she said, "I didn't know anyone was there."

I apologized and told her how much I had enjoyed what I'd just heard. Then she must have recognized me. She introduced herself as Elizabeth Lauren, who taught languages at the school. I knew that the following semester she'd be teaching me as well, in a class on music appreciation. I guess I was getting an early sample. I was also getting an early sample of how absolutely gorgeous she was.

I had never encountered such emotion in a person's eyes. When she stood up to extend her hand, I was completely transfixed by her gaze. She was so beautiful, so youthful, I found it difficult to believe she was a teacher.

We spoke for another ten minutes. For some unknown reason it was the very first time in my life I felt I was able to talk with someone about what I was really feeling. I began to search for her every day. I knew she'd told me she'd only gone to the music room that day on an impulse. Finally, I saw her again. This time it was I who sat in the music room, playing Bach's Italian Concerto. She appeared suddenly behind me. When I noticed her, I stopped playing. "No, no!" she said. "Don't stop." But I wanted to speak to her, and I had only a few minutes before my next class.

After that, we seemed to run into each other with greater frequency. I had already fallen head over heels in love and had begun to fantasize about her. Then one day I found her again in the music room, but this time something was wrong. When she saw me, she burst into tears and ran out. What was wrong?

The rest of that day I could think of nothing else. After school, I summoned the courage to go to her home, finding her address in the phone book. When I finally worked up the courage to ring her doorbell, she called out, "Just a moment."

She was stunned when she saw it was me, but then she smiled. She invited me in, and I persisted in asking her what was wrong. She kept putting me off, but at one point I saw an almost imperceptible shudder pass through her—like a gust of wind rippling through her body. I put my hand on her shoulder. She began to weep and opened her arms to me.

We held each other for some time. And then I kissed her. My head was reeling, as though I'd tumbled into another world entirely. I kissed her forehead, her eyes, her cheeks. Finally, we moved to the sofa and I learned how to make love. It was my first time. It all seemed surreal and yet so natural.

It was the next time we made love that I saw the bruises. I understood that her husband beat her and that she felt horribly trapped in her marriage.

Needless to say, it was not an ideal romantic situation. I felt I needed to protect her not only by loving her but also by keeping our enormous secret. Revealing our sexual relationship would have instantly destroyed her teaching career. Not that I was eager to discuss it with anyone, but I also came to realize that keeping this explosive information all to myself cost me a lot more emotionally than I knew at the time.

Like my mother weeping over the postcards of misery and dejection from my father, my first lover would cry on my shoulder about the state of her marriage. It awakened unpleasant memories. She even read me bitter letters from her husband and I listened just as my mother had done with me. I'd tell her, "Don't worry," as I tried to cheer her up.

I do believe there was real love between us, despite the disparity in our ages. She was thirty at the start of the affair. I, of course, had difficulty coming to grips with the powerful emotions stirred up in me. I felt guilty, especially when her husband, who was frequently away on business trips, returned home. I hated hearing her cry and complain so much. And I eventually even became resentful that this all-consuming relationship was so filled with problems. Even though I loved her, I couldn't help thinking what it would be like to spend some uncomplicated time with the pretty Texas girls my own age. I was a willing shoulder to lean on, but I knew it was time for another major change of scenery. Fortunately, fate took pity on me once more.

That same year, Adele Marcus divorced her husband and moved back to Manhattan. I, of course, went where my teacher went but was personally thrilled and astoundingly relieved to be able to escape back to New York. It would be difficult to say whether I was happier to arrive in Dallas when I was thirteen or happier to leave when I was sixteen. Many years later after a performance in Dallas, a lovely woman appeared in my dressing room and put a single white rose in my hand. It was Elizabeth. As she held my hand, I noticed she still wore a wedding ring. Before I could say anything, she smiled and said, "I've remarried and I'm now very happy, but I will never forget our time together." Both trips liberated me from weighty emotional traps.

Years later Horowitz told me that when he did catch his train back to New York that Sunday after hearing me play, he said to Toscanini, "I heard this very talented boy, Byron Janis, play Rachmaninoff's Second Concerto in Pittsburgh." Toscanini replied, "But that's the boy I was telling you about." I was so honored and privileged that both of these extraordinarily great artists were to play such important roles in my life and career in the near future.

I was still only sixteen when Toscanini reengaged me to play with the NBC Symphony for a second time. I was to play the Beethoven Fourth, again with Dr. Frank Black conducting. Toscanini asked if I would play the concerto for him privately before the rehearsal. I recall being excited but less nervous than I expected. Even if the greatest artists were gods in their art, they were still just men, I thought. This philosophy was so important in carrying me through a lot of high-powered encounters in the coming years. I know it helped me when, after I'd played just eight bars, Toscanini erupted. "You pianists are all so stupid! Serkin does the same thing." Well, at least I felt better not being alone in my transgression, as such a great pianist as Rudolf Serkin was accused of the same "misdemeanor." What caused the uproar was that I had taken a very slight freedom of tempo during a lyrical upward scale—that was it. When Toscanini's outburst subsided, I quickly played the piece again as a way to stop the tirade. Happily, the rest of the concerto did please him. He even patted me on the head at the end and gave me a warm smile.

We went together to Studio 8-H for the rehearsal, and the entire orchestra snapped to attention when we walked in. The "Old Man," as they often referred to him, was their god.

I started spending a lot of time at the Chotzinoffs' Ridgefield, Connecticut, country estate during the summer. Chotzi asked me if I would teach his young daughter, Ann, whom we all called Cookie, to play the piano. I felt very much a part of their family. Other guests

I recall at Ridgefield at this time included Alexander Woollcott; playwright S. N. Berhman; Joseph Pulitzer II; Harold Ross, editor of the *New Yorker*; and George and Ira Gershwin. I especially remember one dinner at Chotzi's house that I was privileged to attend, given for Chaim Weitzman, who was the first president of the State of Israel. I was very emotional meeting the man who had done so much for that country, a country for which I have always had such special feeling.

And, of course, Jascha Heifetz was often there.

Jascha loved playing games. One day, he showed me another way to play Chopin's famous *Black Key Étude* with which the composer challenged himself by having the right hand play only on the black keys. I played the left-hand accompaniment while Jascha held an orange in his right hand, rolling it back and forth over the black keys, making it almost sound like the real thing! It was brilliant. Sometimes he asked me to play for him. He told me that he liked the way I played. How much I treasured that compliment!

Summering in Ridgefield was idyllic, and as much as I enjoyed and appreciated it, at the time I was far too young to understand just how great my privilege was. My life was about to change dramatically again. It all started with that phone call to Mr. Horowitz.

4

WORKING WITH HOROWITZ

You don't want to be a second Horowitz. You want to be a first Janis.
— VLADIMIR HOROWITZ

IT WAS A WARM AUTUMN DAY in New York when Chotzi and I entered the lobby of the hotel Waldorf-Astoria Tower Apartments. I don't remember exactly what he was saying to me, but I do recall feeling a kind of amusement at how much more nervous he was than I as we headed up the elevator to Horowitz's rooms. Coming back down in the elevator, however, things would be quite different.

We were ushered into a room dominated by two pianos and a sofa. Horowitz rose from the sofa as we entered, and, after some light, brief conversation, he motioned for me to sit down and play. After I finished the first movement of Schumann's G Minor Sonata, he took no time in getting to the point.

"I would like to work with you, but there will be several important conditions. One, I don't want you play for anybody else during first year of working together. And, two, that my lessons would require a fee of fifty dollars an hour."

I remember having goose bumps when he said, "I would like to work with you." But I was stunned by the fact that he was asking a fee for his lessons, and such a steep one at that. I thought he would give me a scholarship as I'd always gotten before. But of course I said nothing beyond thanking him for listening to me play. Chotzi, thrilled with the prospect of this opportunity for me, was all smiles and good humor as we said good-bye and headed back to the bank of elevators.

Once we got outside, however, I must have looked very upset, because Chotzi said to me, "Never mind, By," obviously perturbed as well. "I am going to call Mrs. Rosenwald and ask her for the money." As far as he was concerned, that was that.

It seemed that no movement forward in my career would have been complete without someone coming along and making problems, and this time was no exception. I went almost immediately to tell Adele the good news. But she was clearly less than happy for me. In fact, she was furious.

"This is a terrible choice for you to make," she warned vehemently. "Your own personality is going to get destroyed if you work with him."

Once again, I felt stuck between opposing sides. Not wanting to create any problems between her and me, I hid my own desires behind a mask of almost complete indifference over the possibility of studying with Horowitz. But whatever it may have done to appease Adele, it sent Chotzi into a fit.

"By, I don't understand how you can be so unenthusiastic about the chance you are being given here," he argued with me. "This is an experience that anybody would give their eyeteeth for. You have got to take advantage of this!"

He was right, of course, and I wasn't lying when I told him I agreed with him completely. I was upset because I didn't know how to handle the extreme reaction I was getting from my former teacher. Young as I was, I must have understood that it was fear of losing her star pupil that made Adele act so possessively. I was so desperate to ease the situation that even after all the Lhévinnes had done for me, I took their names out of my biography so she would be the only teacher of record I had prior to working with Horowitz. And I recall feeling tremendous relief when she told me that she had been hired to teach at Juilliard.

All drama completed, the lessons began: once a week, in the late afternoons, usually lasting an hour and a half. I immediately saw why working with him was unlike working with anyone else and far more challenging. Adele Marcus, for instance, had taught me how to play more through her own analysis of what she believed should be played—what this bar needed here, what needed to be done there. But working with Horowitz was totally different. The best way I can describe it is that he never "overtaught" me. He would say, "Something is not right. You know, you should go home and find what is the problem and work on it yourself and bring to me next time," instead of telling me *how* to do it. It was a more difficult process but far more valuable that I had to find my own creativity in these moments—to be my own teacher in a problem I had yet to solve.

His informal manner during the lessons was also different from the manner of other teachers I'd had. Often dressed in a sport jacket and always a bow tie, he would half recline on his big sofa while he listened to me play instead of remaining seated right next to the piano as the others had done. His first comments after listening usually dealt with the tempo, having me try slightly different ones to see if I found one more suited to the work I was playing. It was interesting to me to observe how the very smallest change could make such a great difference in its meaning. In between discussions of music, he would also occasionally remark on my work from a more personal perspective. I found these moments quite generous and very real, like the time he told me that one of the reasons he agreed to work with me was because of a quality in my playing, in my musical temperament and my unbridled passion, that reminded him of himself as a young man. "My nervous energy," he called it, "in good sense of the word," adding that it was a good thing for a performer to have because it brings a greater excitement, another dimension to virtuoso passages, than just a great technique alone could convey. Because the excitement comes from the "nerve," without which even the greatest technical proficiency can seem mechanical.

Another of his reasons for his conditions to work with me soon became clear. Asking such a high price for the lessons, for example, was his way of ensuring that I would take those lessons seriously (how could he ever have thought that I wouldn't?). A year later he would end up giving me all that money back as a fee for a concert he arranged at the YMHA in New York when I was seventeen. He wanted to hear me in performance.

I began to hear rumors that it wasn't only music that prompted Horowitz to accept me as a student. Nothing could have been further from the truth, and we would both laugh about it.

He insisted that I not play for anyone else during the first year because his goal was to make me into a "big" pianist. "You are a pianist who could play more in oils, not just watercolors. So at the beginning, if you exaggerate, don't worry. You see why you don't play for others. They don't understand what happens and will tell you you are taking a wrong track." For him, the best way to get me there was to spend that year having me exaggerate my playing in order to feel that bigness, in order to become the pianist he was certain I could become. "Don't worry, Byronchik," he would say over and over, "you can always subtract but you can't add on."

And he was right, but I would learn the wisdom of his approach only by foolishly breaking my bargain with him.

I was almost at the end of my first year of studying with Horowitz, and throughout that time, Adele had been pressing me to play for her. Finally, against my better judgment, I agreed. When I finished playing, she exploded with rage.

"Oh my God, Byron, he is *ruining* you! You were playing with your own natural talent before and now you are exaggerating everything.

You are on the wrong track. All of that beautiful natural expression I harbored in you is gone, *gone!*"

I tried to explain to her what he had said to me. I tried to make her see, but she was unyielding. I was so upset by the scene that I had to leave. This mistake of mine was beyond an error in judgment, beyond breaking my word to Horowitz. It was a lack of respect for him— something I couldn't believe I was capable of. As I walked the streets, I could feel my head swimming with confusion. Here was my teacher of many years with whom I had shared so much—I couldn't believe that she would react as she had. Why couldn't she see that I was strong enough to fight such a powerful personality as Horowitz? Where was her faith in me to be true to myself? I never played for her again.

But I now began to have serious doubts about myself.

Maybe I was not the strong person I thought I was. Maybe all that felt right about my natural playing was gone forever, crushed under the grand dramatic impression Horowitz had indeed made on my playing. And since I dared not tell him that I had betrayed him in this way, there was no one to whom I could turn to sort it all out. I began to think of my own personality, compared with his, as dull and boring—I began to doubt what I had previously known about my own playing. The question of whether it is possible to have a strong musical personality and still be natural would plague me on and off until I finally broke free from the part of Horowitz that wasn't me.

Yes, I was a pianist who could paint in oils. Horowitz was right. But I did not feel I was Byron Janis again until at least five years after I had stopped working with him. I knew exactly how he thought, how he felt, his way of interpreting, and that was hard to get out of my musical psyche. Nevertheless, though I temporarily lost the sense of my musical self, I knew when something he was telling me was *not* me. But something within me never capitulated to the differences in our thinking, and that was my salvation. I knew his heart was in the right place because he would tell me, "You don't want to be a second Horowitz. You want to be a first Janis." But it was easier said than done.

"Byronchik," he asked me once, "do you want a ten-year career, a twenty-year career, or a lifetime career?" I said, "Of course, a lifetime

I treasure this photo Vladimir Horowitz, the great twentieth-century pianist, gave to his first pupil, me.

career." He said, "Then you have to go slowly and gradually, with very solid foundation. Quick publicity, quick success, and it's the flash in the pan."

He took my lessons very seriously, and when his tours started interfering with my lessons, he asked that I join him and his wife,

Wanda, so that the lessons would not be interrupted. As time went on, the line between being merely a pupil and being almost a member of the family began to blur.

My own touring life was developing according to plan. I was nineteen and had just given a recital in Los Angeles. It was one of those performances at which I took that extra bow onstage to acknowledge whoever was my cocreator that night. I know I had one! I felt I had touched that special place that isn't always at your fingertips—that spiritual place where music moves into another dimension. When the concert was over, I was taken back to my hotel, which reminded me of one of those small-town European hotels where everybody has pulled in the shutters by 9 p.m. All was quiet, and this was a night I actually wouldn't have minded one of those after-concert receptions, but no such luck. What to do? I decided to take myself to a burlesque show. After that especially meaningful evening, my "high" had now been replaced by shame. What sort of a person was I to have sunk so low? A terrible doubt swept over me and guilt had taken its place as my demoralizing companion that night. In fact, I don't think I stayed at the show more than fifteen minutes before I bolted, but the whole thing haunted me.

Fortunately, a few weeks later, at an after-concert reception, I met a highly spiritual person—a Catholic priest, in fact. I found myself opening up to him. "Oh, my dear young man," he said, "you are worrying needlessly about that night. What you're telling me about is really two sides of the same coin. As you were flying so high, you needed to ground yourself. Well, you certainly chose the right place." I didn't know how to thank him for healing my crisis of conscience. Whew. I guess I wasn't so wicked after all.

Back in New York, I would end up staying for dinner after almost every lesson. I got to know Wanda quite well during this time. She was a highly intelligent and very outspoken woman who had an extraordinary knowledge of music—almost inevitable, being the wife of Vladimir Horowitz and the daughter of Arturo Toscanini. We spent many evenings in hysterics as we watched Horowitz, with that wildly animated face of his, tell stories and jokes. Indeed, he would go out of his way to seduce the small audience before him, just as he did the large one in every concert he performed. He truly was one of the funniest men I have ever met, and I was grateful for yet another warm, familial environment to help support me through my teens and through the unfolding of myself as an artist.

We would often go to the movies. Horowitz loved movies, and we all three went to see good movies and bad movies. It didn't seem to make any difference. Afterward, he loved to walk down 42nd Street, but he did not ever want to be recognized. If, when we were walking, someone came up to him and said, "You look like Vladimir Horowitz," he'd always reply, "That's what everybody tells me."

That Horowitzian humor was always present—that Chaplinesque walk, those purposefully exaggerated mispronunciations, and that constant obsession with the weather. Watching that on television had all the earmarks of a sacred ritual. How we laughed!

While my work and practice was as disciplined as ever, I enjoyed attending many elegant New York parties and meeting some of the most beautiful women in the world.

Women and music have long been inextricably intertwined with my life, passion for the one inspiring transcendence in the other—much in the way, for instance, that Picasso's passion for the women in his life inspired his art (not uncommon among artists). Sometimes the musical transcendence takes me to another place altogether—it goes beyond the performer, beyond the audience, beyond everything. I don't know what it is. I'm not thinking of anything. It's just happening.

I remember once when I was eighteen or nineteen years old and a gorgeous young girl came up to my apartment. I was intent on making love to her, but she asked me to play something for her first. I began to play, and I got so involved in the music that I totally forgot about her. That's really transcending! There was this beautiful girl, and I couldn't believe I had absolutely no thought of touching her. She was completely undone by this. She must have thought I was gay, and she left quickly in a huff. If she'd only realized that all I needed was a half hour!

When my mother and sister chose to return to New York in response to some anonymous notes about how I was destroying my life with partying and women, I was livid. Everyone around me seemed to have his or her own idea of how I should live my life, and each was jealous of the other. They seemed to enjoy making things difficult for me. So again, as before, I ended up having to share an apartment with my mother and sister at 140 West 57th Street. One day Horowitz called to tell me he wanted to bring a young lady to visit. He introduced her as J. C. Compton (who today is very active in New York theater). We chatted, had a sandwich, and then he asked me to play Chopin's *Black Key Étude* for her. I had no idea what this was all about, and still don't, but he seemed to be very fond of her. We talked a bit more and they left.

Many years later, Maria and I ran into her and she told me that Horowitz had confessed to her, "I sold my soul to the devil. I should never have become a pianist. I wanted to become a composer. My sister was very, very good pianist, and I guess I got competing with her, and to make money I decided to become a pianist."

Another thing he told her, which I'm sure he has told no one else: "I never knew how to play Chopin! I don't know how to play Chopin." I was amazed that he would ever make such a remark. I argued with her, but she firmly assured me that it was a direct quote. In thinking back, it's strange that I can't remember us ever having really spoken about Chopin.

Going on tour, being away from home, was almost a relief. But I began having trouble with my nerves. I was young and touring alone. I remember even turning on the faucets in the bathroom to give me the feeling of life around me. There was no TV in those days and not every room had a radio. My nerves coupled with my bad eating habits—gulping my food down so quickly during my solitary meals—caused me to develop serious digestive problems, which became more and more difficult to cope with.

When I returned to New York, I told Horowitz that I was having these very troubling problems. He told me, "You must see a psychiatrist." I didn't react at all well to his suggestion, because at that time, I felt seeing a psychiatrist was almost something to be ashamed of. I was in such distress, though, that I decided to go. He sent me to see his doctor, one of the foremost psychiatrists at the time,

Dr. Lawrence Kubie of Yale University. I told him my problem and he asked me if I ever felt dizzy. "As a matter of fact, I sometimes do," I replied. "Which way does the room go?" he asked. "To the left or to the right?" I thought this was some kind of joke, but it wasn't. "To the left, I believe," I answered, trying to suppress a laugh at the question. "Then I know to whom to send you." I didn't realize there were doctors who specialized in left or right! So off I was sent to see Dr. Victor Rosen, whose sofa I occupied off and on for some three years (mostly off, as things didn't seem to be improving much).

While Horowitz wouldn't play for me at lessons, on some evenings he would play for hours, going through repertoire known and unknown to me (at times even to him). On those evenings, I heard what I considered to be his greatest playing. There was no audience to seduce—it was Horowitz being natural, without any affectation, and that was something extraordinary to have heard. I shall never forget those evenings.

Chopin used to say to his students, "Play naturally. Play naturally." It's a simple piece of advice, but one of the hardest things in the world to do. Despite my feelings of conflict and confusion, I finally became aware that when I simply played from the heart and soul, I would play naturally and that my playing was not lacking in personality.

I have always said there are two kinds of great artists. There are the big-personality pianists where one is usually aware of the artist first: Hoffman plays Beethoven; Rachmaninoff plays Chopin. The other kind tries to have the audience be more aware of the *music* first: Schubert played by Richter; Schumann played by Cortot. What is important to me as an artist is to try to get to the *essence* of the composer—his birthplace, letters, biographies—and that is what guides your interpretation.

"Don't worry, Byronchik," Horowitz was always saying to me, as if he sensed the struggle I was up against. "Whatever you do, you will never be bad taste." Fortunately, I did have a strong sense of what I felt was musically appropriate, and I juxtaposed oils and watercolors to help create the music I wanted.

5

SOUTH AMERICA

PIANOS ARE AS IMPORTANT to pianists as the music they play. They are like people. Each one has a different personality, a different speaking voice. Some are bright, some are mellow, and some have different actions. In each city where you perform, one is chosen to be your "blind date," your "one-night stand," and it can be a rewarding encounter or one you'd rather forget. You find out pretty quickly. It is one of the pitfalls of a pianist's profession, unless you go through the great expense of bringing your own piano. I have done so on various occasions, and what a difference to make music with an old friend.

In 1947, when I was nineteen and about to embark on my first concert tour of South America, I was told that neither Argentina nor Brazil had any top-quality instruments and that I had better bring my own. The war had just ended, and the concert venues south of the equator were still unable to purchase any new pianos. So I visited the famous basement at Steinway Hall on 57th Street in New York where all their concert grands are stationed. They were looking even larger than usual, all lined up like so many beautiful racehorses waiting to be ridden. This was very early in my career, and I was as worried about money as I was about finding my best "partner." I wondered if I could even afford to send one to South America. At times like that, I wished my mother had been enamored of the violin! I nervously inquired as to the cost. Four hundred dollars, came the reply, as they are sent by boat. I couldn't believe it. At that rate, I could send two pianos, one to Rio and one to Buenos Aires. As a reference, I should add that today the cost of moving a piano across 57th Street from Steinway Hall to Carnegie Hall is a thousand dollars.

I spent many hours down in the basement with those instruments, trying to find the two I wanted. As the hours passed, Bill Hupfer, Steinway's chief technician, said in exasperation, "You pianists are all nuts. There isn't much difference between these pianos—why all the fuss?" I voiced my ardent disagreement. "Okay," he said. "I'll tell you what. By this time you must know the numbers [numbers inside the piano used for their identification] of most of these pianos." There were about eight in all. I nodded my head. "I'll cover up the numbers on five of them, and if you can tell me three of the five, you win." The battle lines were drawn and I took on the challenge gleefully. I hopped from one piano to the next, playing each several times until I was ready. Well, I correctly identified all five. Poor Bill didn't look very happy. I think I'd proved to him that we pianists are nuts—about pianos.

Sadly, the piano I sent to Rio de Janeiro fell victim to shipboard humidity, and its voice was reduced to just above a whisper. I had no choice but to use the local instrument, which I remember was eminently lacking in pretty much everything. Fortunately, the piano sent to Buenos Aires suffered no ill effects. I felt so lucky to have with me a friend I knew so well.

My concerts in Buenos Aires were held in the grand, twenty-five-hundred-seat Colón Opera House, patterned after the wondrous La Scala in Milan. I marveled at its beauty and its sound. My opening concert was a truly great success, so much so that the last three performances were completely sold out. Both the public reaction and the press were more than I could have hoped for. My personal success surprised me even more—girls, girls, and more girls! Some of my new admirers even started an official Byron Janis Fan Club. I never thought I would tire of taking all those flirtatious phone calls, but I did. I admit that battling the Spanish language could have had something to do with it.

I decided to give my ego a rest and advised the hotel to kindly screen all my calls. However, a few young ladies managed to make it up to my room regardless, one proclaiming, "No virgin, no virgin!" Another señorita called me on the house phone asking if she could come up and meet me. I told her it would not be possible because I was still in my dressing gown. This news did not seem to deter her in the least, and a few minutes later there came a knock at my door. I thought I would give her a good lesson, and not a musical one. It was the "man" who opened the door for her, and I quickly let her know what was expected. Horrified, she protested, "But I came to see the artist, not the man!" I retorted, "The man is upstairs, the artist downstairs!" It didn't take her long to make her exit.

There was one caller I was in fact dying to meet—she had the most beautiful voice, spoke English, and told me she'd been to every one of my concerts. Despite my many requests, she was reticent about a rendezvous, but I finally convinced her and we agreed to meet at a nearby coffeehouse. She was there when I arrived, and when I walked in I must have visibly blanched. Before me sat a disturbingly unattractive middle-aged woman whose only alluring feature was that deceptively beautiful voice. The smile on her face quickly vanished. I obviously had not hidden my shock. "You see," she said, "I told you we should not meet. It's best you go back to your hotel." I tried to protest, but I knew there was no way I could possibly keep up the charade, and I hurried back to the hotel. The beauty of a Brahms intermezzo helped me forget my shattered illusion.

Just before my last concert in Buenos Aires, the cultural attaché at the American embassy called and asked to see me. He sent a car, and I went over to the embassy puzzled as to what this was all about.

He said, "Byron, we had a call from Mrs. Perón's secretary, asking that an Italian conductor—I don't remember his name—conduct the Gershwin concerto for you in your farewell concert." I had chosen three concertos for a *Despedida* (Farewell), of which the Gershwin was one.

"What do you mean? I've already got my conductor!"

"Yes, but that doesn't matter. You must do this," he said.

"What do you mean, I must do this?"

"You must do this—it's Mrs. Perón."

It was my first encounter with dictatorship, and I was outraged. I would not accept it.

I said, "I will cancel this concert."

"No, no, no, you can't. You have to play."

Well, I realized finally that I had no alternative. At the rehearsal, this young conductor appeared, one of the handsomest young men you could possibly imagine, and he appeared quite nervous. I thought, "Good! A plus."

He started to conduct, and before we had gone through two pages, I got up from the piano eight or ten times to go over to him and say, "We're really not together. Can we try it again, please?" He was already rattled, and I must admit that I did exaggerate a bit to heighten the effect. I had to find a way out, and I succeeded. After about five minutes, he put down his baton, shouted "*No puedo hacerlo*" (I cannot do it) in exasperation, and stormed off the stage for good.

What a relief! And no one ever heard another word from Mrs. Perón.

On my South American tour, I had played fifteen concerts in Rio, Montevideo, and Buenos Aires, and thus I'd completed the fifty concerts that Horowitz and Chotzi felt I needed to play before performing at Carnegie Hall.

When I returned to New York, my father was so thrilled with the success of my South American tour that he came to visit me, and I could see that he felt that all his sacrifice had been worthwhile. What a good feeling that was for me.

6

CARNEGIE HALL

AT LAST, CARNEGIE HALL! How many years of preparation I had done in anticipation of this evening. As the only pupil of Horowitz, I had a lot to live up to.

As Carnegie Hall was just around the corner from where I lived on 57th Street, I must have been one of the few people who ever walked to their Carnegie Hall debut. Warming up in the backstage green room, I remembered Heifetz telling me that that was the time that would determine how the concert would go. I had also already learned that nerves were mostly caused by thinking about the public rather than the music. I must admit that, at times, it was not a very easy task. Before the concert, Horowitz came backstage and said, with a bit of a nervous smile, "Remember, Byronchik, it's not an examination." But he knew, as did I, that his reputation was on the line, too. I wasn't about to let either of us down. It was a heavy responsibility.

This program is from my concert debut at Carnegie Hall in 1948 when I was twenty.

The stage manager knocked on the door of my dressing room and said we were ready to go, and at eight o'clock on Friday evening, October 29, 1948, I walked across the stage in Carnegie Hall and sat down at the piano. It looked as if every seat in the hall was filled and I knew many of the greats of the music world were there. I took a couple of deep breaths while the audience settled down and began playing the opening notes of the Bach–Liszt A Minor Prelude and Fugue.

Horowitz sat in a box with my parents, and when I played one of the "Songs Without Words," the Mendelssohn piece that I was to have played on the radio the week I slashed my little finger, my mother told me he turned to her and said, "I couldn't have done that better myself."

Horowitz came to the green room at intermission looking quite pleased. "It's going well, it's going well. Just keep playing the way you are. Remember to play from your stomach," something he often would tell me. I don't think that was the best time to remind me of it, because after he left the green room I threw up! My suppressed nerves had now surfaced. I was so glad that I had come to that concert with fifty others under my belt, those important out-of-town tryouts during my tours of South America and the United States. They certainly helped me handle whatever the Fates threw my way.

I went back onstage for the second half of the program. From the ovation I received and the numerous encores I played, I knew I had had a big success. The green room after the concert was crowded with old friends and many new ones and I was so happy with their enthusiastic reactions. Horowitz came in, looking very happy indeed, but he stayed only briefly because, as usual, I'm sure he probably didn't want to be recognized.

The Rosenwalds gave a party for me after the concert at their home in the Waldorf Towers, and the musical world was well represented—Chotzi, the Horowitzes, Nathan Milstein, and Rudolf Serkin. Mrs. Rachmaninoff was there, too, and I was thrilled with her remarks about my concert. She mentioned that her husband practiced every single day, but if he was composing and didn't have enough time to work on repertoire, he would just work on technical exercises to keep his fingers strong. I found that wonderful advice. Talking to her made me think of Horowitz telling me that he always thought of Rachmaninoff as his musical father, and therefore he would be *my* musical grandfather. That was a pretty heady notion to ponder.

I was much too excited to go home and go to bed, so after leaving the party, I said to a friend, "I can't wait until tomorrow to read the reviews. Let's go downtown and be there when the paper comes out." We went to a coffee shop not far from the Times Square Building on 36th Street and had tea while we waited for the first edition of the Saturday *New York Times* to appear at 4 a.m.

I opened the paper, and when I read the first line of the review, I said, "I've made it!" As we scanned the article, we saw that Olin Downes had written:

JANIS, 20, PIANIST, SCORES IN RECITAL

"Making Debut at Carnegie Hall, He Impresses With Ability to Interpret Music"

Not for a long time had this writer heard such a talent allied with the musicianship, the feeling, the intelligence and artistic balance shown by the 20-year-old pianist, Byron Janis, who made his New York debut last night in Carnegie Hall.

One thing that made me happy about this review as I read on was that it sounded as if *I* was playing, not Horowitz—me, with my own personality. It also made Horowitz happy—that was what he had been striving for.

After that review in the *Times*, my career was set. Professionally, I could have as many concerts as I wanted, and my touring began in earnest.

7

WANDA

THE TWO DAUGHTERS of Arturo Toscanini couldn't have been
more different. Wanda was handsome; Wally (pronounced "Vali")
was beautiful. Wanda was extremely musical. She knew every word of
every opera she had heard her father conduct, and she married one
of the world's greatest pianists and became Mrs. Vladimir Horowitz.
Wally was extremely social and knew everybody who was important
to know. She managed to combine art with aristocracy when she
married Count Emanuele di Castelbarco, who was a painter and poet.
She was widely known for her many charitable works, most notably
with orphans.

My life with the Horowitzes changed greatly after I made my
Carnegie Hall debut. Horowitz said to me, "Well, I've taught you
everything I can. Now you will make mistakes, but they will be your

mistakes." He was right about making mistakes, and my mistakes were not all to do with music.

After Horowitz and I stopped working together, we remained good friends, and I was often invited to dinner as before. But now, for the first time, he began to tell me things about his personal life—how he had been in love with a beautiful ballerina in Russia and was devastated when she rejected him. That, he said, was a turning point in his life. The trauma of being rejected affected him so deeply that he developed a profound mistrust of women and began looking for affection in homosexual relationships.

When he met Wanda, he found himself attracted to her, and his demons seemed to vanish. Despite her family's concerns, they were married a year later. He told me that for the first year of their marriage,

For my twenty-first birthday in 1949, Eugene Ormandy and the Philadelphia Orchestra surprised me with a birthday cake onstage at the Lyric Theater in Baltimore.

he was a perfectly normal husband, and they were very happy together. When Wanda gave birth to their daughter, Sonia, something within him changed. The constraints of being a husband and a father had created a new dissonant chord for him in their relationship. He said it became more one of friendship. It was now twelve years since Sonia had been born, and you may imagine that they were not very happy ones for Wanda.

I became troubled by some of the things he was telling me. In spite of my great affection for Volodya, how could my sympathies not be with Wanda? How would I be able to deal with the man in front of me, for whom I had such enormous respect and admiration, and who, at the time, certainly was just about the most important person in my life?

What made it even more difficult for me was that Wanda also began confiding in me at the same time and would weep and pour her heart out about how difficult it was to live with her husband. But she lost all control when she spoke about Sonia, who obviously was very affected by all the upsetting discord around her. Finally it was decided that it would be better for her to live away from home, so she was sent to a special boarding school that was not too far from New York, and Wanda would be able to visit her more often.

I felt the pain of her difficult situation, and I empathized with her. I told her how much I liked Sonia, what an exceptionally bright girl she was, and how surely with her mother's love and support, she would be able to get through this difficult period. One day Wanda asked, "Would you like to drive out with me sometime and visit Sonia?" "Of course," I told her. "I would love to."

Horowitz didn't help the potentially complex situation any when one day he suddenly asked me, "Byronchik, have you ever had a homosexual experience?"

"No," I replied. "You know it's just not my thing."

With a mischievous smile he said, "You knows you should try it one day; you might like it," and then we both broke into peals of laughter as we went downstairs to join Wanda for dinner. It was more of his impish game playing.

On Christmas Eve, I was happy to receive an invitation to attend a party at the Toscanini home on 252nd Street in Riverdale, which overlooked the Hudson River. Wanda called to offer to drive me up to Riverdale, as Volodya was at another party and would come on his own.

I was having a wonderful time at the party. Toscanini talked about the concert he had conducted at the Chatham Square Music School with the orchestra members all dressed in short pants. The concertmaster was Heifetz, the first cellist was Piatigorsky, and other top-notch musicians all played their roles. Maestro had a large hobo handkerchief flailing around in his back pocket. It was truly hysterical. And Toscanini was dead serious about the whole thing, which made it even funnier.

Wanda got more and more tense as it got later and later and her husband still hadn't arrived. He never did appear. I had seen flashes of Wanda's temper before, and I could see it smoldering this time, but she didn't let it catch fire. Her father's house was not exactly the best place for that kind of display, but apparently the car on the ride back was. I'm glad my Italian wasn't very good. But my English was. "I've had enough. I am going to leave Volodya," Wanda declared. I couldn't believe my ears, but I assumed her remark came from a moment of temper. However, nothing much changed except that the situation at home seemed to worsen.

Again, Wanda asked me if I wanted to visit Sonia with her. How could I refuse? Not that I didn't want to go, but I knew it would make our relationship become more intimate. I was being cast in a difficult role that I knew would eventually present me with terrible problems. I saw no way out because by now I was beginning to have strong feelings for Wanda, as she had for me. One day, despite all my fears and terrible guilt, the inevitable happened. It didn't take long for one of my own mistakes to come home to roost. After several months of living with beauty, fear, happiness, and guilt, after several months of playing a necessary game of deceit, my phone rang. It was Volodya asking me to come over. I had had dinner with them the night before, so I had supposed he had forgotten to tell me something. But why couldn't he have done that on the telephone? Once

I arrived I quickly understood why he wanted to see me in person. His message was simple and to the point: "Sam Barber [one of America's great composers] told me you and Wanda are having an affair." I stopped him; I simply had to deny it, and I did so vigorously even though I couldn't look him in the eye. He briskly interrupted me. "I do not wish to see you again." He led me to the door and slammed it shut as I left.

This was the bombshell of my nightmares. All my fears had come to pass. I could no longer hide from the truth, and I wondered what further punishment might be lying in store for me. Yes, I deserved it, but once again loving and rescuing the woman I loved seemed deeply embedded in my romantic nature. It was a pattern that appeared to define the nature of my relationships with women, and the price was too high. I had lost my teacher. I had lost my friend, and I had been shown the door by someone who was irreplaceable to me.

Now it was Wanda who tried to comfort me. She was much less upset than I. After all those years of an unfulfilling marriage, she must have felt her actions were quite justified. Nevertheless we both agreed it was best not to see each other. Wanda suggested I go to California, where they were planning to spend the summer. Perhaps he might change his mind about seeing me. But it was not to be. All the stress and guilt caught up with me and caused me to develop some strange physical symptoms. It was as though my body was moving sideways though I was standing still; what a fitting physical manifestation of having literally been pushed aside. Not feeling well, I didn't want to travel alone when my concert tours resumed, so I engaged someone to travel with me. It helped.

When the Horowitzes returned to New York, it seems that he began disappearing more and more, and Wanda finally did ask him to leave the house. It was some time afterward that Wanda and I started seeing each other again. There was a new intensity to our relationship that, I suppose, wrapped me in a cloud of unrealistic happiness. It was some months before the second bombshell hit. Without warning, one day she calmly declared, "I've decided to go back to Volodya." That was it. There was no point in having any further discussion.

I stared at her in disbelief. I was absolutely crushed. I wanted to throw myself under the nearest moving car. Why is it that despite knowing the inevitability of an unhappy ending we are still so devastated when it comes?

I was stunned at the effect her decision had on me. I had really fallen in love with her.

I was still seeing that psychiatrist. One day he threw me an unexpected question: "Suppose she said yes, she wanted to marry you? What then?" That thought had never entered my mind, though at one point she told me she wanted to run away with me. Just like the classic romantic I am, she would also take things to the brink but never take the leap. Could I marry her? Neither of us would have taken *that* leap. But I still couldn't get over her. Thank goodness, this time love chose to think, and I was very grateful to Wanda for saying, "Byron, if it helps you to talk with somebody, tell Alfred about us."

Alfred Katz, our mutual friend and a public relations person, made it his business to know everything about everybody. I don't know if he knew about my relationship with Wanda, but he didn't act surprised when I told him. "Listen to me," he said. "I will give you the telephone number of an extremely lovely girl. I want you to call her today and make a date." His advice proved prescient. I called Paula that very day, and we made a plan to meet. She was beautiful, intelligent, fun—it was balm for my wounded soul, and as our relationship blossomed, the impact of my time with Wanda slowly faded into the past. Life taught me later that one may or may not remember a romance but one never forgets a love.

Horowitz and Wanda didn't resume their relationship until several months later. In the meantime, one day I had a wonderful surprise: I picked up the phone and heard Volodya's voice on the other end. How wonderful it was to hear from him. There was no talk of anything in the past. I was even more surprised when he asked me if I could find a nice young lady for him so we could all go out together—my God! Double-dating with Horowitz!

How tremendously grateful I was to realize that he had forgiven me. Paula asked a girlfriend of hers to join us, and we drove up

Maria and I with the Horowitzes, Valdimir and Wanda, at their home in 1987.

the Hudson River to a lovely romantic place for dinner. Everyone had a happy time. Volodya was at his best—utterly charming. His Horowitzian humor of deliberately mispronouncing words was very much in evidence. He certainly impressed my date with his lavish praise of me—even I was impressed! Horowitz, however, was not impressed, as I had wished he would be, with my beautiful, brand-new Buick convertible: "You knows, I only like Rolls Royces."

It made me very happy to hear that shortly after that double date, Horowitz and Wanda had reconciled. Even though we didn't speak for many years, it was good to know we were friends again. One night Maria and I ran into them at a restaurant. They invited us to join them. It seemed like old times. After that, we began to see them quite frequently for dinner. One day, they came to our apartment, where we have two pianos, and he and I played the Rachmaninoff *Symphonic Dances* together. What a special moment, especially when he told me that the last time he had played them was with Rachmaninoff himself!

One evening, we invited the Horowitzes to our home for dinner. After we sat down, he looked at me with an impish grin and said, "I listened to you on the radio last night. You knows? You're good!" He seemed to be happy that he had "rediscovered" me.

One morning Wanda telephoned to tell us that Voldya had had a heart attack and died the previous night. The tragic news came as a great shock. The world had lost one of its greatest pianists, and I had lost one of the most meaningful people in my life. Death is always a shock and a loss, but for me, it is never a final chapter. I have felt his presence on many occasions.

After Horowitz died, Maria and I stayed close to Wanda and continued to see her. I was so touched when she came to celebrate my seventieth birthday with us.

By 1998, Wanda was in her nineties, and she was frail and mostly housebound. I asked her one day if she would like to hear a new recording I had just made of the two Liszt concertos. I was so thrilled when after listening to it she said to me, "You're the pianist who keeps the Grand Tradition alive."

She liked Maria so much and even gave her some very personal and lovely mementos. One day, it became evident that she wanted to see me alone, and a few days later I went to visit her for what turned out to be the last time. She motioned for me to come closer to her bedside and quietly asked me, "Does love last?"

I said, "Yes, Wanda, real love does!" I took her hand and leaned over to kiss her forehead. She started weeping and asked me for my handkerchief. After she wiped the tears from her eyes she handed it back to me and, with a look that was hard to forget, said, "Now you have my tears."

She died less than two months later.

8

A FEW MORE TURNS OF THE WHEEL

IN 1952, TOSCANINI CONDUCTED a series of concerts in London. Chotzi, I, and an entourage of Maestro's friends and admirers made the trip. I was invited to a party one night at which I met a young lady named Heather Dickson-Wright, the daughter of a prominent British surgeon, who invited me to their house to practice, assuring me, "Yehudi Menuhin works at our home whenever he is here, so I trust you'll find the piano up to your standards."

Their piano wasn't the only grand feature of that lovely drawing room. I immediately noticed an intriguing portrait of a beautiful young lady whose image exuded both strength and femininity. A few minutes later, to my surprise, the subject of the portrait entered the room. Immediately I was smitten. Her name was June; she was Heather's younger sister. We saw each other every night for a week and fell in love. But our romance was interrupted by my departure for Milan and my debut at the magnificent opera house, La Scala.

While I was in Milan, the Toscanini family invited me to stay at their flat on the Via Durini. The Maestro was not in residence, and his daughter Wally, the Countess Castelbarco, and her daughter Emmanuela were at Salso Maggiore, a spa not far from Milan.

I was to take the train down to meet them, then drive back with Emmanuela and have lunch with Luigi Visconti, the famous Italian actor, at his château in Grazana.

Walking through the main building at Salso Maggiore, I passed a group of women whose faces were totally encased in mud, with only their eyes showing. I managed to suppress a chuckle, which was increasingly hard to do, when a few of these "raccoons" winked at me. I don't think they had seen a man in weeks. Finally, I located a "mud-free" Emmanuela, and we quickly headed for Grazana in her tiny Fiat Topolino, with her maid squeezed into the backseat.

Emmanuela, a blond, blue-eyed, and extremely beautiful sixteen-year-old, asked, "May I drive?"

With some misgivings, I looked at the maid, who volunteered, "She has a permit."

"Well," I said, squelching the odd foreboding I was suddenly feeling, "all right, fine." I knew I would have a problem turning down this beautiful young lady.

So off we went. It is well known in Italy that any vehicle that comes from the right has the right-of-way, even on entering the autostrada. Suddenly out of nowhere a truck came barreling out of a dirt road on the right, and I cautioned, "Careful, Emmanuela. Watch that big truck." Well, she overreacted and turned the wheel much too sharply, and we flipped over.

In that split second I was sure we were going to die. And then time ceased to exist. Images of my life passed in front of me, as people who've had such an experience will tell you. In that frozen instant in time when I was reliving my young life, I could step into any part of it and feel as though I was actually there in real time. I can still remember the feeling moment by moment, frame by frame—the emotion as well as the experience. The very next second, I found myself lying on my right side with Emmanuela sprawled on top of me. We were alive! The maid, still wedged into the backseat, kept muttering, "*Meno male! Meno male!*" ("It could have been worse!") It most certainly could have, but I did suffer a serious whiplash, which didn't become apparent until a few years later. My neck has never been the same since.

People driving by stopped their cars wanting to help, and were able to pick the little car up and turn it over, righting us onto the road. "*Miracolo! Miracolo!*" ("Miracle! Miracle!") they were saying. Where had I heard that public cry before? Many years earlier, near the bottom of a steep hill in Pittsburgh. That time, the miracle intervened a second earlier, sparing my mother, my sister, and me from plummeting over the cliff to a certain death. But both times, in both cars, the Fates had spared our lives.

Happily realizing that we were all in one piece, we cautiously continued on to join Wally for lunch. It was agreed we'd say nothing to her about the accident. But Wally greeted us with, "What happened to you?"

I tried to be nonchalant. "Oh, nothing," I said. "Traffic held us up a bit."

Wally didn't buy it. "What do you mean, nothing?" she said. "You all look as though you've seen a ghost."

Seeing a ghost would have been far more preferable. Eventually, we told her the whole story, and I had to admit we were damn lucky to be alive.

"*Miracolo!*" she said. Again, that word, "miracle."

Back at the Villa Durini, once my nerves had settled down, I began to feel the excitement of living in Toscanini's apartment. He had known Verdi, as well as Puccini. He had conducted the premier of Puccini's famous opera *La Bohème*, as well as three one-act operas called *Il Trittico*: *Il Tabarro*, *Suor Angelica*, and *Gianni Schicchi*. He also conducted the first performance of Verdi's *Four Sacred Pieces*. He considered Verdi to be one of the greatest composers; some say he compared him to Beethoven! My sensations in that apartment were almost like those I felt when touching a composer's manuscript.

It was always dark when I would go into his study to get to the piano and I would have to fumble for the light switch. During those few awkward seconds, there was something that I touched in the dark that turned out to be a life-size cardboard replica of Verdi. But touching a manuscript didn't compare—I was touching the composer!

Wally Toscanini took me to meet an Italian professor who possessed an extraordinary collection of manuscripts. They were astonishing—Beethoven, Mozart, Wagner, it went on and on. Then he brought out a large packet of letters written by Verdi. "I will never, never allow these letters to be published."

"Why?" I asked.

"Because these letters are totally pornographic, and his image could be seriously damaged. Remember, they had no telephone in those days, so Verdi would have to write to the women his fantasies about them. Sometimes at La Scala, I see an aged diva in the audience, and I blush knowing what Verdi had written to her!"

I had practiced so hard for my debut that about three days before the concert, my whole right arm went numb. I had overdone it. I was very concerned, but Wally, long accustomed to living with men of artistic temperament, obviously had a knack for calming one down. She soothed, "Oh, don't worry, Byron. Don't play anymore. Let's go to a movie." A wise suggestion, as I undoubtedly would have kept testing that arm and only made it worse. She then found a doctor for me who happened to be a surgeon. "It's nothing," he said. "You're just overworked." He gave me some exercises and told me to practice very little.

The day of my debut, I took a nap before leaving for La Scala. Emmanuela came into the dark room and woke me, saying it was time to get ready. She seemed to linger a bit. What a romantic moment— that was all it took! Having fallen in love with June in London, I now found myself starting to fall in love with Emmanuela in Milan. That I could even think about Emmanuela a few days after leaving June was a good warning that I was certainly not ready to settle down.

My right arm revived in time for the concert, but the physical problems I had felt during the few days before were only a fore-shadowing of what would become a way of life in little more than a decade. That glorious evening, however, the concert went extremely well; I felt it was one of the best I'd ever given.

When I returned to New York, Wanda mentioned to me that her mother had told her of a letter her father had just received from Milan. It was from an old friend of his who wrote, "I have just attended Byron Janis's concert at La Scala, and I was moved to tears by his playing." Nothing could have meant more to me than being told that this came from someone whom Toscanini so highly admired and respected.

I found that my psychological woes had increased as I tried to understand my quixotic behavior with women. I was still seeing Dr. Rosen. As a strict Freudian, he had hardly ever said a word, but he broke his quasi-silence one day when he finally asked, "What about that girl in England? You seem to have a feeling for her."

"Yes, I do," I answered. And added that I had not called her in all that time.

"Well," he said, "why don't you call her?"

I decided to call June from Holland, where I was playing with the Concertgebouw for the second time, and invited her to Paris, where I was to make my debut with the Orchestre Lamoreux play-ing the Rachmaninoff Third Piano Concerto.

She accepted, and when I met her at the Orly airport, I immediately noticed how different she seemed from a year earlier. She wore more makeup, seemed more sophisticated, and appeared to lack some of that natural simplicity I had loved when I first knew her. I wondered if, since I had not been in touch with her for a year, someone else had come into her life. However, despite my concerns, after spending just one week together in Paris and one week together in London the previous year, I asked her to marry me. We were married in London in June 1953.

It was wonderful having someone in my corner, someone to help fend off those people who had conflicting emotions about me, someone to travel with—and, of course, most important, someone to love.

That same year, we were in Buenos Aires when I received a call from my mother informing me, in sobbing hushed tones, that my seventy-two-year-old father was dying and had asked to see me. I immediately canceled the remainder of the tour, and June and I flew to Pittsburgh. Trying to comfort my distraught mother distracted me from feeling my own grief. She told me the doctors had given dad a spinal tap and discovered a malignant growth in his stomach. The prognosis was not good. Because of his age and his overall health, he would probably be with us only a few more days. I can't say why, but this medical conclusion somehow did not entirely convince me. I wanted another opinion, so I asked several important doctor friends, including my medically renowned father-in-law in London, if they could speak to the Pittsburgh doctors to confirm their grim diagnosis. They did, and it was confirmed. I suppose for anyone else that would have been the end of the matter, but not being a doctor allowed me to still have hope.

I asked my mother to fill me in on what had been going on at home. My sister, Thelma, had been suffering from a serious emotional disturbance and had been wreaking havoc around the house. It was obviously something for which she should have been hospitalized. Why hadn't my mother seen to that? "I just couldn't do it. How could I? Poor girl," she answered.

"Well," I said, "you couldn't, but we will."

I hurried to my father's room at the hospital. Seeing him in that oxygen tent, not moving, eyes closed—it was like he had already gone.

"Dad. It's Byron." No response.

Oh, please don't let me be too late.

"It's Byron! Dad!" I nearly roared.

There was a slight fluttering of his eyelids. And then they opened, expressionless but looking directly at me.

"Dad. We're taking Thelma to the hospital. She will not be at home when you return—she will *not* be at home."

I repeated this over and over with all the emotional force I could muster. I knew it was something he needed to hear. It was a beautiful moment when a slight smile creased his face.

A week later he felt much stronger, and the experts were wary but decided to send him home. Their prognosis had not changed. Two weeks later, the doctors took another X-ray. They were flabbergasted at the result. The growth had totally vanished. It seemed I had fortunately struck the right key! Stress can so often deplete our immune system that it posts an open invitation for any disease to accept, and they often do. My instincts strongly told me that the unbearable situation at home had helped cause my father's illness.

Whatever the sequence of cause and effect, a spontaneous remission had now occurred. Time proved that it was more than a remission. He completely recovered and lived fifteen more years. There is a beautiful quote by Plato: "The greatest mistake in the treatment of diseases is that there are physicians for the body and physicians for the soul, although the two cannot be separated."

We returned to New York, and June began traveling on my tours with me. About a year later she got pregnant, and a son was born to us on March 20, 1955, in Chicago. At the time the baby was expected, I was touring the Midwest, so we rented an apartment in Chicago near some good friends. I wanted June to be close to them just in case I was not there when she went into labor. We were so sure the baby was going to be a girl that we had already picked out a girl's name—Lélia, after the title of the George Sand novel. It was one of the times in my life when my ESP decidedly failed me. We also had a boy's name as a standby, and the baby was named Stefan, after the writer Stefan Zweig.

When we moved to our apartment at 525 West End Avenue in New York, I called Horowitz to give him my new address. There was complete silence. I felt shock waves transmitting over the line. Finally, he said, "No! That's the same building Rachmaninoff lived in. That's where we met for the first time." He told me an interesting story. One day, he picked up Rachmaninoff at West End Avenue and they went to the Steinway basement to play his Third Concerto. Horowitz played it through, with Rachmaninoff playing the second piano part. Afterward, Rachmaninoff said to him, "Well, it's not what I meant, but I like it anyway." Interestingly, Rachmaninoff never had the success with that concerto that Horowitz did. Perhaps a composer does not always know what's best for his own music!

My son, Stefan, is seeing me off on my way to open the U.S. Pavilion at the Brussels World's Fair in 1958.

After my Carnegie Hall debut at age twenty, Horowitz had told me, "Well, you don't have to play for me anymore." And for the next six years I didn't. One day he telephoned me. "Why don't you ever play for me?" he asked. There was that old Horowitzian paradox at work again. "Because you told me not to," I answered. It had taken me many years and great strength to finally throw off the unintended influence of such a great pianist. I finally felt I was not "Horowitz's pupil" but rather someone who had studied with him. I knew I had developed my own voice, so I thought, why not play for him?

I found the answer to that the hard way. I played my upcoming recital program at Carnegie Hall for him. All the subtle changes he offered made sense. Yes, I thought, what he suggested might perhaps sound better. Only it was *his* way, and before I could recapture *my* way, I found myself stuck somewhere in the middle. It was one of the worst concerts I had ever played. June said to me, "If you ever play for him again, I am leaving you." She was right, and I never did.

That year, 1955, friends of the Toscanini family told me about a place near Lake Como, not far from Milan, a small village called Lanzo d'Intelvi, with a beautiful view of Lake Lugano in Switzerland. We decided to rent a house there for the summer. It was a good place to work, and for recreation we'd often drive the hour and a half to visit Milan.

One day, as we were driving back home at a pretty fast clip on the autostrada, there came a downpour the likes of which I had never seen—close to zero visibility. But what happened next was the coup de grâce. The windshield wipers suddenly stopped dead. I was terrified that the next thing stopping dead would be June and me! The windshield turned into a gurgling cataract, completely obliterating my view. I was driving blind. The only thing I could do was slow down, keep moving, and pray. I couldn't see the other cars, but I knew that they at least had a slight chance of seeing me.

To be totally out of control on the autostrada is one terrifying experience, believe me. Worse yet, it was late afternoon and rush hour was at full bore. All I could do was hope nobody would hit me or vice versa. But then, after about a minute and a half of sheer terror another "auto miracle" occurred. The rain abruptly lightened a short distance from what became the most beautiful sign in the world: *Lanzo d'Intelvi a Destra* ("Lanzo d'Intelvi to the Right"). It was hard to be lucid after we made it back home. We drank a toast to the Big Man upstairs—He's quite a dramatic choreographer, but I hoped this "ballet of the cars" had had its final performance.

9

COMING TO TERMS WITH THE PARANORMAL

*"Miracles are not contrary to nature, but only
contrary to what we know about nature."*
—ST. AUGUSTINE

THE TERMS "PARAPSYCHOLOGY" or "paranormal" may be unclear
to many. With those terms being very much woven throughout this book, I thought I would like to tell the reader, who might be
curious, a little more about what they really mean—and don't mean.
Parapsychology and PSI research deal with and study events and

behavior that fall outside of the usual experiences our five senses give us. PSI phenomena refer to a variety of situations. As I want simplicity and accuracy, I have taken several definitions from the American Society for Psychical Research (ASPR), the oldest organization of its kind in the United States. For over a century, it has explored with scientific rigor the unexplained phenomenon called "the paranormal" and has delved into the implications of its meaning for our understanding of consciousness and the nature of reality itself. The ASPR has kindly given me permission to reprint its definitions here.

ESP: Extrasensory perception. Knowledge of or response to an external event or influence by non-sensory means.

Telepathy: Extrasensory awareness of another person's or animal's mental activities, thoughts, or feelings.

Precognition: Foreknowledge of or response to something that has not yet happened. This knowledge or response cannot be explained, predicted, or inferred by normal means.

Clairvoyance: Extrasensory awareness/perception of physical objects or events. In contrast to telepathy.

Automatic Writing: Writing that is not under the conscious control of the writer.

Psychic Photography: The paranormal projection of mental images on to photographic plates or film.

Psychokinesis (PK) (Teleportation): A physical change in an object or in its state or rest or motion which cannot be explained by ordinary physical processes and is therefore assumed to be due to PSI (mind over matter).

Reincarnation: A form of survival in which the mind or some aspect of it of a deceased individual is reborn in another body.

Synchronicity: A term coined by Carl Jung to indicate that an acausal principle could account for PSI occurrences, or, as he preferred to call them, "meaningful coincidences."

Healing: An ability to affect positive change in a living organism usually through non-sensory means. (The terms psychic healing and spiritual healing are sometimes used.)

Remote Viewing: Another aspect of ESP, which demonstrates the ability to obtain information, often detailed, about a distant (close or far) and unseen target without the use or help of any sensory clues or cues.

In the back of this book is a short list of relevant reading material and Web sites for those who are interested in learning more.

It's interesting to note that in polls taken of random groups of people, 50 percent or more will report having had a "psychic" experience. I wish the definition of "normal" could be broadened and deepened. Then, hopefully, our perceptions of the possibilities of normal reality would expand equally, and the word "paranormal" would happily disappear. As has been said many times, and in many different ways, our limited knowledge is the culprit.

Sadly, there is resistance by some scientists to this field even though there are "impossible" discoveries being made every day. A *New York Post* article on August 27, 2009, reported that scientists have once again been thrown a curve. The headline read, "New Planet Sends Astronomers into Orbit." They have discovered a planet that "shouldn't" exist. It is believed to be approximately one billion years old and, according to our knowledge today, it "should have been reduced to cinders ages ago." "This is a paradox," says astronomer Douglas Hamilton of the University of Maryland. It is another "impossible" challenge to our limited knowledge.

"It's fun to do the impossible," quipped Einstein. May I add it's also fun to experience the impossible, and after reading some of these stories, I hope you will agree.

There is much information out there about this field. Unfortunately, some of it is misguided and tends to be extreme. I urge anyone seriously interested to proceed with caution as to where and from whom information is received. The field needs good research and good science. It does not need overbelieving or negativity but honest inquiry and a sense of wonder at the possibilities contained within our consciousness and our relationship to the universe.

10

NOHANT

NOHANT IS A PLACE ENCHANTED by spirits very near to my heart, and I had always yearned to visit it. A seventeen-year-old girl named Aurore Dupin inherited this grand French estate from her family in 1832. Some years after becoming its mistress, Aurore Dupin became George Sand, the great female writer who gained infamy for wearing trousers, smoking cigars, and mocking all the traditional conventions of her time. In 1836, George Sand met the great young pianist and composer Frédéric Chopin at a party given by Franz Liszt and his mistress, Countess Marie d'Agoult, and after several years of a Sturm and Drang courtship, the two became lovers. Chopin spent eight summers at Nohant, and some of his greatest music was composed there.

About a century and a quarter later, in 1955, during the summer I spent in the Italian village of Lanzo d'Intelvi, I started reading André

Maurois's biography of George Sand, *Lélia*. I couldn't put it down. I had already heard and read a great deal about Nohant, but *Lélia* revealed details I'd never imagined. Given my lifelong fascination with Chopin, I immediately ached to visit that storied place, and my impatient Aries temperament made it difficult to wait even a day. June and I embarked the following morning and arrived at Nohant a day later.

The house was rather unique in that along with its simple beauty, it seemed much larger than photographs I'd seen of it. The house had been converted into a museum with an entrance fee of fifteen francs. Imagine—only three dollars to visit a place that, for me, held the most excitement of any place on earth.

As the docent escorted us through this hauntingly beautiful house, we tried to drink in all its magical history. It felt so "lived-in," it gave me the sense it hadn't changed much in a hundred years. Bottles of pills still cluttered the bathroom cabinet. The kitchen's service bells still provoked a clang in distant corridors. Each room could still ring for a servant whenever needed.

But there had been some changes, of course. There was no sign of Chopin having ever been there. The relationship with Sand had ended two years before his death as the result of a rather violent argument they'd had about her daughter, Solange, who wished to marry a gruff but talented sculptor named Clésinger. Chopin was very much against it, and Sand was strongly for it. She was irate with Chopin. How *dare* he meddle in her family affairs. The episode ended with the composer leaving the house, never to return. Sand's feelings were so intensely hostile that she went as far as to slash in half the famous portrait Delacroix had painted years earlier of the two lovers. The half depicting Chopin now hangs in the Louvre; the other, of Sand, resides in the George Sand Museum in Paris.

But perhaps this was just the trigger needed to set off a much deeper reason for the rupture. Two years into their eight-year relationship, Sand had denied Chopin any physical intimacy due to his illness. The doctor to whom she had taken him had simply advised moderation. You can imagine Chopin's resentment. He became her "little Chopin," "*mon petit fils.*"

The last thing we saw on our tour was a beautiful portrait of a beautiful woman with extraordinary eyes. I asked, "Who is the lady in this portrait?"

"Oh, that's Madame Aurore Sand, the proprietor of the house," he answered.

"Oh my goodness, of course. I hadn't remembered that," I said. "Is she still living?"

"Yes, of course. As a matter of fact, she's currently in residence."

My jaw dropped.

"Oh, please—is there any way I could possibly see her?"

"I am afraid not. Madame does not see anybody."

I thought a fistful of francs might help. "Please give her this note," I said, and I wrote in my best French, "I'm an American pianist to whom it would mean everything to have a brief moment with you."

The docent replied in a voice curdled with pessimism, "Well, all right. Please wait in the garden, and I'll present your note. Your proposition is highly doubtful."

As we waited, I pictured George Sand and her guests sitting in the garden with all that glorious music floating out to them through the open windows. Chopin playing Chopin! I tried to imagine what that would be like. I knew he'd had a piano in his room upstairs, which he used for working, and a piano in the drawing room downstairs where he'd sometimes play for guests or just for George—whom you might have to look for lying under the piano, her favorite listening place.

Shortly, a gentleman appeared and introduced himself as George Smeets, Aurore's adopted son. He said, "Madame Sand will see you for five minutes. Not a moment more." I would have been thrilled with five seconds! We went inside the house and entered the drawing room, and there was Aurore Sand—petite, gray haired, highly made up, and with the most extraordinary huge brown eyes I have ever seen. Flaubert was reported to have said when he picked the child up after her grandmother's death, "Thank God the eyes of Sand will be preserved in little Lolo [Aurore's nickname]."

The now elderly granddaughter of George Sand said to us, "Please, sit down, sit down."

*Aurore Lauth Sand, the granddaughter of George
Sand, for whom I played in Nohant, in 1955.*

We started talking, and our five minutes turned into an entire
afternoon I will never forget. She said, "Grand-maman raised me until
I was eleven years old, before she passed on." Aurore so loved and
respected her grandmother that she said she had dedicated her life to
her memory.

I asked her what she thought about Maurois's *Lélia*.

"It's a good book, but he paid much too much attention to my
grandmother's sex life, rather than to the life of the great woman and
writer that she was."

I offhandedly brought up the subject of Chopin. The outcast. I
held my breath.

"Oh, Chopin, you know he was an ingrate."

"What do you mean?" I inquired, restraining as best I could my
natural impulse to rush to his immediate defense.

"Well, you know Grand-maman did everything for him," Aurore answered. "She ran the house for him—she gave him her room upstairs, which had been her study, and even had it enlarged to accommodate his needs. She moved downstairs, where she rearranged a small room in which to do her writing. Then when he left, he never even sent a letter. Nothing. Not a word!"

She then related a fascinating story. Her grandmother had told her about a dinner party at Nohant at which the guests included the painter Delacroix, the poet Heine, the Russian writer Turgenev, and Jérôme Bonaparte, the nephew of Napoléon. Solange, Sand's daughter, was also present and seemed to be flirting with Chopin, who was sitting across the table. Solange was then sixteen or seventeen, a rather voluptuous, beautiful blond creature who had a difficult relationship with her mother, one in which jealousy was to play a major role. Her mother confronted her afterward: "Look, I saw you flirting with Chopin. If you are so mad about him, why don't you marry him?" Whereupon Solange replied, "What? Marry that sick old invalid? Why on earth would anybody want to flirt with him?!"

There was just one little piano left in the house, but it was not Chopin's. He had arranged for his own pianos to follow him shortly after his retreat from Nohant. This remaining one had been sent to George Sand by Pauline Viardot, one of the great singers of the day, after Chopin's death in 1849. She said, "Nohant should never be without a piano." Chopin and Pauline had always been very close. He was known to proclaim, "Whenever I lose my musical faculties, I call Pauline, and when she comes to me, somehow I regain them."

The one thing in that great house that didn't feel lived-in was that piano. It was enshrouded in a large silk cloth with two ropes tied around it for good measure. I felt it was treated with such care and respect, almost as though it *were* Chopin's. And then something very special and unexpected occurred. Perhaps Aurore looked at that poor neglected instrument and had a change of heart. In any event, she turned to me and asked, "Could I ask you to play something for me?"

"It would please me very much to do so," I said. I answered her very formally, as was my wont, a way of attempting to control the intensity of my emotions.

She walked over to the piano, slid off the silk drape, and waved off any help in unfastening the ropes. A little ivory oval on the wood above the keyboard identified it as an 1849 Pleyel, Chopin's favorite make of piano.

I could not describe the feeling it gave me to play in that house— not in words, only with music. Chopin's Nocturne in D-flat, which I decided to play, would hopefully give me that chance. After I finished, she waited a moment and then said, "He would have been happy." I involuntarily shuddered, something that often happens to me when

I had the unique experience of playing on Chopin's piano in Valdamossa, the monastery in Majorca where Chopin lived with George Sand for three months.

I am strongly moved. This more than moved me. Then she asked, "Would you play a piece of Liszt's for me?" I was soon to discover that she adored Liszt. (No doubt Grand-maman had regaled her with many a laudatory story about him.) His *Sonetto del Petrarca* seemed to make her very happy. She covered the piano again and tied the ropes back around it and said, "Please have some tea." And we had tea. "Artists need sugar; you must always take a lot of sugar," the mistress of the house advised at one point as she added an extra spoonful to my cup.

The surprises were not yet through for the day. Aurore told me she earned her living as a medium in Paris but was not happy with the French. "Did you see that street in Paris where Grand-maman lived, and on her house it says 'George Sand lived here'?" she asked. "Who do you think put up that plaque? I put it there, not the French government. Did you see the fire extinguisher in the house? Who do you think put that there? Not the French—me! I put that there." She was quite indignant about it all. She felt strongly that George Sand had never been given her proper due as a writer. Yet many contemporary prominent writers, including Victor Hugo, had held her grandmother in very high esteem.

Finally it was dusk, and I thought it time to leave. "We have imposed too long on your hospitality," I said, standing. Aurore's adopted son joined us in the drawing room, and the four of us walked to the front door. June and I each hugged Aurore with a strong embrace that she graciously returned. It was so hard to leave.

No more than ten seconds out the front door, June and I looked at each other, startled. We had both heard a piano playing. Surely, it would have been impossible for anyone to have undone the knotted ropes around the piano so quickly. What could it have been?

11

SOVIET UNION,
1960–1962

I SPENT THE SUMMER OF 1955 in Lanzo d'Intelvi, and my concert
tours resumed in the autumn, taking me all over the United States
and Europe. In 1958, I was chosen to represent the United States and
to open the Brussels World's Fair. Later that year, I went to Cuba to play
in Havana and Santiago, the birthplace of Fidel Castro. In Havana,
Batista's machine-gun-toting soldiers were everywhere and almost
outnumbered the music devotees at the concert there. It was even
more apparent in Santiago. It didn't take long to find out why. I was
told that Castro was in the hills above Santiago waiting to make his
move. Interestingly, everyone I spoke to was excited and eagerly
awaiting him.

Luckily, the morning after my performance, I caught an early morning flight to Havana and then continued on to New York, where I was greeted by the screaming newspaper headlines, "Castro Takes Over Santiago—Marches Toward Havana." I got out just in time.

I was the last American artist to play in Cuba before the revolution and the first classical musician to return forty years later at the invitation of the minister of culture.

Speaking of revolutions—cultural ones, that is—in 1960, I was again honored to be chosen by our government to be the first American artist to open and perform in the cultural exchange between the United States and the Soviet Union. In October 1960, I was backstage in the artist's room of the Great Hall of the Tchaikovsky Conservatory in Moscow. I was about to launch the opening salvo of the new cultural exchange with a piano recital of Mozart, Chopin, Copland, and Liszt. After the midday rehearsal, my Soviet hosts inquired whether I'd care for any backstage refreshments before the concert. My custom was to drink a cold Coca-Cola to charge me up with a jolt of caffeine and sugar if I felt I needed it. I realized, of course, that the Real Thing would be impossible to procure behind the Iron Curtain, but an impish impulse goaded me to have a little cross-cultural fun. I ever-so-politely replied, "Just a cold bottle of Coca-Cola, thank you. That's what I usually drink backstage." Honestly, I expected their collective jaws to drop at this request or at the very least to receive a lecture on the evils of brand-name capitalist beverages. But my hosts did not bat an eye. Just before my performance, I was presented with an ice-cold, sparkling bottle of Coke, unmistakable in that famous beveled hourglass bottle. I learned after the performance that they had actually sent a plane to Finland to honor my request. Now that's really hospitality!

But that's where the niceties came to a screeching halt. Moments after quaffing the miracle Coke, I stepped out onstage amid shouts of "U2! U2!" and "Cleeburn, Cleeburn" (Van Cliburn, whom the Soviet public felt they'd discovered, was now "one of them"), echoing loudly throughout the auditorium. The concert was completely sold out—at prices double those charged for their great pianist

Sviatoslav Richter. The organizers knew the public would pay extra to hear the "enemy American." (Richter, incidentally, was touring the United States just then as my cultural exchange counterpart.) All that shouting was not exactly the welcome I had dreamed of. The hostility was palpable and the atmosphere was charged. For one frozen moment, I felt the ugly shock of being utterly alone, despite the presence of our ambassador, Llewellyn Thompson, and the entire U.S. embassy staff. (The official Soviet box remained empty for this performance, as it would at every concert I gave on this tour.)

Nor was the hostility confined to the concert hall. In the street, a man rushed up to me, firing an imaginary machine gun. He must have read in the paper that my wife was English because he shouted "Englishanski, okay, Americanski, nyet," as he kept firing away at me. Of course, it was because of such international tension that the idea of a cultural exchange had come about, to help melt those arctic Soviet-American relations with nonpolitical artistic heat. But standing on the stage of the historic Great Hall that evening, I was the object of the collective Soviet outrage over the recent Gary Powers U2 spy-plane debacle. It was no fun. Where was John Foster Dulles when I needed him? I am a sensitive person to begin with, but to have what felt like an entire nation mad at me was an extremely unpleasant experience. The more I was assailed, the more difficult it was for me to handle the audience's intense reaction to my presence. I am, after all, half Russian by blood. But, I suppose, in their eyes I had nothing in common with them; I was just another hated American. I could offer them nothing.

Buffeted by those ringing insults, I walked slowly to the piano and steeled myself. I waited until the shouts died down. I waited not with anger but with this thought: "I am not your enemy. I just ask you to listen to my music, which I want to play for you without rancor but with love." They quieted down, and I was able to start playing—the Mozart Sonata in G Major, a little Schumann, Schubert, and then the Chopin *Funeral March Sonata*. Russians are a passionate people. They revere music, and I could feel their hostility melting away as they listened to beautiful music. To my great relief and delight, I received a long ovation after the Chopin sonata, the last piece before intermission.

A glowing Ambassador Thompson raced backstage and excitedly gripped my arm, "You've got them!" he exclaimed. "Thank God you've come!" Then, somewhat to my surprise, he embraced me, and I realized that he was even more on edge than I was. "I'm sick of hearing that all America can produce is cars and that the only pianist we have, they had to discover for us." The Soviets claimed that the United States had originally been cool to Van Cliburn before he won the coveted Tchaikovsky Competition that brought him international fame. Their devotion to him was, as a result, fanatical. I was more than gratified by the ambassador's excitement and returned invigorated to perform the second half of my program.

At the end of the concert, pandemonium broke loose. Audience members thronged the edge of the stage, some weeping. The cheers and applause were deafening, lasting some twenty minutes. Seeing the tears of joy and gratitude streaking down those faces that only a short time earlier had been twisted in hate, made me understand more deeply than ever the power and mystery of music. Thanks to music, I was no longer the enemy. I was a human being, just like them. I blinked back tears of my own as I heard one woman shout, "You make us love America."

That night was one of my life's greatest triumphs. I had always wanted "more than music," and here before me was a perfect example of that transcendent power. My tour of the Soviet Union appeared to be actually helping change people's minds, literally making friends of enemies. It was reported in the *New York Times* that I could consider myself "an ambassador in breaking down 'cold war barriers.'" The rest of the tour—Leningrad, Odessa, Kiev, and Minsk—followed the same pattern of helping reduce the animosity between our two countries on a very personal level. Though I have never believed that music could stop a war, I was beginning to see how it might make one a little more difficult to start.

I also spoke to students and faculty at many of the conservatories. Most had never heard an American play. They had no idea of the number of performing pianists we had or how many U.S. cities provided enthusiastic concert audiences. This information astounded

I am accepting a standing ovation in Moscow at the final concert of my 1962 tour of the Soviet Union, part of a cultural exchange between the United States and the Soviet Union.

them. Soviet propaganda had painted the United States as a nation with no interest in the arts. I ached to show them how wrong they were.

When I reached Kiev, I placed a phone call to Horowitz. Kiev is the city of his birth, where people who had known him as a young man came backstage to tell me all sorts of stories about him. One had been his tuner, another went to the conservatory with him, still another was a good friend of his sister's who lived in Kharkov. After a dramatic delay, the transatlantic call went through. "Volodya, this is Byron," I exclaimed. In reply I heard only static. Had the call been lost? It had been so long since I'd spoken to my great mentor. Did he refuse now to speak to me? My heart was racing. And then came the surprised retort, "From where you calls?" "I'm calling you from Kiev," I said. There was another long silent pause. "From Kiev you calls me, from

I thank the audience in Kiev on my 1960 tour of the Soviet Union.

New York you doesn't!" It was a remark so indicative of Horowitzian humor that in an instant I realized how much I missed him.

Something quite special occurred after my performance in Minsk. My mother was born in the small village of Chedrin (now a big industrial city) not far from Minsk. As I left the auditorium, there was a line of many people standing outside applauding and shouting, "Give our love to your mother." I don't know how they knew, but it touched me deeply.

Then there was the Odessa concert and the mystery woman. When I walked into my dressing room, I found a very attractive woman, about forty, wearing a long black dress, standing in front of the mirror primping and rehearsing something in Russian. I thought there might be a theater connected to the concert hall, but no. I had dressed before arriving, so I didn't need privacy, and, not knowing who she was, thought it would be rude to ask her to leave. When I returned at intermission, she was gone. I assumed it was to be yet another of those mysteries in my life that would never be solved. But after the concert, she reappeared, this time accompanied by a gentleman. As the applause continued, he came over to ask me what my encore would be. Meanwhile, the mystery woman was back at her primping. He then went over and said something to her in Russian. As I started to walk onstage, the gentleman stopped me, "A moment, please." The mystery woman regally swept past me, waltzed out to center stage, and intoned, "Nocturno, Chopin." Then she walked off. The mystery was solved. She was the auditorium's *official encore announcer*! I don't think they could ever have found a more dedicated one.

The Soviets sent me a telegram asking me if I would return in May and June 1962 for a three-concerto evening honoring the winners of the Tchaikovsky Competition, to be followed by a seven-week tour of the Soviet Union. Even though I knew they would pack my schedule with more concerts than I ideally wanted to play, I so loved the Russian public that I simply couldn't say no. Music is such a natural part of the Slavic heritage that even the Russians with little exposure to classical repertoire were tuned in somewhere deep in their hearts.

My first concert was with the Moscow Philharmonic Orchestra, led by one of the Soviet Union's great conductors, Kirill Kondrashin. As an accompanist, I put him on a par with Eugene Ormandy, the legendary conductor of the Philadelphia Orchestra, who was at the top of my list. This time the audience greeted me with great warmth and excitement; Gary Powers and his spy plane were no longer part of my entourage. The elite of the Russian music world were in attendance, including Madame Sergei Prokofiev, pianist Emil Gilels, and Vladimir Ashkenazy, who had himself just won the Tchaikovsky prize. Also in attendance were a decidedly different kind of elite from the Soviet espionage world—Guy Burgess and Donald Maclean, the famed British diplomats who had defected to the Soviet Union in 1951, causing an international furor.

After the Rachmaninoff First Piano Concerto, the cheering began. There was even more cheering after the Schumann A Minor Concerto. But it was hard to believe that the audience was only warming up. After the Schumann, I went backstage and munched on a Hershey's chocolate bar (chocolate also did the trick; no need for plane trips to Finland!) for some quick energy. I would need it for what lay ahead—the Prokofiev Third. If you play its many virtuoso passages with that nervous energy Horowitz spoke of, they will never sound fast and mechanical (and boring). You should be utterly spent when you finish, and I was. Not that playing the two concertos earlier helped any! The audience began to applaud and shout, surging toward the stage even before I struck the last notes. After a while, they shifted to that slow, rhythmic clapping that conveys their highest praise and tells you they have no intention of going home.

After twenty minutes of this, Kondrashin said to me, "They will never leave. You have to play an encore."

"An encore?" I said. "After three concertos? You must be joking!"

"Let's do the last movement of the Tchaikovsky," he suggested.

I hoped I was hearing things, as every muscle in my body ached.

Before I could protest further, he had already dispatched someone to the library to get the orchestral score, and before I knew what was happening, the last movement of the concerto had been distributed to the orchestra. He turned to me: "What's your tempo?"

I took a couple of deep breaths and gave him my tempo, the audience sat back down, and off we went. The twenty minutes of "rest" I'd gotten during the last ovation was a blessing and replenished my reservoir of energy. Somehow I still had enough of that energy needed to play the Tchaikovsky finale. Well, after that, the applause never ended. At least, I never heard it end because I raced back to my dressing room to collapse on the sofa with the thunderous acclamation still ringing in my ears.

The electrifying response from that Moscow audience was something I'd never experienced anywhere before. It was a beautiful feeling, starting with excitement, turning into love, and ending with utter exhaustion. My body language said, "I love you, but please, I'm tired, please let me go . . . thank you, thank you!" Only when the lights were turned out did the audience finally accept that there'd be no further encores.

Only Kondrashin, Gilels, Ashkenazy, Mrs. Prokofiev, Ambassador Thompson, and a few reporters were allowed into my dressing room afterward. I was so gratified by their comments (at least the ones I understood), which spilled spontaneously from those crowded around me. *Time, Newsweek*, and the *New York Times*, along with a few Russian reporters, were also on hand, asking for any statements.

I was traveling with Peter Gravina, my personal representative and press agent, as well as the Mercury records team of Wilma Cozart, Robert Fine, and Harold Lawrence. Alone among the big American record companies, Mercury had somehow managed to work out an agreement with the Russians, making their label the first one to record in the Soviet Union.

The trip was not, however, without controversy and intrigue. After seemingly being embraced by the entire nation, the Soviet people's hero, Van Cliburn, unexpectedly arrived in Moscow, apparently having made his own concert arrangements with Anatole Mikoyan, the Soviet foreign minister. Sol Hurok, who represented us both, happened to be there at the same time and was startled because he knew

Cliburn was scheduled to be concertizing in Europe at that time. The American press tried to get me to comment on this awkward and highly unusual situation. What could I say? "No comment."

But it didn't end there. I was supposed to record with Kondrashin in the Great Hall of the Tchaikovsky Conservatory. It had taken a lot of persistence on Mercury's part to arrange for me to make three recordings in the Great Hall, but the byzantine workings of the Kremlin had not yet played their last card. An unctuous Mr. Belotserkovney of the Ministry of Culture informed me that my last concert in Moscow was to be moved from the Great Hall to what I knew was the inferior and acoustically dry-sounding Tchaikovsky Hall. He deeply regretted to inform me that, sadly, Cliburn would be performing in the Great Hall with Kondrashin that very same night. It was, unfortunately, he said, a simple mis-understanding. He was certain I would understand, and he confided sotto voce that Tchaikovsky Hall was the crown jewel of Moscow's concert auditoriums (which it certainly wasn't). It took me not a moment to reply that I would not accept the crown jewel, thank you all the same. As the pleasantries and politesse grew grimmer and more strident, Mr. Belotserkovney called Kondrashin to apprise him of the delicate situation. A short time later, a gentleman approached me: "Mr. Janis, there is a phone call for you." It was Kondrashin. "Janis, the recordings are in jeopardy. You must play in Tchaikovsky Hall or there will be no recordings," he said and hung up. I was now in a cloak-and-dagger film, with our historical recordings—my recordings—the intended victims. Finally, I told Mr. Belotserkovney how much I appreciated the chance to discuss this opportunity with him and that I'd like another day to think it over.

I knew I was not going to accept the inferior hall, and we all (the Mercury people included) decided to turn the Russians' tactics back on them by throwing a big vodka and caviar party of our own. I had my two lovely allies, June and Svetlana, our very attractive interpreter, each sit on one of Mr. Belotserkovney's knees as he quaffed huge quantities of vodka. When the alcohol level seemed right, I blithely told him I intended to cancel the concert.

"Janis, my dear Janis, everybody in Moscow loves you. You cannot disappoint them," the somewhat inebriated minister protested.

"My dear Mr. Belotserkovney, I'm afraid I can and I will," I retorted.

The two girls kept working their diplomatic magic, and finally, after a few more shots of 80 proof, an agreement was carved out. I would play an extra concert in the Great Hall in Moscow as my farewell and I would still play the concert in the other hall as scheduled, but I would be allowed to make my recordings in the Great Hall. Thankfully, the recordings were now ensured, but as Cliburn was performing at the Great Hall that night, we couldn't start recording there until midnight—and that after my having played a full-length recital with five encores at Tchaikovsky Hall. Moreover, as Kondrashin had to leave in two days for South America, it was imperative to get started as soon as possible so we could complete at least two of the concertos scheduled to be recorded with him.

Mercury's unique sound truck was parked in front of the Conservatory. It was an incredible sight—huge cables snaking right across the lawn, up the windows, and into the building. When it was time to begin, the engineers plugged a cable into the auditorium's outlet. There was a loud click, and out went the power. The Soviet circuitry couldn't handle it; the Mercury sound truck had knocked out the auditorium's entire power grid. "Oh no, no, no!" I thought in horror. "Does that mean we can't record? My God, after all that . . . it can't be!" We all fell silent.

Then, Bob Fine, one of the greatest recording engineers ever, had an idea. Though it seemed pretty far-fetched to us, he asked for several lightbulbs—for what conceivable purpose none of us laymen could fathom. He attached one to the cable going into the hall and turned on the power. There was a huge click, and out went the power again. He tried the same thing with two bulbs. Same result. Then he tried three—by God, it worked! The power stayed on. The three little lightbulbs siphoned off just enough electricity so the power could hold. It was amazing. We could record!

Prokofiev wrote a famous little piece called "The Love for Three Oranges." After my exasperating experiences with the recording in the Great Hall, I decided I should write one called "The Love for Three Lightbulbs!"

Despite all the excitement, terror, and aggravation, I liked the way I felt—I was tired but not depleted, relaxed but not too relaxed, and had energy enough to play with nerve and without tension. Fortunately, the lightbulbs didn't take any power away from me! We finished recording the first two movements of Prokofiev's Third Piano Concerto around 3 a.m. Of course, there was no food available at that hour, but the peanut butter and jelly sandwiches Wilma had brought along tasted better than caviar. The cleaning people and other hall workers wouldn't go home. They stood out by the sound truck, listening to the playbacks until we finished recording. You couldn't find a better audience than that!

The following morning we dove again into the Prokofiev and devoted the rest of the day and evening to the Rachmaninoff First and one of the Liszt concertos, racing against the clock to finish before Kondrashin had to leave for South America. The next day, with Kondrashin in Rio, I recorded the other Liszt concerto with another leading Russian conductor, Gennady Rozhdestvensky, and continued with the third recording of *Piano Encores*. Three LPs in three days! Our recording marathon must have been a record in itself. We were all thrilled when the Prokofiev/Rachmaninoff became a best seller and then won the prestigious French Grand Prix du Disque award as the best record of the year.

There was one amusing coda to this story. Wilma gave the finished Prokofiev tape to an Associated Press correspondent returning to New York so studio work could commence immediately. At the airport, the Soviet customs people spotted it in his luggage and were understandably suspicious. "What's this?" one agent challenged. The correspondent answered, "That's the Prokofiev Third Piano Concerto." The man hesitated for a moment, looking him in the eye, and then, incredibly, simply said, "Da." ("Okay.") And off to New York it went.

Meanwhile, we were off to tour the provinces for seven weeks. And what a time we had. The audiences in Georgia and Armenia fascinated and gratified me the most. At one outdoor concert, some of the young people in the overflow audience were sitting up in the trees. It was the first time I had literally been showered with flowers. Without a doubt, the Georgian custom of rhythmic applause has no competition; they are surely the leading virtuosos in the field. It has the sound a freight train would probably make if it were going a hundred miles an hour. But the greatest reward, personally, was the critic who called the recital "a precious contribution to furthering Soviet-American friendship."

In Armenia, men would crowd to the apron of the stage and kiss my hand. I had also never seen that before. In Yerevan, the capital, the service at mealtimes was extraordinary. The 21 Club in New York might have had difficulty competing. No wonder, as it turns out that Yerevan was the number one training ground for all waiters in the Soviet Union. The caviar, fresh from the Caspian Sea, was unparalleled. We ate it virtually straight from the sturgeon's belly, and then they served us the charcoal-broiled flesh. God, it was good.

Armenia had its own pope, Vasken II. The Armenian patriarch was evidently very musical but never ventured into Yerevan because he was virulently anticommunist. When I was offered an audience with him I accepted with alacrity. The conductor of the Yerevan orchestra drove us over an incredible high mountain road to the monastery. He told me Pushkin had been exiled in that region. When we passed a little church on the right, someone said, "That's where Christianity started." According to them, Christ had visited there.

Not that there wasn't a price to be paid for all this high living. The variety of Russian foods, coupled with my very tight schedule, suddenly began to wreak havoc on my stomach. Unfortunately, this occurred just before my audience with the Armenian patriarch. I whispered to one of my hosts, "I must use the bathroom immediately." He in turn appealed to the pope's assistant, who replied, "Well, we don't have a bathroom as such. There is a facility behind the pope's room that you can use." However, to reach it I had to pass through his room. It was a most embarrassing moment for me, but I had no choice. He was having an audience with someone and happily ignored me as I scooted past. The facility was nothing more than a hole in the ground, but nothing I hadn't seen before. I had to pass through the pope's chamber again and, moments later, returned with June for our own audience. What a very charming man he was, with a warm expressive face and a long beard, and I couldn't help wondering what those twenty-five or thirty keys hanging from his belt were for. We had a wonderful conversation about music. His face took on a special glow as he told me his favorite symphonies were the Ninth of Beethoven and the *Pathétique* of Tchaikovsky. When it was time to leave, he gave flowers to June and a photo to me. Leaving the chamber, I turned the photo over to read, "Gregarian, Hollywood, California." We laughed.

Peter Gravina had been to the Soviet Union before, traveling with the American soprano Dorothy Kirsten. He had taken snapshots of the beautiful old section of Tiblisi, the Georgian capitol, not realizing that photography by Westerners was strictly forbidden. This time the authorities kept him under a watchful eye. After downing a few vodkas, Svetlana, our interpreter, confided, "Be careful. We already have bad information on you from your first trip." In one city on our itinerary, Peter was assigned such a terrible room that June asked them to change it. When we returned sooner than expected from sightseeing, we bumped into two men stumbling out of Peter's old room draped in audiotape trailing like spaghetti behind them. I'm afraid Peter's change of room played havoc with the state's own recordings.

Back in Moscow, we asked Bob Fine to see if there were any bugs in our rooms. He found one in the telephone and another in the chandelier. There was one unexpected boon to all of this. We no longer bothered telephoning room service. I'd just shout, "We need more toast tomorrow morning," and there it would be.

In Leningrad, I received a note in English from a group of students who had pushed their way to the stage front. It was this kind of deeply moving popular response that kept me going on a tour that was physically, emotionally, and, on occasion, politically draining. "We can't find words to express our feelings; our admiration and words are helpless in this case. We follow you from Yerevan to prolong the highest and unrepeatable enjoyment. You are absolutely extraordinary and remarkable phenomenon for us. You gave us the greatest and biggest a man can transmit to a man." It brought tears to my eyes.

It might not have been so bad if the Russians had been the only ones giving me problems. When I was asked to inaugurate the cultural exchange, I brought with me the expected classical repertoire, but I also intended to smuggle a little of what the Soviets considered to be contraband into my performances, in the form of an American composer I passionately wished to share with my hosts. My farewell concert in the Soviet Union was to be with Benny Goodman in the first performance there of Gershwin's *Rhapsody in Blue*. The Sports Palace in Leningrad, with twelve thousand people in attendance, was the scheduled venue. My Soviet hosts were appalled when they learned of the inclusion of this composer non grata and did everything they could to stop me. They considered Gershwin to be an inferior composer. How could an artist of my stature play such music? It seems Prokofiev himself had graced the same stage playing an American jazz composition and hardly escaped the wrath of the government for doing so. I, of course, had no intention of changing my program, and I eventually won out. I think they privately feared this famous modern piece by an American might just be too successful.

The other problem was that Benny Goodman was an incredible clarinetist but not the greatest conductor, which made the rehearsal a stop-and-go affair. I was really worried. Teddy Wilson, the great jazz pianist and a member of Goodman's famed trio, was aware of my concerns and confided to me, "Don't worry, Byron, we'll keep looking at you. We'll pull this off."

The concert certainly was a gala affair. The band wore bright red jackets and fired up the teeming crowd in no time. After taking a large swig of what I am pretty sure was vodka, Benny strolled onstage. But instead of standing next to me as we had rehearsed, he went to the other side of the piano. I couldn't even see him, as the lid of the piano obscured my vision. But by standing there he was certainly more visible to the audience. I was furious. "I can't see you," I called out before we started, but he ignored me. The King of Swing charged

Benny Goodman and I are rehearsing Gershwin's Rhapsody in Blue *for its debut in the Soviet Union in 1962.*

into that opening glissando to Gershwin's jazz masterpiece even as I protested. Fortunately, with the support of his great band and a little help from the powers above, we pulled the music together, and somehow our debut was a hit.

I returned to Moscow to give that much negotiated extra recital. I knew it would be exhausting, but I did not want to leave Moscow with the taste of that dry-sounding hall in my (as well as the public's) ears. By contrast, the Great Hall has just about the best sound for music anywhere, and it was worth the effort.

At last the day of my planned departure back to the Riviera for a much-needed rest was approaching. However, the day before my flight, a telegram arrived from La Scala that said, "Would you be available in five days to play a concert that was canceled by Van Cliburn?"

He was still performing in the Soviet Union. I needed to think about it because La Scala is not a lady whose invitation one turns down easily. As weary and homesick as I was, I decided to accept. Happily, it went very well.

During my whole trip to the Soviet Union I felt at times like I was moving through a dream—it was sometimes fantastic, other times horrifying, but always a little unreal. And if I'd known what troubles were around the bend when I returned home, I would have savored the experience all the more.

Within the next few months after my return home, I began to experience serious problems with my right shoulder. Doctors informed me it was bursitis. I have always wondered if the super-human schedule I was forced to meet to record in the Great Hall and the extra concert I had to play in the bargain had something to do with my affliction. Dr. Charles Christian, one of the leading rheuma-tologists in the country, who treated me for many years, told me that bursitis was usually a precursor of arthritis. Time would unfortunately prove him to be right.

12

A RIVIERA DREAMSCAPE

THE SOUTH OF FRANCE has always captivated me, as has the Mediterranean Sea. The lure of its Odyssean Siren remains undiminished after many centuries. When I needed a home base for my 1962 summer concerts at the various music festivals in Europe, it was to the resplendent Riviera that I turned my longing gaze. Nor was it long before I fell in love with Villa St. Sophie, situated on the Moyenne Corniche, halfway up the mountain and overlooking the picturesque village of Villefranche and the splendid Cap Ferrat. For the next three years, this magical abode, this nurturing place, was to be my family's idyllic summer retreat.

As I would be traveling quite a bit, I wanted foremost an atmosphere that June and our son, Stefan, would enjoy in my absence, and this was it. When you strolled out onto one of Villa St. Sophie's terraces at night, it was as though you were on the deck of a snug ship with nothing between you and that glorious expanse of sea.

Each of the villa's three levels spilled out onto its own terrace. How differently you saw the same view from each promontory—same night, same house, same viewer, but each level gave a different perspective. Those architectural outcroppings stimulated my thinking about the importance of different perspectives in life and art. Your perception of a painting can be strongly influenced by the distance you stand from it, just as your perception of a concert can be affected by the seat you're in. At a play, you can watch a vastly different scene unfold depending on your sight line. Some theatergoers see things others can't see, and everyone sees everything from a slightly different angle. And your perception of life? If "all the world's a stage," then your choice of seating in life's pageant can make a profound difference. Unless you try to look at life from different perspectives, you may never see much beyond the back of the head of the person in front of you. Too many people hold onto the same subscription seats decade after decade, thinking they are protecting their turf, but in reality, they are losing the chance to see life from all sides.

Villa St. Sophie's greatest gift was the precious time it allowed me to spend with Stefan and his fertile seven-year-old mind, which saw everything as new and wonderful. We might better enhance our own lives by paying attention to the awareness of children and their capacity to live creatively. All of the great artists I have known have possessed this childlike quality of infinite wonder. It is a wonder that never wearily condescends to say, "Oh, I've seen that before."

Once while in London dining with Osbert Sitwell, of the renowned Bloomsbury family, we were discussing the derivations of words. He challenged me to define the original meaning of "sophisticated." "It meant spoiled in Chaucerian English," he explained. "You would say I don't want to eat that fruit because it's 'too sophisticated.'" The only defense against sophistication is learning to remain fresh. A sophisticated person to me is usually a spoiled person—one who has lost that inner child. I learned so much from my son during the time we stayed at Villa St. Sophie. Seeing the world through his eyes was the greatest shift in perspective of all.

Another great appeal of the house was that it came with its own staff—a cook (who claimed she'd posed for Renoir) and a maid (who couldn't have). In the past, June had complained that her problems would be solved if she only had help at home. Sadly, the help didn't seem to help her level of happiness—or, rather, unhappiness—to any observable degree. It seemed that there were deeper forces at work. I believed her emotional upset mostly stemmed from her difficult childhood. But perhaps it was quite simply her basic unhappiness in our marriage. "If only" is usually a prescription for misery; when the essential condition is supplied, it often doesn't take long before another "if only" takes its place.

In 1962, after finishing my tour in Russia and the concert at La Scala, I raced back to the Villa St. Sophie, which was as beautiful as I remembered it. As I knew a good rest would be needed after my tour, I planned to perform a minimum of summer engagements. I just wanted to luxuriate in the beauty nature had lavished on that part of the world.

Though the La Scala concert had drained me further, it brought with it at least one unexpected dividend. Not long after I arrived at the villa, there was a knock on the door, and out on my doorstep I found a man in a chauffeur's uniform. "Good afternoon. I represent Alfa Romeo," he said, tipping his cap. "Our president attended your concert at La Scala, and he wishes you to have this car for the summer." I couldn't have been more surprised by this extraordinary gesture. I had already shifted my gaze from the chauffeur to the beautiful black Alfa Romeo still purring in our driveway. What a perfect gift for racing around the Côte d'Azur. Despite Chotzi's long-ago admonition, I still loved driving fast almost as much as playing fast when it was needed. Honestly, I think the two activities are one and the same. If a concert pianist has the ability to be a daredevil, he will take the chance and attack the awesome g-force curves of the perpetual octaves in Liszt's Sixth Hungarian Rhapsody with lightning speed just as a Le Mans competitor must open the throttle all the way to have a chance at winning.

I spent the rest of that first summer at Villa St. Sophie recuperating from the Soviet tour by musically immersing myself in new repertoire and absorbing the inspiring beauty around me. The following year, 1963, was dedicated not only to work but to having more fun à la Riviera. Rebecca Hamilton, an old friend from my early days in New York, now lived in Paris, and she introduced June and me to Rosita and Norman Winston. The Winstons owned a most beautiful home on Cap Ferrat, that exquisite tract of land jutting out from the Riviera mainland, and were known for hosting some of the best parties on the coast. Their houseguests and friends were not only top jet-setters but interesting people from every walk of life. Rosita was everything you could ask for in a hostess—intelligent, amusing, and straightforward. She often proudly invoked her Cherokee Indian heritage. One night in response to a snobbish guest hautily boasting about her Mayflower ancestors, Rosita shot back, "Well, mine were there to greet ya, honey!" Norman, though no match for Rosita's effervescence, held his own by being a brilliant real estate tycoon and a most generous philanthropist.

Rosita invited us to a luncheon given in honor of Elsa Maxwell, a preeminent international party hostess based in New York, whose society column was the most widely followed of its kind. Rosita informed her I'd just returned from a benefit concert for the victims of the terrible earthquake in Skopje, Yugoslavia, and Elsa was keen to know about my experience. She was a great opera fan and a close friend of the two greatest singers of the day, Maria Callas and Renata Tebaldi. Before leaving, she asked if June and I were free to attend a small dinner party she was throwing at Monte Carlo's beautiful Hôtel de Paris the following Sunday. We accepted with pleasure. In any case, I accepted with pleasure. At that time most distractions appealed to me simply as an escape from my increasingly unhappy marriage.

June and I arrived at the party just as our hostess was making introductions. Elsa grabbed my arm and guided me to a strikingly beautiful lady, "Byron Janis, meet Miss Greta Garbo." Now, *there* was a distraction. I found Great Garbo to be even more beautiful in person than on the screen. Dear Elsa then became even Dearer Elsa as she escorted me to the best seat in the house, the one next to "Miss G." I was too awestruck to even attempt "sophistication." I did manage to speak to her somewhat intelligibly about her films. I told her how she was so great in *Ninotchka* that it was the only movie that I had ever seen twice. She was delighted. She steered the conversation to music, telling me how much she adored Chopin.

At one point, Elsa asked the question I knew was coming. "Oh, Byron, won't you please play a little something for us?" For once I didn't hesitate to comply. A white grand piano was rolled onto the terrace. It was a romantic setting I'm sure even Darryl Zanuck could not have improved upon. I stole a look at my screen-goddess dinner companion, and our eyes met; I wanted her to know I was playing the Chopin for her. When I returned to the dinner table, she turned to face me with a deeply penetrating look. She clasped my hands, broke into a most Garbo-esque smile, and whispered, "If I were ten years younger, I wouldn't ask you where, I wouldn't ask you how, I would just ask you when." I was stunned, but without missing a beat I answered, "Do you really think in moments like this age means anything?"

She just smiled that famous enigmatic smile. A few weeks later we met again on the Riviera. She told me the film role she coveted most was to portray George Sand, that famous writer and political agitator—and Chopin's lover. I was more than intrigued. I said to her, "I am sure Chopin would have loved it if only she had been as beautiful as you." She really laughed at that. She was such fun to be with, and it was wonderful to continue our conversations back in New York.

I met Maria Callas first through our good friends Baron and Baroness von Zuylen, with whom we often stayed when I played in Deauville. How surprised I was when she appeared at my concert in France at the Festival of Menton, just across the border from Monte Carlo. She was staying at the palace in Monaco and came to the concert with Princess Grace, and my heart skipped a beat when the princess told me that Callas had flown in expressly to hear me play.

Maria Callas and I next met at dinner in New York as guests of Senator Jacob Javits and his wife, Marion, at Luchow's, that famous

Princess Grace of Monaco (left), Maria Callas (right), and Eunice Kennedy Shriver (background) greeted me during the intermission of my 1969 concert in Menton in the south of France.

German restaurant on 14th Street. The only other people present at our table were my wife and Aristotle Onassis. Callas and I got along famously, talking, artist to artist, passion to passion, and Onassis became more and more annoyed by our artistic liaison. Eventually, shouting broke out between them. "Why are you doing this?" she snapped. "I have a right to speak with anyone the way I want to." But he grabbed her arm and pulled her away out to the waiting limousine. I found I liked her so very much, both as a person and as an artist. She had a passion and a charismatic stage presence that was unequaled. Indeed she was the greatest singer-actress of them all.

13

ADIEU À LA BELLE FRANCE

ONE EVENING, JUNE and I drove down to Villefranche with some visiting American friends. The port had quite a honky-tonk environment back then. Sailors behaved there as they usually do on shore leave, and the crew of the USS *Springfield,* temporarily stationed in the harbor, was no exception. Music from the jukeboxes in every bar and bistro was blaring out onto the street, providing the perfect accompaniment for their rowdy merry-making. As we all piled out of my car, we were in such high spirits that we started singing, too. It was just good fun until an angry little man raced over to us and commanded, in French, "Make less noise!"

At first, I was merely puzzled. Who was this man? If he was a policeman, he certainly was not in uniform. "Make less noise?" I said. "It's the jukeboxes that are making the noise." Studying him a bit closer I could sense his mounting resentment of my racy red Lancia and our affluent manner of dress. Suddenly he hollered, "Arrest them!" Instantly, the street seemed filled with angry bullies, the little man's cohorts. June, walking in front of me, was grabbed with such force by one of them that she lost a shoe and her handbag. I tried to protect her, but another man grabbed my left arm and wrenched it behind my back. It was all I could do not to scream in pain. "Please," I pleaded, "don't hurt my arm. I am a pianist." But he simply twisted it even harder. Now I was really frightened. I realized that these monsters were capable of doing anything to us. They were true thugs.

Our visiting American so-called friends, much to my surprise, chose not to get involved and just kept walking. The men loaded June and me into a police van. By now I was shaking with both fear and rage. June, of course, was also in a fury. When street thugs are in charge of police vans, society has completely disintegrated. As angry as I was, I felt sad about France, a nation that until that moment I had respected as well as loved. How could I generalize about a country as a result of one specific incident? But I felt France was changing.

These men turned out to be Compagnies Républicaines de Sécurité, or the CRS, and were not standard police officers. They were soldiers who'd been fighting in Algeria against the local uprising, where some of them reportedly committed acts of great cruelty. If one wishes to see how a nation can sink into the pit of "necessary" torture and lose its soul in the process, one need look no further than the French experience in North Africa during the 1950s. When the Algerian War ended in 1962, de Gaulle didn't know what to do with these brutes, so he imported them to France and deployed them as an adjunct paramilitary police force. But they weren't policemen, they were trained killers. The angry little man, though out of uniform, was clearly CRS.

But they were soon to learn that they'd bitten off a bit more than they could chew. One of them must have been told who I was, because they now gathered around the back of the van, shouting, "Get out! Get out!"

June said, "We're not getting out. Take us to the police headquarters in Nice."

As he brandished his machine gun, one of them threatened, "If you don't get out, I promise you a ride that you're never going to forget."

Though I confess I was relishing the sudden turn of events, I didn't think we should press our luck any further. "June, get out," I said. "We must exit here *right now*."

She was all for sticking it out and seeing their comeuppance in Nice, assuming France's court system had not completely disintegrated along with its national police. Yes, I thought, if we ever make it alive to Nice. At last, I got her to leave the van. A man I'd never seen before hurried over to us, saying, "Ah, this was a stupid thing that happened. Come, and we'll have some champagne and forget it."

"We most certainly are not going to forget it," I said. "My arm has been badly hurt."

He could see I was serious, and he became almost as enraged as his cronies had earlier that his cheap blandishments had not succeeded. I suppose he was connected to the police in some fashion, hoping to buy us off.

My shoulder was so sore I couldn't play for several days, nor could I play at the upcoming festival at the royal palace in Monte Carlo. After I regretfully canceled my scheduled appearance, Prince Rainier sent me a lovely telegram of commiseration, saying, "Now you can see why we have such trouble dealing with the French." I heard he sent them a fiery letter of protest.

I remained deeply upset by the incident and vowed never to return to France. You can imagine what that decision meant to me. France had been more than a source of great personal inspiration; Chopin and so many other great artists had lived and worked there. And it was for me one of the most satisfying places on earth to perform. Since my first concert in Paris, we had had a mutual love affair. I could not, however, let this outrage pass, and June understood my feelings.

I called René de Chambrun, a renowned international lawyer who'd represented me before. As a direct descendent of Lafayette, René enjoyed the family privilege of automatic dual French and American citizenship. "Just sit tight," he told me. "I will call [American ambassador] Chip Bohlen." A short time later our maid dashed excitedly into the room crying, "*C'est la Maison Blanche!*"

Pierre Salinger, President Kennedy's press secretary, was on the phone. "Byron, what's happening?" he inquired. So I told him, getting hotter by the second as I recounted the events of that night. "Well," the ever-politic Salinger counseled, "just let René and Chip Bohlen handle this." All my initial fury had returned, and I exclaimed, "This was an outrage! I'm never coming back here."

The diplomatic intervention succeeded! I received a letter of apology from the normally vitriolic Roger Frey—de Gaulle's minister of the interior—saying, "A man of your talent should not have such an experience. It is something to be regretted. You know how you are loved in France," and so on. I was told this was an unprecedented action on his part.

Newspapers in both France and the United States had strongly played up the story. Stymied, the CRS must have hired its own public relations people, because soon afterward articles began to appear describing all the wonderful, noble things the CRS had done—rescuing people from mountaintops and other daring deeds. Incidentally, the "angry little man" was apparently never again seen in Villefranche. I also took a long time before wanting to see those "walk-away acquaintances" again.

Political revenge was sweet, but the pain in my shoulder in fact persisted and increased to the point where I had to take the painkilling drug butazolidin in order to practice or play. Having that arm and shoulder nearly dislocated by the CRS was yet another excruciating link in a lifelong chain of events that might have ended my career. My understanding of the biblical character Job grew by the day.

14

MEETING
MARIA

THE FOLLOWING YEAR, the Villa saw me through some of the happiest and some of the saddest moments of my life. My marriage to June was disintegrating, and my life was in turmoil. I felt in desperate need of a friend to talk to. It so happened that my close friend Boris Chaliapin, the superb painter and son of the great basso Fyodor Chaliapin, was in Paris at the time. Boris and I first became acquainted after Steinway commissioned him to paint my portrait.

I managed to track him down and immediately placed an SOS call: "Could you possibly come down to Villefranche to visit? My marriage is breaking up, Boris—I am truly in bad shape." Noble friend that he was, he flew down the next day. I loved Boris dearly.

He was one of the sweetest and most complicated people I've ever known. Through our years of friendship, the Smirnoff always flowed freely chez Chaliapin, and he was such an expert in drinking vodka, I decided to make him my personal vodka-drinking instructor. On the rare occasions when I'd down a shot—or two—*zakuski*, Russian hors d'oeuvres, came to the rescue. That was my first lesson: straight shots of vodka without *zakuski* can be lethal.

The first night of his visit we sat on the terrace of my house and hashed out the whole drama of human existence, and his spirited company gave me a real boost. I ignored my usual two-drink limit, and mercifully the *zakuski* worked their magic.

A few nights later, we were invited to a dinner given for Rocky, the widow of Gary Cooper, and her new husband, the renowned plastic surgeon Dr. John Converse. There was one added inducement to this evening's invitation: accompanying them would be Rocky's daughter, Maria. The photograph of Maria I'd seen in the local paper showed how beautiful she was, and her interview intrigued me even more.

In the early summer dusk, the air saturated with scents of the sea and orange blossoms, June, Boris, and I arrived at the party. I recall strolling out onto the long terrace, where an enormous grape arbor flourished. It was so lush it formed a dense canopy framing a view of the sailboats dotting the harbor far below. From the end of the terrace I watched the sunset surrender to a full moon that covered the sea in silvery iridescent light. It would have been impossible to arrange a more romantic setting. "What a waste," I thought, "for a man in the throes of imminent divorce."

Rosita introduced us all with her usual exuberance, and soon we met the bride and groom. A tall, slim girl with her right arm in a cast stood talking to another guest. I failed to recognize her at first because her hair was piled atop her head. "Maria," Rosita said, "I'd like you to meet Byron Janis." She turned around. She was even more beautiful than the photos of her in the newspaper. I don't remember any of the other words, though there must have been some, but all I remember to this day is that as we shook hands (as much as her cast permitted) and our eyes met. I have never reacted to anyone so quickly, so intensely. Time was erased. There was only recognition; there was knowing; there was love, strength. I felt sure I had known her in another time. I felt a "yes" to something that had not yet even been thought, much less uttered. It seemed a lifetime was encompassed in that moment. She later showed me her journal entry for that day, and her feelings had exactly mirrored mine. But there was a postscript: "Damn! He's married!" She couldn't have known my marriage was all but over.

Guests kept arriving, introductions came and went. Fate and my hostess obliged, and I was seated next to Maria at dinner. We spoke of many different subjects, none having to do with music, which actually pleased me. Maria later confided that she was a nervous wreck because the world of classical music was foreign territory to her, and to conceal her lack of familiarity she'd kept up a running commentary on just about everything else. She appeared to be totally unspoiled. It was most surprising, given her Hollywood royalty background.

Somewhere in the middle of dessert, my left cuff link leapt—there is no other way to describe its arc—out of its cuff and nearly disappeared into the soufflé. Although I think I know why this happened—at that moment every atom of my being was aching to inch closer to my charming dinner companion, but I still don't comprehend how it could have happened. I was totally baffled. The clasp of those particular cuff links required force and finesse to insert and remove. It simply couldn't have "de-linked" itself. It had never happened before, and it has never happened since.

I would rather have been asked to play the most demanding work of music that very moment than try to reinsert that soufflé-filled cuff link while sitting next to a woman I wanted to impress with my savoir faire. Damn that PK. Why did it choose this moment to play games? While I realized it was helping me get to know Maria a little better, I wish it had taken a slightly more dignified approach. Happily, my dinner partner took pity on my predicament and, with her good hand, restored it to its proper place. Our eyes met again for the second time that night, and the pitch darkness I'd been stumbling through for so long was effortlessly deflected by the light in her eyes. For the first time in a very long time, I felt a very strange sensation— I felt hope.

The next day, I called as early as propriety would permit to invite the Winstons and the Converses and Maria to dinner at our house later that week.

During dinner, Maria confided to me the reason for her cast. David Douglas Duncan, the great photographer, had given her my record of the Prokofiev Third Piano Concerto, the one recorded in Moscow that had just won the Grand Prix du Disque. The Prokofiev is a mostly fast, exciting, virtuoso piece, and Maria loved it. She said she had played the record so often while painting, compulsively rotating her hand and wrist in time with the music that over a period of two or three months she frayed the tendon in her right wrist. She could no longer use her hand and had required major surgery to repair it.

I should have realized that the physical manifestations stirred up by the sparks of Maria and me meeting would continue. Every summer during the dry season on the Riviera, the idyllic beauty of the region was often marred by brush fires, most commonly spring- ing up by the roadside. The firefighting equipment available to the French at that time was rather pathetic and consisted of small fire extinguishers that spurted a trickle of foam that couldn't put out a cigarette butt. It was the American sailors of the USS *Springfield* who came to the rescue much of the time. Maybe the French had a hidden agenda when they allowed our naval ships to anchor in their harbor!

About 1 p.m. the day after Maria and I met, I spotted a little fire at the bottom of our hill. A bizarre thought popped into my head. "Boris, how would you like to see me bring that fire up here?"

"Yes, sure, you do that, Byron," he replied in that deep, gruff, basso voice, chuckling with a cynical grin.

I don't know what demonic impulse came over me, but there was not the slightest doubt in my mind that I could summon that fire up our hill. I sat at the piano and started playing de Falla's "Fire Dance." In fact, I had never played it before. I just played it by ear. About five minutes into my performance, the little fire slowly crept up the hill, growing more and more aggressive. And it was on a direct path to our house! "Holy . . . !" I suddenly thought. "What am I doing?"

There was a pounding on the front door, and I raced up the stairs to answer it. Two American sailors from the *Springfield* barked: "Evacuate immediately. You're in danger of fire destroying your house." I raced back down and grabbed—some music! I don't recall what June took with her besides our son, Stefan. Boris, dear Boris,

The artist Boris Chaliapin, son of the great opera star Fyodor Chaliapin, was the best man at my wedding to Maria. Here we are at the ceremony in which I was made a Chevalier in the Legion d'Honneur in 1965.

nonchalantly picked up his suit, carefully folded it over his arm, and leisurely strolled up the staircase. "Hurry up! Hurry up, Boris!" we yelled as we stood by helplessly in the street, waiting for the catastrophe to happen. Thank God a light wind sprang up and the fire slightly altered its course. Incredibly, it came within two yards of our house and only the beautiful oak that shaded our terraces was badly singed.

The evening of the dinner at last arrived. Besides the Winstons, the Converses, Maria, and Boris, our guests included George Schlee, the constant companion of Greta Garbo—who couldn't come herself because of another engagement—and his wife, Valentina, as well as Prince Troubetzkoy of the famed old Russian family. They all commented on the eerie "snow effect" encircling the house, courtesy of the blanket of fire-resistant foam laid down by our compatriot sailors. After dinner, we left the terrace and went inside. Several of the guests wanted to meet nine-year-old Stefan, so we asked him to come downstairs. He required not a minute's coaxing to show us his pièce de résistance—a virtuoso performance of "The Twist," the song that inspired the latest dance craze of the time, with Chubby Checker on the record player booming in the background. Needless to say, Chubby and Stefan brought the house down.

Rosita then asked if I would play something. I thought Stefan would be a heck of a hard act to follow! The piano room had quite large windows that opened onto the terrace. Maria perched herself on the low windowsill between my piano and the terrace—beyond her I could see the moon, the starlit Mediterranean, and the USS *Springfield*, which was festooned with its multicolored lights. I hoped she knew I we playing just for her that night—all I could offer Maria was the beauty of the music. But I prayed she heard my sentiments. As we shook hands to say goodnight, our eyes met. I knew she did.

One of Maria's closest friends—in fact, they are like sisters—is the former actress Dolores Hart. They met in the late 1950s when her career was taking off. Her two films with Elvis Presley, as well as the spring break favorite *Where the Boys Are* and the dramatic movie *Lisa*, put her on the fast track to Hollywood stardom. She abruptly left the film world and became part of another—that of the Benedictine Order of Contemplative Nuns at the Abbey of Regina Laudis in Bethlehem, Connecticut. The friendship of Maria and Mother Dolores only deepened, and after we were married, Maria wanted me to see the letter she had written from France to Mother Dolores right after we had met. She asked for a copy of it, and Mother Dolores gladly complied. Following is the letter:

Dear Sis,

I sit writing this on the shaded terrace of Villa le Clos, part of a compound of houses gracing Cap Ferrat and at the further most tip by Villa Fiorintina whose gardens boast plants who continue exhibiting every shade of green possible.

Le Clos is smaller, more intimate with a beautiful dense grape arbor arched over the terrace giving complete shade and protection from the Mediterranean sun.

Three nights ago our hosts—Norman and Rosita Winston—gave a welcome dinner party for my mother and her new husband who is the famous plastic reconstructive surgeon Dr. John Converse. They were married three weeks ago, went to Germany for a medical convention and then spent their "honeymoon" in the south of France at this lovely home of the Winstons.

There was a lot of drama for my mother getting remarried, a lot of ambiguity I think but she is a woman who does not like to be alone, who is wonderful with "her" man and has very "wise ways." She invited me to come over and join them there as they hardly needed to be "alone." . . . She is more fragile and scared inside than anyone could imagine and I think I'm a kind of security blanket. How many people go on their mother's honeymoon?

Rosita invited about 20 guests for a wedding celebration party and I arrived barely one hour before it was set to start. I missed my nonstop flight in New York City—the only time in my life I read the departure time wrong and being at the height of summer travel, could barely find a seat on a connecting flight from Paris to Nice.

It didn't land until 6 p.m. I found the Winstons' chauffeur and we raced from the airport to Cap Ferrat, getting there just in time to change clothes for the party. Wish I could adequately describe the beauty—visual and sensory—such a combined aroma of orange blossoms, olives, eucalyptus, the sea and whatever varieties of flowers lined all the paths. To complete the landscaping, trees and bushes representing every possible shade and tone of green framed the surrounding villas—amazing.

I raced downstairs literally five minutes before the first guests arrived.

Now, I'm kind of shaking as I write you this—I think my life has been changed. I don't know how else to put it. A couple arrives and Rosita introduces me to Mrs. Byron Janis who shortly moves off to talk to some friends. Rosita takes me over to meet Mr. Byron Janis. "My dear, this is the great young American concert pianist, Byron Janis," she says. I don't know what my face showed because shock is what I felt—because there is this man whose picture I had seen over the past eight months on the album cover of his performance of the Prokofiev Third Piano Concerto and the reason for my hand surgery last month.

But that is not what is important, Dolores—what happened next as we were introduced and shook fingers, as mine were protruding out of white plaster, is that when we looked at each other—into each other's eyes (how else to say it) I was catapulted into another world—time dropped away and all I can describe is the overwhelming feeling of "recognition"—it felt like a torrent of information passed between us in that one first moment and we were not strangers. I would say as I sit here writing this—love at first sight, but no, that really doesn't tell it right—such another world showed itself, so much happened and we had only barely shaken hands. I don't know how to put words to this. After I guess several seconds, I came back to earth and did find the word, DAMN—as there I had just met his wife! Not being a home wrecker type, I felt shattered inside but still excited about this incredible moment that had just occurred.

Then I find our hostess had seated us next to each other and his wife at the far end of the table—was she psychic or what? You know my classical music background is zero so in order not to doubly embarrass myself—not to show Mr. Janis how ignorant I was about his world—when he quizzed me on the origins of the cast, I was really reluctant to explain the Prokofiev story. I bravely tried to avoid/evade and keep the conversation going on any other subjects but music and my painting gymnastics. More later . . .

This afternoon there was a big lunch given for all of us at another villa. Tables set in the gardens and my frustration that Byron's table was about as far away from mine as one could get. Was I mad! I subtly tried to find him to chat a little but it didn't work out. After lunch, I went up to change into a bathing suit. It was a leopard print suit (my favorite) and I must admit I did take one action. I positioned myself on the top of the stone wall that framed the Winston's terrace. The roadway to and from all the villas ran at the bottom of that 20 foot or so old moss and vine covered retaining wall. The guests were leaving the luncheon and I sat there with my book watching carefully for his car. Thank goodness I finally spotted it—a red Lancia, about to drive past our villa. I was looking down, Mr. Janis was looking up and our eyes met again. Oh so brief, oh so potent, then he was gone. Double Damn.

Last night we all were wined and dined by the Byron Janises at their house—a charming villa they rented for the

summer perched between the little village of Ville Franche
and Cap Ferrat. Their house is very high on the Moyenne
Corniche, dead center overlooking the harbor. The water is
rimmed with fishing boats and smack in the middle is the
USS *Springfield* cruiser on maneuvers. The Janis house overlooked this all. It was a very special night—tell you all about
it when I see you. The three terraces, indoor and outdoor, are
cooled by the natural winds blowing off the sea. Byron played
for us—it was so beautiful. But at one moment after playing
a Chopin waltz, Byron stopped, looked at me very strongly
and quietly started another piece of music. It wasn't "classical."
It was a lovely, almost single note song, quite like a folk song
that sounded very Russian. I learned it was called "Moscow
Nights." He had heard it being played when he was in Russia
the year before. This single little folk melody was so romanti-
cally haunting. I sat on the stone wall that ringed the terrace.
I could see Byron and he could see me. I became aware only
of him, the others melted away. And again that bond I felt the
other night was all I knew. He looked at me while his fingers
released the music into the evening air and it was one of those
total moments we have spoken of that happen spontaneously
and is more complete than anything else one can relate to.

When we left and said goodnight, I was in a turmoil, darn,
I didn't want to say goodbye but there it is. Onward! Life is all
very mysterious, something powerful happens and there is no
place to go with it. . . . What to do except trust that there will
be an answer somewhere, someday. Is this called faith?

Thanks for listening to my saga.

YS

When the summer was over I went directly from Paris to Boston
for a recital and then returned to New York. There was a message
from Rosita at my hotel inviting me to dinner the following Friday.
When she told me Maria Cooper was going to be there, I jumped
at the invitation. By now June and I were separated and living our
independent lives.

When I arrived at the Winstons' house on Sutton Place, in came Maria, but she was not alone. The gentleman with her was a prominent lawyer. I was furious at Rosita for not telling me that Maria would not be alone. I later found out that Maria also hadn't been told I would be there—I didn't know how mischievous Rosita could be. I must not have been a very congenial guest at cocktails, but Rosita somewhat redeemed herself at dinner by seating me directly across from Maria while putting Maria's friend at the opposite end of the table. Our conversation took me back to those magical moments we had spent together in the South of France. Only now there was a big difference. I told Maria that June and I had separated and down the line divorce was inevitable. I couldn't detect her reaction, but I don't think she was displeased! I boldly asked her to join me in drinking a toast to the future. She did, and with a smile we clinked glasses.

I called Maria the next day, and she asked me to come by for a drink. We quickly plunged into an animated discussion about creativity in art and music. I was admiring the beautiful paintings I saw—Renoir, Picasso, Gauguin. There was one in the library that I particularly liked, and I asked who had painted it. "Oh, I did that," Maria answered. I then realized what a wonderful artist she was and that she had been a serious painter all her life. I also learned Maria loved skiing, horseback riding, scuba diving, and a whole host of other sports. "Well," I thought, "it will sure give me plenty of time to learn a lot of new repertoire!"

When I left the apartment, I knew our adventure had begun.

15

SYNCHRONICITY

IN THE FIRST CHAPTER of this book, I wrote about synchronicity, a
word used by Carl Jung to describe "acts of creation in time."
Because of the importance of this concept I felt a few more
stories would be beneficial to explore its meaning. Perhaps the most
famous example of synchronicity comes from Carl Jung himself,
who described one of his patients, a woman who was difficult to
treat because she was totally rational in her approach to life. After
several sessions in which he felt they were getting nowhere, she told
him of her dream about a scarab. Jung was aware that the scarab
represented rebirth in the Egyptian mythology, and he wondered
if her subconscious was trying to show her that something of a
psychological rebirth was about to happen. He was on the verge of
bringing this up to her when he heard a strange noise. Something
was tapping against his windowpane. He looked up and saw a gold

and green scarab on the outside of the glass (he had never seen a beetle at his window before). He opened the window and it flew into the room as he and his patient were discussing her dream and its possible meaning. She apparently was so shocked that her compulsive rationality was greatly reduced, and they were able to proceed therapeutically.

I was reading a book about Edgar Cayce, one of the greatest trance mediums of our time, called *The Sleeping Prophet*. It includes a story of how Cayce, in trance, once recommended that a client go see a healer and body therapist, a person whom Cayce had never met or even heard of. Cayce's client was told that he should go and see Dr. Harold Reilly, who had a fitness center at Rockefeller Center. I was intrigued by this story and wanted to meet him, so I set out to locate Dr. Reilly but had absolutely no luck. He was no longer at Rockefeller Center, and no one knew where to find him.

The next night Maria and I were invited to a dinner party where we met a writer named Ruth Broad. Somehow talk turned to my struggles with my hands and arthritis, and Ms. Broad said, "Oh, the man you must see is Dr. Harold Reilly. I've just finished writing a book about him. I'll call tomorrow and give you his address and phone number—be sure to tell him I referred you."

Coincidence? No—that's synchronicity.

Dr. Reilly now lived in New Jersey, and Maria and I made an appointment to see him. I received many treatments from him, and Maria even took lessons in therapeutic massage from him. Indeed, here was a most remarkable man/healer. I have never met anyone quite like him. He was so extraordinarily psychic. I would think to myself, "I wish he would go to my right arm." He would immediately stop what he was doing and move those incredible hands directly to my sore right arm. In the following months he helped me more than I could have ever dreamed. After each treatment, his associate would serve us large bowls of delicious, healthy mushroom barley soup. We seemed to leave there healed both inside and out.

•   •   •

The wardrobe department for *The Wizard of Oz* unknowingly purchased a coat for the character Professor Marvel from a second-hand store. It was later verified to have originally been owned by L. Frank Baum, the author of the very novel on which the movie was based!

An amusing synchronicity occurred as I was on the Internet the other night. I noticed a book I had never seen before about Chopin and Jenny Lind, the so-called Swedish Nightingale and one of the greatest sopranos of the day, claiming that they had had a close secret relationship from 1848 to 1849, the last two years of his life. While she had certainly met him, I have found there is no conclusive evidence to support the claim that they had a relationship at all.

A concert tour brought her to the United States in 1850, and she had such a spectacular success that she soon became a household name. Apparently, a group of Swedes who had emigrated here at the same time and settled in a small town in Pennsylvania paid tribute to their Swedish Nightingale by naming its main street after her. That town happened to be none other than my birthplace, MeKeesport, Pennsylvania.

And then came one of the most meaningful synchronicities of all. What patterns were being woven beneath the surface of the everyday that caused two people of very different worlds to meet? Connections we couldn't see were moving Maria and me toward each other all the time.

16

AT LAST

With a kiss let us set out for an unknown world.
—ALFRED DE MUSSET

THEY SAY OPPOSITES ATTRACT—my impetuous nature was clearly the opposite of Maria's tranquil one. I was being true to form by asking Maria to marry me barely three weeks after our second meeting in New York. Her concern about it being a rebound situation was, indeed, understandable. But how could I assure her that this time I *knew*. I had no doubts. Time provided the answer. After a year and a half of courtship, she knew.

Maria very much wanted Mother Dolores and me to meet, so we chose a date and drove up to the abbey. I was instantly captivated by her, and we all spent a beautiful day together.

*Maria and I are cutting our wedding cake on April 11, 1966, in Woodbridge,
Connecticut.*

A short time later, on one of Maria's visits, she asked Mother Dolores what she felt after meeting me. Maria showed me her beautiful response.

My first impression of Byron, when he walked in the room for my consecration, was complete light, like a man dressed in light. He communicated such a sense of energy, and artistry, and intent.

I was not in small concern about the man that Maria married, particularly since she married after I had entered the monastery and I really didn't know Byron and we had no relationship. The worry I had was "What if Maria would marry someone that I didn't relate to?"—but then it would be absurd to think that could possibly happen, because people who love one another always love one another and love one another, and there is a round, there is a transmission of energy, there is an aura of wholeness that love communicates.

As Maria's mother had misgivings about our marriage, we decided it best to elope. Maria told our plans to her close childhood friend Susan Granger, a syndicated movie and drama critic, who immediately said, "Oh please, let us give you the wedding at our home." We were both delighted by the idea. There was a bit of a time problem, as my concert tour of South America was scheduled to start mid-April, so we decided on April 11 for the ceremony.

Susan and Dr. Donald Granger, a prominent Yale neurologist, lived in Woodbridge, Connecticut, and we drove up there a day before to get our license. Susie met us at Woodbridge's tiny town hall, really just a one-room house. Things didn't start off too well. The lady behind the counter said, "Okay, now what kind of a dog would this be for . . . or is it a hunting license you're wanting?"

We broke up laughing, and I replied with a chuckle, "No, as a matter of fact, my hunting days are over. You wouldn't by any chance have a marriage license?" "Oh, honey, you bet we do," she replied. She gave us the papers to fill out, and when she noticed that in the box marked "Father's name" Maria had put "Gary Cooper," she turned to the elderly man in the rocking chair behind her and said, "Huh, Gary Cooper, what a coincidence. Her father must have been named after that famous movie star." As we started laughing, she smiled and said, "Oh, it's so nice to see such a happy couple." Well, she had that right, anyway.

April 11 arrived, and our two excited godchildren, Janet, six, and Donnie, four, were sequestered in the kitchen and allowed to peek through the door but were given strict orders not to make a sound during the ceremony. My dear friend Boris Chaliapin, who had seen me through so many difficult times in the South of France, stood beside me as my best man. Susie, Maria's matron of honor, led the bride to where I should have been. Except I wasn't quite there at the beginning. I decided we needed some music, so I went to the Grangers' piano and launched into the "Wedding March." The Grangers' beloved bassett hound, Pierre, who always looked so miserable, almost looked happy. He was my piano companion, and he rested his big head and long ears over my feet, not making my pedaling any easier. It was probably one of the fastest wedding marches on record, as I was in a hurry to get to Maria's side. Our wedding kiss promised "everything" as we set out to explore that unknown world.

We spent the weekend at a rustic country inn called Stonehenge. Maria got a little taste of life with me when at 5 a.m. some "early bird" burst into song outside our cottage window. I couldn't help but mutter, "B-flat," as I pulled all the covers over my ears.

After a couple of crazed days back in New York, we were off to South America and Buenos Aires, which was the opening concert of my tour. Seven weeks later it ended in Rio de Janeiro, and not by chance. I knew Maria would love it and find Rio to be a glorious place to spend our honeymoon. And it was.

17

THE ABBEY OF REGINA LAUDIS

SHORTLY BEFORE WE MARRIED, Maria introduced me to the Abbey of Regina Laudis, a Benedictine monastery in Bethlehem, Connecticut. I was not prepared for the effect it was to have on my life. I met her very best friend, the former actress Dolores Hart, who was on her way to becoming a major star in Hollywood when, at twenty-three, she chose instead the cloistered life of a Benedictine nun. Maria was insistent that the two of us meet.

I felt an instant connection with her and the monastery's residents, particularly its founder, Lady Abbess, Mother Benedict Duss. She had been a surgeon by profession and, like me, was born in Pittsburgh.

*Lady Abbess, Mother Benedict Duss, the founder
of the Benedictine Abbey of Regina Laudis in
Bethlehem, Connecticut, was my very close friend.
Here we are at the abbey in 2003.*

In World War II, she had operated on injured members of the French Resistance deep in the bowels of a church in Paris. The Nazis had put a price on her head, but she kept on with her work until the liberation.

After the war, she came back to the United States and founded the abbey as an act of thanksgiving for the American soldiers who had given their lives in the war and to pray for oppressed people everywhere. Regina Laudis is not a place where women go to run away and hide from the world's problems. What is so unique about the nuns there is that Lady Abbess requires each of them to have excelled at some profession before entering the monastery. Also, as all Benedictine orders do, the sisters grow almost all of their food, take care of the herd of dairy cows, make incredible cheese, and even drive their own tractors. Still, these nuns possess a femininity that many women today lack. One of the things they emphasize strongly is the importance of both our masculine and feminine sides and how important it is to realize that we are both. That strikes a knowing chord in me—it's a thought I have often had. Women pianists who try to play like men are in the same category as the "macho man"—they both have abandoned their feminine side.

One of the specialties of these Benedictines is counseling, and people go to the abbey to talk to the sisters about their problems. The nun who seems best suited to help with a particular problem will have a "parlor" (a private meeting) with the person seeking help.

I went to the abbey on many occasions just to drink up the beautiful feeling of love and spirituality that is the heart and soul of that community. They also saw me through some very difficult times, and I have since realized that Lady Abbess was one of the first besides Maria to recognize that I had a special gift beyond music. Mother Dolores also understood things that are hard to put into words, but she had an immediate window into my deepest feelings and questions about the mysteries of life. I had never expected the abbey to have the impact on me that it did, and in a mysterious and wonderful way it became a beacon of light to me in the ensuing years.

One day, I performed a small concert for Mother Dolores to celebrate her Feast Day. As I walked into the room where the program was to take place, my Jewish heritage was greeted with joy and sensitivity by the community of forty-five nuns, who had placed a beautiful menorah on the piano in my honor. Another day when Mother Daniel, who was of Jewish heritage, greeted me with a big hug and a rousing "Shalom," it made me feel even more at home.

I played some Chopin, Schumann, and Liszt, followed by a song I had written especially for the occasion. It gave me such deep joy to be able to give Mother Dolores that musical gift. For a finale, we all joined in singing a chorus of "Happy Birthday." She wrote Maria about that moment:

> After yesterday, my knowledge of Byron has just been expanded.
> He walked into the room, and sat down at the piano, and began
> playing this music. And it was, to embarrass him, a sacred presence.

Mother Dolores Hart, Prioress, with me on the grounds of the abbey in 2002.

It was a sense of a person walking into your life who came from another place, who came from a place that was interior to your whole past and your whole future, and you knew it. And this person embodied a statement of love. And when Byron played, I knew a soul communication had taken hold, and that has never left in all the years of our friendship, that lock of interiority and that lock of sense of understanding who the other was without even knowing.

And I think that was for me a great privilege, to feel that I not only participated in your own choice of husband, but that I would be somehow taken into your marriage and that was a privileged position to be inside the gift that one person is to another.

I began to sense as the years unfolded that the abbey was in a very mysterious way significant for Byron as well.

The peace I feel when I'm at the abbey, I liken to being in the eye of a hurricane. The sisters create for their visitors a zone of quiet in a chaotic world, maintained by their intense prayer and work life and by their reaching out in love to any and all who come, whether for a day's visit or a week of introspection.

I soon looked on Lady Abbess as my spiritual mother, and with Mother Dolores being a spiritual sister, the monastery gradually became more and more an important part of my life. Lady Abbess was wise and fierce. She was a woman who wasted neither time nor words. Her training as a surgeon in no way interfered with her knowing how it felt to be the patient. Her conversations reflected both perspectives, and if emotional or spiritual surgery were needed, she could quickly detect the source of the trouble like a laser beam homing in on a target. We spent many wonderful hours together in conversation on topics ranging from music to religion, to why-get-up-in-the-morning-at-all, to the normality of the paranormal, to practicing the art of medicine as well as its scientific demands.

When paranormal events occuring around me began to multiply, I at first hesitated to tell her about some of the unbelievably extra-ordinary things that were becoming an important part of my life. But there was no need to worry.

She knew. She understood.

How comforting it was to hear that these phenomena were in no way foreign to her. She told me it was important to keep any gifts in their proper perspective, to keep open and stay well grounded so that these gifts could grow. She told me I just should "be." She told me at various times, quoting Jesus, "You must be wise as serpents and innocent as doves." "Keep making beautiful music," she would say. "That is the other talent you have been given to help others." I felt so privileged and grateful that this extraordinary person had entered my life.

My eighty-six-year-old mother also took great pleasure in visiting the abbey. I performed for the community on many occasions, and my mother came to one of my concerts there. On that occasion, the community had prepared a special surprise for us. When I finished playing, they gathered around us and chanted some beautiful psalms from the Old Testament, their thank-you to me.

In those moments, I experienced a connection with love that was incomparable. My mother, who always said, "It doesn't matter where you pray—church, synagogue, anywhere—as long as you pray," had a look of peace and happiness on her face that day that I shall always remember.

One day, after a nap, I woke up with a feeling of love that I had never experienced before. Love for everyone—I wanted to call everyone I knew and tell them how much I loved them. I felt a transcendent love for everything. It was so overpowering I had difficulty in restraining myself. I decided to call the abbey. Mother Dolores answered and I told her what had happened. "Byron," she said, "you are living in what we call a state of grace." I don't think I could have continued in that state of loving for too long—I felt as if I would burst. It was a feeling of such ecstasy that there would be nothing that could contain it. I knew I had to do something menial to let it go. I went to the kitchen and started washing dishes. Slowly, the intensity of the feeling started to fade away, and love was love again—still the strongest power on earth.

18

A POWER
TRIP

PRESIDENT AND MRS. JOHN F. KENNEDY had twice invited me
to perform at the White House. I was in Montreal, and shortly
before I was to leave for Washington I received the following telegram
from the White House: "We very much regret we have had to cancel
the State Dinner at which you were to perform, due to the Bay of
Pigs situation. We regret any inconvenience to you. Most sincerely,
Jacqueline Kennedy." It was hard to equate the Bay of Pigs incident
with "inconvenience," particularly when a nuclear war might be
in the offing, but I appreciated the eloquence of her note. When
Mrs. Kennedy invited me a second time, I had to decline because the
French would not free me from a previous contractual obligation.

I received a letter again from Mrs. Kennedy, saying, "Third time lucky." Sadly, that was not to be.

Years later, when President Ford invited me to perform, again I had contractual obligations in Europe that could not be broken. So it was not until 1983, when Ronald Reagan was president, that I finally played at the White House for the first time.

On July 19, 1983, I was honored by being invited to celebrate the fortieth anniversary of my orchestral debut by playing at a state dinner. Being honored as well that evening were the emir of Bahrain and the five astronauts on the *Challenger* crew, which included the first female shuttle astronaut, Sally Ride. The president's entire cabinet was present. It was a very dramatic occasion and was visually stunning.

The emir and his entourage were dressed in full formal regalia— flowing gold and black robes, ceremonial sabers hanging from their waists.

That evening, I decided I would use the piano that was first given to the White House in 1938 by Steinway. It had a beautifully elaborate case with gilt stenciling and stood on highly unusual gilded American eagle supports. After a short forty-minute program, one of the encores I played that night was Debussy's *Clair de Lune*. I hoped most of the audience understood the reference—even though these astronauts had not actually been to the moon, they were close enough.

Maria told me what she was thinking while she was waiting for me to begin the concert.

> Look at all the power in this room, with the president, the man with the red phone at his side, all the cabinet, all the country's key decision makers sitting here, and the foreign guests, and then—our astronauts—man is breaking free from gravity, getting off this planet, exploring the universe! Collectively, what an extraordinary nucleus of power under this roof!
>
> I thought of all the things you and I have seen and experienced, that speak of a power so much greater than we here on this planet can imagine. "Do they really know what power is?" kept running through my head like a mantra. As I listened to

To Byron Janis — With appreciation for the magic you brought to us. Very Best Regards Ronald Reagan

President Ronald Reagan honors me after my performance at the state dinner at the White House.

you play some particular virtuosic passages I noticed a pain in the fourth finger of my right hand. But I was so caught up in the music, I ignored it until finally it hurt so much I had to look. I was shocked. You know, I was wearing a favorite ring that my grandmother had designed and worn—an emerald set in thick twisted gold ropes and as I looked at the bottom of my finger I could see the entire band had not only broken but was gradually bending and pushing itself into the flesh of my finger. I also realized this had started at the same time as my thoughts about "the true meaning of power."

After my performance and some eloquent words of thanks by President Reagan, we all filed into the East Room for coffee. Maria caught up with me, and I said, "What's the matter? You look upset." She said, "No, no, I'll explain in a minute. You won't believe what just happened—wait here." She flew down the stairs to the ladies' room. Five minutes later, she reappeared looking slightly more relaxed, and I noticed she had something grasped tightly in her right hand. She motioned for me to step behind a couple of potted ficus trees so we could have some privacy. "What's going on?" I asked. She said, "This!" She opened her hand, and resting there in her palm was the broken ring, and as we looked, it kept on bending! Then suddenly it

This is Maria's gold and emerald ring that broke on her hand during the concert at the White House.

stopped and the metal became rigid again. If she hadn't gotten the ring off immediately with soap and hot water, her finger would have been in serious trouble.

We quietly hugged each other as we contemplated the meaning of what had been shown us on this special night.

After we returned to the hotel, we looked again at Maria's ring, which was now unwearable, and wondered—will we ever understand?

19

ARTHRITIS

I WAS IN LONDON in 1973 when it began—a strange red patch on the inside of my fourth finger. It was slightly swollen and very painful, particularly when I was playing. The doctor's initial bafflement resolved after nearly an hour's examination. "You have psoriatic arthritis," he finally declared.

"What's that?" I asked.

His response shot through me like a bolt of lightning. "It's a form of arthritis. I'm afraid it doesn't get any better." And he was right. It didn't.

Thus began my pilgrimage from one specialist's waiting room to another. But the initial diagnosis would not yield. Once again, my hands were under attack. This affliction might have threatened my career more than that severed nerve. Truth be told, it could very easily have ended it. But that was a truth I refused to tell myself or accept from others.

I entered a state of conscious rational denial. I knew all the facts. I'd met every specialist. I could have written a textbook on my condition. But I lived moment to moment, behaving as if arthritis was some kind of modern superstition to which I simply could not afford to subscribe. Living in denial is viewed today as a serious psychological disturbance. That's a shame, really, because deliberate conscious denial is sometimes the only option one has aside from surrender. "At the stroke of midnight, God will win," wrote the legendary Irish poet William Butler Yeats. But who can say when midnight will come? Who knows when to call it quits? So I strongly recommend denial to you the next time an authority figure intones, "There's nothing to be done." Sure there is. Deny it! And if, at some point, you must accept it, read the famous Serenity Prayer, which says:

God grant me serenity to accept the things I cannot change,
Courage to change the things I can,
And wisdom to know the difference.
Amen

But I would like to take the liberty of altering the first line to read: "God grant me the serenity to know *when* to accept the things I cannot change." That's to make sure you've given it your best shot before you quit.

I returned to New York earlier than planned and called a family friend, acupuncturist Dr. José Corcus. He had previously been an internist at New York Hospital and referred me to the renowned rheumatologist Dr. Charles Christian, the head of the rheumatology department at the Hospital for Special Surgery. Of course, I rushed to see him, and the verdict was bleakly the same. He told me I should begin taking anti-inflammatory medications right away.

I've always been a cutting-edge person, so I decided to try to deal with the pain in my fingers with acupuncture treatments with Dr. Corcus. At this time, acupuncture was still relatively little practiced in the West, though it had achieved many successful results. I also wanted to avoid the potential gastrointestinal side effects of the anti-inflammatory medications prescribed by Dr. Christian. Happily the acupuncture treatments were extremely successful in controlling my pain. Dr. Corcus even placed a small, almost invisible pin at an acupuncture point in my ear that could be left in indefinitely. During a concert, if my pain increased, I could squeeze the pin and it would reduce the pain. I was amazed. It did, however, have a bit of a downside. The press observed that during a concert, "Mr. Janis has developed a strange, new nervous habit—he pulls at his ear quite frequently." Little did they know.

Over time I learned that everything that helped at first would eventually lose its effectiveness. And so it was with acupuncture. Dr. Corcus next tried injecting cortisone into the distal (top) joint of a finger that was particularly inflamed. That was not a pleasant experience, as those of you who've had it done know. But it kept me playing.

As the disease crept up on me, like a vampire trying to suck the music out of my hands, I realized I would have to start the course of anti-inflammatory medication Dr. Christian had prescribed, and I became his patient.

Unfortunately, as the disease spread, every finger became inflamed, and Dr. Christian had to start giving me those dreaded but effective injections. I was constantly changing fingering, using a comfortable finger in place of one that was hurting. And so it went until none of my distal joints would bend. During this time, I had also accumulated an arsenal of alternative medicine treatments to supplement Dr. Christian's medications, but always with his approval.

"I must have been a sherpa in another life," Maria would laughingly say. Along with the usual change of clothes for after the concert, at intermission she would sprint backstage to the dressing room, part of which had come to resemble a traveling medicine show, trying to help treat my arthritis. The short massages she gave me prior to performances were a major blessing. Next came the hot packs, the cold packs, and fluorimethane spray (a topical analgesic), then DMSO (dimethyl sulfoxide, another topical analgesic first used on horses' legs) was rubbed into my fingers and joints. The clear topical liquid helped alleviate pain but had an immediate and unusual side effect: it created a strong garlic taste in my mouth. I played many a concert inspired by the flavor of some nameless Italian spaghetti sauce!

This flurry of activity at intermission had to take place hidden from the eyes of managers, stagehands, guests, and even my piano technician—who might have been the most likely to suspect something, as I was unusually particular about the action of my instruments being very light. Obviously, the heavier the keys were to play, the harder they would be for my fingers to push down.

I saw to it that no one knew of my condition. For me a secret has tremendous power, and if I hid reality from myself, then why shouldn't I hide it from others? The ultimate keeper of the secret was the quality of my performance. If I had ever played more than a few successive substandard concerts, I would have stopped immediately. I could deceive myself, but I would never betray the music.

The whole elaborate charade became a death-defying game, like a trapeze artist working without a net. The cost was very high. The daily struggle with my nerves was, at times, intolerable, but I chose to continue.

After a while, I discovered I could no longer tolerate all of the medications and their side effects. In anguish, I said to Maria, "For God's sake, Maria, why don't you tell me to stop?"

"Byron," she answered, "that decision has to be yours. I cannot—will not—make it for you."

I was enraged—how cruel of her not to intervene—but I realized if Maria had told me it was over, that it was time to stop, I wouldn't have listened anyway. At age eleven, I'd discovered that mind over matter is a very powerful tool—that if we don't think something is impossible, it won't be.

In 1983, my condition deteriorated so badly that I had no choice but to take a break. I needed a recuperative interlude—just enough time to get over a slight case of "tendonitis"—the word we used as a cover. However, I noticed that after even a short time off, I would usually return to being in good form. I'd think to myself, "You can't stop when you're playing as well as this." It was more than gratifying that the press never noticed any problems other than the occasional off night.

Throughout this torturous time, I rode a seesaw of conflicting emotions, and that was the most difficult thing of all to handle. This was the life-and-death struggle for me—so crucial was my career to my very survival that it colored every minute of my life.

From early on, my experiences in the paranormal were a powerful and welcome reminder that the impossible was possible and that truth has embraced me many times.

In addition to everything else I now began being hindered by bouts of fatigue that prevented me from functioning at my usual level of intensity and creativity. In the past I would sometimes utilize one area of the paranormal called automatic writing to help me with problems I couldn't understand, as it was a technique I had used with often positive results. I would sit down, sometimes with my eyes closed, put pen to paper, and without conscious guidance let my hand be free to write or draw whatever it wished.

I wanted to see if automatic writing might provide me with some clue as to what was going on. One day the message I received read: "Go to the Museum of Natural History." That was it! I wondered, "What kind of communication is this? I must not be 'on' today." Maria's expression told me she agreed. "What a strange message," she concurred. But after a moment she suggested that we go to the museum. "What do we have to lose? We haven't been to the museum in a long time, and it is an interesting place."

The instant we stepped inside the museum, our visit became very interesting indeed. It felt as though I was in a jet stream that was pushing me forward so strongly that I had to follow its lead—occasionally even ricocheting off the walls! People started looking at me as though I were some kind of nutcase. I couldn't blame them, really, but I had to see this through. Maria was struggling to keep up with her "off-the-wall" husband when I was suddenly coerced into going down one level, to a hall where various exhibitions of the human body were on display. I was repeatedly "pushed" in front of one that read "The Thyroid Gland." The case contained an extremely detailed model of the thyroid and how it controls the way the body burns energy. "Well, that's interesting," Maria said. As we moved away, my "jet stream" suddenly abandoned me, and we were able to visit other exhibits without it. When we got home, I promptly phoned a doctor friend, who suggested I see a top endocrinologist, Dr. Eugene Cohen. My friend also advised me to keep the details of my "inspiration" from the great specialist, or I might find myself sitting in a psychiatrist's office instead.

Dr. Cohen's diagnosis didn't take long: "You have an extremely underactive thyroid. No wonder you're feeling so fatigued," and he handed me a prescription. The automatic writing had steered me right. Maria and I were dumbfounded. "I can't believe this," she said. Neither of us had known anything about that exhibition at the museum.

After about a week of Dr. Cohen's pills, my thyroid and I were back in sync. It was a happy ending, at least to that chapter of my story.

Over the following years, I resorted to anything and everything to keep playing while the public and the profession, including my most trusted managers, remained in the dark about my condition. I started visiting a famous hypnotherapist to help with the pain and the anxiety brought on by the constant hour-to-hour uncertainty of how my hands would respond at the keyboard. We had several strong, very helpful sessions. Once just before heading off to a European tour starting in Paris, I was especially apprehensive, and the therapist said, "Mr. Janis, don't worry. We can have a session on the phone from Paris just before your concert if need be."

I was to call him in the late afternoon, Paris time, just before dressing and going to the Théâtre des Champs-Élysées for my recital. I was lying on the bed with the phone next to my ear as he started counting me "down"—one, two, three, four—to induce a hypnotic state prior to giving me the posthypnotic suggestion that the pain could be ignored, that it would not hinder me or interfere with my playing in any way. In the middle of this countdown, I stopped hearing his voice—silence. I roused myself and called his name—no answer. I hung up and ordered the operator at the Hôtel Plaza Athénée to ring his number. It was busy. After about ten minutes, I finally got through. "What the devil happened?" I exclaimed, more than a little annoyed.

"What happened to you?" shouted the doctor. "I'm in the mi of counting down, and suddenly I hear some strange man's vo. groggily saying, 'What the hell are you doing to me? Cut it out. Who is this?'"

The hotel operator obviously had crossed lines. "You had better call the gendarmes to be on the lookout because somewhere in Paris, there's a hypnotized zombie on the loose, and he's not happy!"

At critical times, the right person has been led across my path. Synchronicity? Just as Dr. Harold Reilly came into my life, so did the amazing Dr. Moshé Feldenkrais. His techniques of physiotherapy came out of his particular and unique understanding of the human body. "Awareness through movement" became his credo. With his assistance, I was able to keep pushing back against the lock-down arthritis was trying to impose.

After Dr. Christian retired no one could have been "righter" than Dr. Steven Abramson, my superb rheumatologist and revered friend. His medical wisdom then and now has seen me through so many troubling times.

And I had the great good fortune to be in the care of the eminent hand surgeon Dr. Charles Melone III, whose five operations on both my hands made it possible for me to continue performing.

After surgeries, the many long hours of slow, tedious hand therapy given by the expert and sensitive Anita Simmons kept me from getting discouraged when regaining the use of my hands again seemed impossible.

Arthritis has a mind and a schedule of its own, yet after months of despair I found I was able to resume playing again in between flare-ups and sometimes despite them. But I had been coping with my hidden condition since 1972, and as the serious flare-ups grew more frequent, I felt as though the walls were beginning to close in on me. It was now next to impossible to hide all that it took to play. I knew I couldn't keep my secret much longer. One memorable night, Maria and I had dinner with an old friend, the head of public affairs for the New York Philharmonic, Frank Little. I broke my ironclad silence and told him about my arthritis and that I had come to the end of my rope in the game of subterfuge I had been playing. It was exhausting just fending off the new concert dates offered by my manager, Shelly Gold. Every excuse and outright lie left its mark on me. I was lost and didn't know where to turn or how to handle what felt like the dissolution of my life. No piano, no music making, meant no Byron.

It was Christmastime, and as the three of us walked back from dinner toward Fifth Avenue along 57th Street, I was blind to the glittering crystal star high overhead that illuminated the street during the holidays. We walked past Carnegie Hall and my old apartment building, 140 West 57th Street, from where, many years earlier, I had walked to my Carnegie Hall debut. Wonderful memories flooded through me, but at that moment my usual gratitude for my incredible life was obscured by pain and an overwhelming sense of life-sapping loss. Then I heard Frank say something, but with the car horns and other holiday street noises, I wasn't sure that I heard him correctly.

"Why don't you offer yourself to be a spokesperson for the Arthritis Foundation?" was what he'd said. I stopped short. "What—a public admission? Out of the closet? Absolutely not!" I exclaimed.

But as we continued walking and were now almost directly underneath that huge reflecting star, I became aware of not only its light but of something even brighter inside me. It felt like a new road was being illuminated for the first time.

"I'll call the foundation tomorrow as your representative and talk about the possibilities," Frank continued. I could hear him now loud and clear. "What a great spokesperson you would be for them."

Going public about my arthritis was a far bigger hurdle to clear than recovering from my little finger accident. But once the decision was made I went, as always, full speed ahead. The Arthritis Foundation decided to make the announcement in a big way with a special White House luncheon concert for all the governors' wives hosted by Nancy Reagan. I was thinking about a thirty-minute program and decided to include a difficult new piece filled with Americana that I would learn especially for the occasion, Louis Moreau Gottschalk's *The Union*. I knew I'd be playing under the Lincoln portrait and that this very work had been performed by the composer at Lincoln's

At the 1984 White House concert for First Lady Nancy Reagan and all of the governors' wives, I announced that I was becoming ambassador for the arts for the Arthritis Foundation.

funeral. It would be a fitting connection. After my performance, Mrs. Reagan called me to the podium. Her words were so moving: "Byron Janis, whom you have just heard play so beautifully, has been suffering with arthritis for twelve years. He has been struggling privately with the physical and emotional agony of psoriatic arthritis in his hands and wrists, which is particularly shattering for a pianist. Today, he becomes the ambassador for the arts for the Arthritis Foundation." (Which I continue to be.) I responded with my own heartfelt emotions, finishing with the slogan I used for an upcoming public service announcement: "I have arthritis, but it doesn't have me." Many of the governors' wives knew me and had attended my concerts when I played in their states, and I was so happy to hear them say that they never would have known that I had arthritis.

To my amazement, having lifted the burden of secrecy, I found that somehow I could play without any medication, and after my next concert the press commented, "You would never know he has arthritis." To achieve this was what I had hoped and prayed for. I was beginning to feel a new surge of confidence —and it frightened me. I did not want to lose grasp of the reality of my situation this time. I did not want to go through—or put Maria through, as I had before—the living hell it took to continue playing, even though it had given me a heaven that nothing could replace.

It had not been the applause that kept me going, nor had it been the press when it was glowing. It was my passion, my ability to never stop persevering, and the feeling of creating beauty that was necessary for my soul to exist. Whenever I bowed on stage, I always felt a "presence" and made a special bow, sometimes visibly, sometimes invisibly, to something beyond the public, besides the music and the composer. I suppose that was my way of thanking God, and this was my way of communicating with Him.

Music for me was indeed the closest thing to a feeling of God, an unspoken reverie to and from beyond. To lose music to me was like losing my most intimate contact with Him. "Believing" was not the issue, but if I could no longer play, what then?

My sense of self and identity came along with my gift, and since I was five years old I had been a performer. But if I couldn't play, who was I? What would people say to me? What would I say to them? I was terrified. I was a man who had lost his identity. But shortly afterward I remember a dinner partner saying to me, "That is one of the most interesting conversations I've ever had with anybody," and I realized that even away from the piano, I was someone whom people liked, liked simply for who I was, piano or no piano.

As I continued to play my scheduled concerts without medication, a new freedom seemed to enter my being. Having gone public about my twelve-year struggle with arthritis truly seemed now to have lifted the terrible burden I had been carrying all those years. I practiced less than before and with quicker and better results. I felt my psychic abilities were stronger again. I felt at peace—joyous—and at the beginning of a new life.

But this fruitful period would only last eight months, and sadly I had to resume taking my medications.

I then embarked on a new kind of tour, sponsored mostly by Searle and Pfizer Pharmaceuticals. I still played regular concerts and recitals, but I also traveled to other cities and performed short programs at functions to benefit the Arthritis Foundation and research fund-raising. I received in return the priceless gift of being able to help others. I remembered Horowitz once asking me when I was a teenager, "What is more important for you, to give or to receive?" It hadn't taken but a moment for me to answer, "To give." And now I felt that I was giving in a new way. I met children who had juvenile arthritis, and they would say, "I wanted to be a baseball player or a basketball player or a ballet dancer, and now I can't." "Look," I told them, "don't have one dream, have *dreams*. Don't have one goal. Have various goals. You could still be a sportswriter, an announcer, a choreographer, a trainer . . . there are endless possibilities. There are so many ways to use your talents and interests. You will surprise yourself."

About a year and a half after I played at the White House and became a spokesman for the Arthritis Foundation, one of my journal entries states:

When it is necessary to accept your Fate, something seems to change that which you feared most. Your Fate in fact, becomes a very different one. This time I truly accepted my Fate and that gave birth to a new feeling. Not one born of fear, but of meeting my adversary head on—confronting him—one of us had to lose. I took all his blows—blows to the soul—the heart—the body—the guts—and when he was finished, I found that I was not. I was still there—perhaps really there for the first time.

I had not just conquered fear. I had reached a new understanding of other people's lives and consequently my own. I had learned that you cannot put yourself in other people's shoes until you have filled your own. I had listened, really listened, to others as I never had before, as some may have listened to my music. I had talked to others as I had never talked before. With no piano to speak for me, I had to use words. And as I opened up verbally to people, they opened to me. I had discovered a new place for meeting, a place I had never been before.

I now saw that conscious denial was not the only option open to me before "surrendering"—before saying, "I can't." Any battle requires an adversary. But if you *deny* its existence, as I did with arthritis, there is nothing to fight. You can keep it a secret from others, but not from yourself. In *acceptance* is where I started to find my answers.

There are brief moments of celebration before they become the past where we seem to understand so much, but they are brief, and we must start all over again. But I found each time we go a little farther, and as we struggle, suffer, and enjoy life, those moments of understanding grow, not in length of time but in an ever-enlarging vision that celebrates and unites all of them.

By 1990, the top joint of my left thumb had disintegrated. I couldn't put any weight on it whatsoever. Never mind playing the piano, holding a fork was impossible. It became clear that surgery to fuse the joint was needed.

What a bizarre sight: me walking into the office of hand surgery at the Hospital for Special Surgery carrying an electronic keyboard. "Ah, a concert for the staff?" someone inquired. No, I simply needed to demonstrate for the doctor what exactly my hands and fingers needed to do at a keyboard. My doctor reassured me that all would be well. He'd rotate the tip of the thumb a bit outward, so my reach would not be adversely affected. But when the bandages came off and I could touch the keyboard again, I noticed something was horribly wrong: I couldn't reach my normal nine to ten notes. With a sinking feeling, I measured my two hands and discovered that the left thumb was now a half inch shorter than the right one. I sat at the piano and wept. All the years of struggle since the early seventies to keep on playing, overcoming one obstacle after another, were suddenly meaningless. I did not see how I could overcome this setback.

I spiraled down into a severe depression that imprisoned me in my room. Weeks turned into months before Maria was finally able to coax me to see a doctor for help.

At the time we were both so consumed by my depression that we neglected to look beyond it to an obvious issue: the nature of the surgery and its options. A few years later—too late to do anything about it—several surgeons informed us that there were a couple of different ways of doing that procedure that would not have resulted in a shortened thumb. It is best that I remain silent about my thoughts. Then and now.

Ask anyone who has moderate to severe arthritis, ask any family member who lives with someone who struggles with the disease on a daily basis, and you will hear of lives significantly changed and challenged. Simple everyday things, such as buttoning shirts, putting on cuff links, and tying a tie feel like playing three concertos in one evening. When your body, which all your life has been able to go from 0 to 60 in three seconds like a Ferrari, becomes a Model T Ford that has to be hand cranked just to get started, high-level adaptive skills are called for. As in the animal kingdom, we too must follow that law of nature that states adapt or die. We must be flexible even if our bodies aren't or lose that many-splendored thing called life.

The will to adapt, create, and keep growing is available to anyone who has to reorder his or her life due to an illness. And adapt I did! When I finally crawled out from under the bedcovers after months of depression, a new spark ignited my life, courtesy of the father-in-law I'd sadly never met, Gary Cooper.

At the time, TNT was making a documentary called *Gary Cooper: American Life, American Legend*, and Maria wanted a special theme song to represent her father in the film. On a particularly bleak morning, she burst into our bedroom, pulled the shades way up, and insisted, "Byron, please write the theme music for this documentary. I know how you can compose, and this would be so wonderful."

I muttered something like, "I can't do that . . . well, I'll try," and went back to bed. But the idea intrigued me, and I had such love and respect for her father, both as I have come to know him through his daughter and through the roles he portrayed on the screen. I agreed to give it a try. When I played the newly composed theme for Maria a few days later, tears welled up in her eyes. "It was as if Poppa had walked into the room," she said. It was not only her words that made me so happy, but the fact that this was the first time I had touched a piano in eight months.

A few months later, hoping to find a lyricist for the music, Maria showed it to an old friend, the brilliant singer Judy Collins. She loved it and suggested we get the advice of a legend in the world of pop music, Frank Military, who'd walked and worked among the giants of that era, including the legendary Rat Pack: Frank Sinatra, Dean Martin, Sammy Davis Jr., and the rest. Frank watched the film, listened to the music, and proclaimed to Maria, "He can write!"

Not long after, Frank and his wife, Pam, came over for dinner. He wanted to meet me and hear more of my songs. At one point, he reached into his briefcase, pulled out a script, and dropped it in my lap. "How would you like to do something big?" he asked. As I mumbled, "I don't know if . . ." He continued, "Here's a property we [Warner/Chappell Music] own, and we need a musical score written for it. Want to give it a try?"

I glanced down at the script in my lap. It was titled *The Hunchback of Notre Dame*, based on the Victor Hugo masterpiece. A moment later I heard my otherwise depressed being saying, "Yes, I'd love to try my hand at it."

And so began a marathon of composing and doing what I had thought impossible.

Quasimodo may have been ugly to everyone else, but he was beautiful to me. He felt like my best friend as I tried to give a voice to his heart and his dreams. The crippled bell ringer of Notre-Dame, not too unlike a certain newly crippled concert pianist, was still able to sing and dream and love. I wanted to tell that story.

In a torrent of creativity, I wrote twenty-two songs in six weeks. Although arthritis is not good for pianists, the piano is good for arthritis and probably is the best exercise for arthritic hands.

After I finished the last song, with some trepidation I asked Frank to come and hear them. And when he said, "You've written a great score," I said, "You're joking." "I never joke about music," he replied. Not long afterward, I began to play again. Now that I was told I could write, my motivation and confidence returned. It's amazing how the long depression almost made me forget my powers of the mind, my persistence, my own strong abilities, and my paranormal experiences.

Almost nothing is impossible, and it was time for me to prove it again. I looked at that shortened thumb and said, "I'm not going to let you stop me from playing. I'm going to find a way around you." And I did. I worked out various ways to compensate for it by using different hand and body positions, using more of my arm and my elbow and, when possible, my right thumb or another finger in its place. I was driven by the power of the story, the force of the characters, and, probably most of all, the need for my own creativity to break out of its psychological prison.

Maria and I were in Paris having a drink with a friend. I asked if he, by chance, knew whether Victor Hugo had any close descendants. "He most certainly does," was his reply, "and Pierre Hugo, his great-great-grandson, is my good friend. He is an extraordinary artist, jeweler, and goldsmith." Again synchronicity! I immediately telephoned Mr. Hugo. We had a wonderful chat, and I told him about *The Hunchback* musical and he asked if I could send him the music. I did and got a letter back that thrilled me to the core—he loved it and felt it was just the right music for the story and he would do anything he could to help me. Music aside, after that first telephone conversation, I felt we were kindred spirits, and indeed, we have become good friends.

Frank and I recorded a demo CD of six songs, and our close friend David Douglas Duncan, the great photojournalist and author, asked to hear them. He seemed highly taken with the music and asked, "What is needed?" We replied that $120,000 was needed to have a showcase production. When he reached into his pocket and pulled out a check, we thought how wonderfully kind of him to make a contribution. He then handed us the check and we nearly collapsed. It was not just a contribution—it was a check for the full amount!

From the first time we spoke, I felt that Pierre Hugo, Victor Hugo's great-great-grandson, and I were kindred spirits. The two of us are at Bouterin for my seventieth birthday in 1998.

"David, you're mad! You can't be serious. Come on, that's ridiculous!" we protested. He was a successful artist but hardly a Wall Street tycoon. We tried and tried to dissuade him but to no avail. It is hard to ever win an argument with David.

We now had a producer, and a showcase production of *The Hunchback* was launched.

Living with arthritis may have deformed my life and my hands, but I still drew strength from the discipline of daily practice—and now from a new source, the joy of composing. Though it now took me a lot more time to choose concert programs that my hands could handle, at least now I no longer had to keep my arthritis a secret. In interviews I was free to talk about all the challenges I had to face and the different ways I had managed to overcome them.

Learning to live with a limitation can give new intensity to life. I couldn't control the fact that I had arthritis, but I could control how I coped with it.

It is said that a great scientist begins with a dream, then makes the equation afterward. What I've had to do is make my technique fit my condition as well as my dream.

Here, too, is where the power of love plays such an important role. In living with me and my chronic condition, Maria's attitude, her unconditional love and understanding, were essential to my professional and physical survival. She even learned hypnosis to help me with the pain before concerts on the road. There was only one problem. She herself is such a good hypnotic subject that in the process of "counting me down" she would occasionally put herself "out" as well. I would hear, "Twenty, nineteen, eighteen, seventeen . . . ," a long silence, then, "Seventeen, sixteen, fifteen, fourteen," and she would be out again. Unfortunately, I wasn't! Ultimately, a shot of caffeine helped solve that problem.

Through the whole of my trial with arthritis I have never asked, "Why me?" Rather, I have asked, "What do I do with this pain?" Through that question came a new relationship with that higher power. Music had long been my way of speaking to God, and I'd never thought much beyond that until confronted with the reality that my "voice" might be taken away from me. Arthritis taught me to look inside myself for new sources of strength and creativity. Somehow I kept finding them.

20

MEETING URI GELLER

IN FEBRUARY 1973, Maria received a phone call from a friend who was an executive at CBS television. He recently had attended a healing seminar that Maria had conducted. "Come down to my office. I'm having a meeting with Dr. [Andrea] Puharich, a physicist who's just come from Israel, and he's just brought this young Israeli psychic named Uri Geller. I thought you might be interested to meet them." We had already heard of both from Dr. Robert Laidlaw, the forward-thinking head of psychiatry at Roosevelt Hospital.

Since Maria was interested in scientific research, Uri said he wanted to do some telepathy experiments with her. For one of them, Uri said, "Do a drawing." They went into separate rooms, and each drew a picture. Most people seem to draw a house or a sailboat for such experiments, but because of my problems with recurring bursitis, Maria did a line drawing of my shoulder, right arm, and hand. Uri, who had never seen or met me before, did not replicate Maria's drawing, but instead continued where she left off at the top of my shoulder and then drew my head in an exact profile. He said this was the first time he had added anything to what had been an original drawing—usually his telepathic drawings are reproductions down to the last detail. What was also amazing was that it was on exactly the same scale as Maria's. She was equally amazed when he gave an example of psychokinesis in which he took a key, lightly stroked the side of it, and said, "Bend. Bend," and it did.

As Maria explained a little about me, Uri asked, "Can we come over when we're finished here?" Maria called me to check if my practicing for the day was finished. I said, "Yes. And I would love to meet them."

The minute Uri walked in the door, he said, "Let me show you what I do." He asked me to bring him a spoon. He took it in his hands and again voiced the words, "Bend. Bend." The spoon quickly bent, curling itself into a ninety-degree angle.

I didn't need to see anything more. I immediately understood what it meant and how powerful a thing it was. Some people whom I invited to meet him would say afterward, "So he can bend a spoon, so what?"

So what? What it means is that the mind is capable of affecting matter, and his mind can do it on command. If the mind can affect a piece of inanimate metal such as a spoon, it can affect almost anything. I have been proving that since I was eleven years old—playing the piano with, for all intents and purposes, only nine normal fingers.

I gave him a recording of mine as he left. I knew that a deep friendship had begun.

New York City had just hosted a parade celebrating the twenty-fifth anniversary of the founding of the State of Israel. The next day we joined Uri to have our own little celebration, when we suddenly became aware of a small object slowly floating down from the ceiling just above me. I couldn't see what it was until it embedded itself

This photo was sent to us by our close friend Uri Geller, the famed Israeli psychic. He's standing next to a poster for one of my concerts in Paris.

into the right shoulder of my jacket and stopped just short of penetrating my skin. It was a small blue and white pin with the Star of David on its face, over which was written, "Israel: 25th Anniversary, 1948–1973." The first thing that came into my mind was a quote from the Old Testament (Psalms 137): "If I forget thee, O Jerusalem, let my right hand wither." The phenomenon stunned us. Despite my deep feelings for Israel, I had sadly, not as yet, ever been there. When I was in my early twenties, the Israel Philharmonic Orchestra had asked me on two different occasions to perform with them. It was required that I play fourteen Tchaikovsky concertos on fourteen consecutive evenings! My doctor told me that I could seriously damage my little finger if I attempted this marathon. I was heartbroken, but I thought it wise to decline. Only a very few people knew about my little finger and it was important to keep it that way.

As time went on, Uri and I realized that our gifts seemed to intensify when we were together.

A fitting example of this happened one day with Uri when he called me from Ossining, New York, where he was living at the home of Dr. Puharich. He said, "Byron, come quickly!" I didn't need to think twice. Maria and I got a car and drove straight to Ossining, a little over an hour away. As we entered the house, Uri introduced us to Dr. Russell Targ and Dr. Hal Puthoff, two of the leading physicists at Stanford University. Uri was holding a bean in his hand, which he could cause to sprout on command, an experiment that he had often done. The physicists were trying to capture that extraordinary phenomenon on their video camera, but for some reason they weren't able to film it. Uri said, "Byron, you've got to sit down and play something." I went to the piano and, for a reason I can't fathom, I started to play the first movement of a Beethoven sonata known as "The Tempest." I must have been playing about a minute when suddenly there were shouts: "We got it! We got it!" They could finally capture the bean sprouting on camera. My enthusiasm must have gotten the better of me, and I said, "Okay Uri, now make it go back in!"

"You're crazy. That's impossible."

I said, "No, it isn't. Try it." I started to play again and, a moment later, it did the "impossible."

Uri came to dinner one evening and was intrigued by something he saw on my piano. He said, "Who is that?"

"That's a death mask of the composer Frédéric Chopin. It was in vogue at that time for someone who had just passed away to have a layer of wax molding put over their face, which an artist would then cover with plaster in order to make an exact likeness."

"Oh, I know who Chopin was," exclaimed Uri. "Can I see it?"

"Of course," I said, "but be very careful it doesn't drop, because I believe it is one of only three originals in the world."

I carefully took it off the piano. Maria; Stefan, who was then seventeen years old; Uri; Uri's future brother-in-law, Shipi; and I were

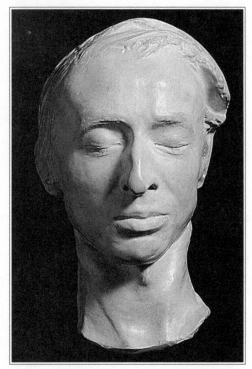

Chopin's death mask.

standing in the middle of the living room and were all holding the mask with one hand. No more than ten seconds later, a clear liquid suddenly started coming out of the left eye of the mask.

We froze in shock. Uri's eyes got larger than flying saucers. But that wasn't all. Before very long a liquid started coming out the left side of the mouth so strongly that it began to *bubble* on the surface of the lip. I decided to put my finger in the substance that was coming out of the eye and tasted it. It was salty. Tears! Maria did the same. "My God, these are tears!" she exclaimed. For well over a minute we watched in utter amazement before placing the mask back on the piano. As soon as we put it down the phenomenon immediately stopped. We collapsed on the sofas in utter disbelief; it was hard to comprehend what we had just seen.

Were these tears of sadness or joy? I believed they were tears of joy at having been able to make contact with another dimension—this dimension—and with someone who had such a deep love for his music and his persona. Was it because I felt so close to him, even as a child? It brought back the memory of when I would ask my mother why she cried when I would tell her something wonderful and she would answer, "Remember I told you, Slavs always cry when they are happy." Chopin must have been happy.

Dr. Puharich told me that with all the research he had done on Uri's pyrotechnical abilities, this was the first time he had been in touch with a soul. Uri was very shaken up and awed by the experience.

On a trip to Paris, I had one of those moments of absolute knowing. Uri happened to be in Paris also, and we asked him to come with us to Père-Lachaise to visit Chopin's grave. We walked to the peaceful shaded grave site, which was perfumed with the aroma of the many layers of flowers that were strewn around Chopin's tomb. Carved into the side of the base of the monument is a marble medallion about twelve inches high, and set inside it is a wonderful bas-relief sculpture of Chopin. As we stood together, I said to Uri, "Please do me a favor. Would you please place your hand on the side of Chopin's face?"

"No way," he replied. "With all these people around?"

"Uri, there's absolutely nobody around at this moment. Come on!" It took a moment, but he reluctantly climbed over a small iron fence that surrounded the grave and placed his hand on the sculpted marble face. It didn't take long. We watched as liquid rivulets started streaming out of the left eye with such force that they discolored the marble with a slightly yellow tinge. Uri was so unnerved by the experience that he leaped back over the fence, taking off like a frightened deer. "Let's get out of here!" Maria and I didn't move. I was half smiling and half crying—I wasn't surprised.

21

PÈRE-LACHAISE AND MARIE D'AGOULT

E VERY YEAR WHEN WE are in Paris, I make a point of visiting Chopin's grave site. On one visit, we were dining with a very close friend, Robert de Barrat, the editor of *Paris Match* magazine, and his wife, Stephanie. He was a rare breed—a hard-nosed journalist with a prove-it-to-me attitude who was nonetheless open to the possibility of the paranormal. He was certainly curious—even eager—to learn about such phenomena. As it happens, we had just returned from another startling experience at Père-Lachaise cemetery and welcomed an empathetic and interested ear.

I told Robert that we had gone with our son, Stefan, to Père-Lachaise to visit Chopin's grave site. We brought flowers, paid our respects, and were walking to the broad corridors that take you back out to the front gate. Maria's high heels were making it hard to walk on those lovely but somewhat treacherous old cobblestone bricks. She said she was looking down, walking carefully so as not to catch her heel and fall. Suddenly, she heard a voice cry, "Maria. Maria." She looked up; there was absolutely no one there. Then the voice called again. Stefan and I heard it as well. It was neither male nor female but compellingly human. She turned and steadily made her way about thirty feet over the cobblestones toward its source, with us following close behind her.

Soon we were brought up short by a low iron fence. When I looked up, a shock wave rumbled over me. We were standing directly in front of an ornate grave site with the inscription COUNTESS MARIE D'AGOULT.

Maria turned toward us and exclaimed, "Byron, look. I can't believe this!" "Oh my God," I blurted out as my pulse rate tripled. Stefan said, "Cool—but what's going on, Dad?" What was going on, indeed?

Maria told me she realized that the voice seemed to emanate from this very spot and that she felt the very least she could do was acknowledge it: "I felt the only gesture that came to mind was to leave a note as an offering, so I dug into my purse for a scrap of paper to write on. I didn't stop to think how silly this all might seem. I just knew I had to do it." Poor Stefan, being young and agile, was pressed into service to scramble over the fence and place the note in a deep crevice at the base of the marble. It felt right.

The three of us silently made our way out of the cemetery, very much lost in thought. Why had we chosen that particular path out of many? We had absolutely no idea where Marie was buried and, in fact, had not been thinking about her at all. And why, if indeed it was the voice of Marie d'Agoult, was she calling out to us?

Hearing that disembodied voice was extraordinary enough, but the fact that she had been such a dynamic force in the lives of Liszt, Chopin, and George Sand added to its poignancy. She had been

Liszt's mistress for nine years and gave him three children. Her close-
ness to Chopin and George Sand made this occurrence all the more
intriguing, especially given the fact that we had just come from visiting Chopin's grave. Chopin and George Sand were one of the most
visibly romantic couples of their time. Yet, it is quite a mystery why
Chopin dedicated his opus 25 études to Countess Marie d'Agoult only
a year after they met. How strange it was that he had never dedicated
anything to George Sand, who was his lover and friend for eight years.
Persistent rumors of a *ménage à quatre* continue to hound the four of
them. True or not, their lives were fraught with drama. A letter Marie
wrote to Chopin in 1836 certainly shows great warmth and affection:

> I learned from Liszt that you are gravely ill. I hastened therefore
> to remind you that Croissy [Marie's summer château] would be a
> perfect infirmary for you. . . . You would [breathe] in good air.
> I promise wonderful milk and the music of the nightingales . . .
> I adore your études, they are absolutely wonderful.

In another letter from this period, she wrote:

> I was ill, and am still ailing; I think that one of your nocturnes
> would cure me completely. Pray do not refuse.
>   P.S. If you cannot tomorrow, then Saturday, if not on
> Saturday, then on Sunday, etc.

Once she visited Chopin every day while he was ill in Paris, and
then would write George Sand to tell her of his condition.
    Marie d'Agoult stirs the pot again in a letter to a friend about
George Sand:

> I have recognized how childish it was of me to have believed
> (and this thought often filled me with sadness) that I alone
> could give Liszt everything necessary, that I was an unhappy
> barrier between two destinies made to fuse with and comple-
> ment each other.

After we told Robert about our cemetery saga and some of the background of the relationships, he ordered another bottle of wine and we spent the next two hours intensely discussing not only what had happened but *why*. Our story bumped up against his pragmatic mind-set, yet he knew Maria and I were not crazy. Proceeding as the journalist he was, Robert asked Maria, "Well, what did you write in your note?"

She answered, "Well, Liszt and d'Agoult used to affectionately refer to themselves as 'Mr. and Mrs. Fellows,'"—Liszt forever loved using nicknames; he called Chopin "Zopin"—"so in my message I addressed the 'Fellows' and said that we kept the memory of their lives in our hearts, and that I offered a special prayer for Marie. There had been a time when I felt a strong affinity for her, but then that evaporated."

"Why?" he prodded.

Maria seemed embarrassed but continued, "Well, I had read a lot about her complex life, and I felt I knew what I needed to know and didn't delve into it any further. Whatever Madame d'Agoult's purpose, she certainly got my attention."

In fact, Robert loved science, and after spending more time with us and hearing more of my experiences, he became increasingly interested in investigating various areas of the paranormal. Some months later, we introduced him to Uri Geller and had him witness some examples of psychokinesis. We all arranged to meet in an Italian restaurant, Les Trois Frères Righi, just behind the Hôtel Plaza Athénée. Before Robert's eyes, Uri used his mind to bend a large thick pasta serving spoon. Robert was so intrigued that he later put Uri on the cover of *Paris Match* as part of an article investigating psychic phenomena.

22

A PATH TO SPONTANEITY?

SPONTANEITY ISN'T THE SAME as creativity, but it's an ambiance in which creativity flourishes—a state some have called being in "high carelessness." It's a feeling of letting go from the bottom of your toes. Some veteran practitioners are said to enter a playground of "passionate indifference," a phrase coined by Teilhard de Chardin, the French Jesuit theologian and paleontologist. If you're feeling "Oh, what the heck" as you toss a splash of Chopin vodka over your poire Hélène, you're approaching the realm of spontaneity. If you're checking on your soufflé every five minutes, you can expect mud pie for dessert.

One of the best songs I wrote for *The Hunchback of Notre Dame* came upon me when Maria and I were strolling after lunch near a little Parisian bistro tucked in the shadow of that beautiful, mysterious cathedral, Notre-Dame. We were walking along one side looking up and pondering the gargoyles, wondering whose faces had inspired the sculptor, when I suddenly said to Maria, "Go on ahead of me, I'll be with you in a minute." I reached into my jacket pocket and found a cocktail napkin from our lunch. The notes spilled out of my head fast and furiously. My only difficulty was preventing the napkin from disintegrating under my fingers as I wrote down all the letters of the melody. I have developed my own musical shorthand, which came about as a result of my arthritis. It is difficult for me to put notes onto a musical staff because of the small space between the lines. I use letters, as Mr. Litow, my old piano teacher back in Pittsburgh, used to do, designating which note is to be struck—A, B, C, and so on. After five minutes the napkin looked like it was covered in hieroglyphs, but a song was born—unpremeditated, spontaneously. I was relaxed—both open and focused—and grateful. But was it good? That I still had to determine.

Speaking of napkins, Maria's uncle, Cedric Gibbons, an art director at MGM for decades, designed the famous "Oscar" statuette on the back of a cocktail napkin in a Hollywood restaurant. Why do you suppose so many sketches and drawings are started on napkins—and used ones at that? Why are so many memorable songs first scribbled on the backs of electric bills? One of the most important currents in the world is Spontaneity, with a capital S. If you cherish it too long or start to polish it, watch out. Usually even noticing spontaneity has the same effect as it does in quantum physics: the very act of observing something alters it. In the case of spontaneity, attempting to scrutinize it can eliminate it. As a matter of fact, the existence of even the possibility of observation without it ever having taken place will theoretically alter its position. To ponder that is staggering.

Spontaneity is a charge of imagination that seems to strike out of nowhere. You cannot light a fuse to ignite it. It is not an island you can visit when you're all caught up with your chores. It's more like a floating island that visits you.

So what good is spontaneity if it's so precious you cannot mine it and if you find it you cannot hold onto it? It is definitely a mercurial presence you had best take advantage of and be comfortable with if and when you are lucky enough to have it strike. And at the piano, an artist's ability to spontaneously deviate from exactly what he has practiced so religiously and be creative is walking a fine line—great actors know this feeling in their guts. The words (or the notes) will be the same, but oh, the variety, the range of feeling that can spontaneously burst forth.

When Cy Coleman, the famous composer of many Broadway shows and songs, and I would play two pianos together, we would have so much fun improvising and enjoying the surprises that only spontaneity can bring. Our collaborations gave birth to the "By and Cy Classic/Jazz Variations" on the famous *Rhapsody on a Theme of*

Cy Coleman (left) and I are performing for the first time our two-piano "By and Cy" Classic/Jazz variations on a Theme of Paganini. *This photo was taken at my fiftieth birthday celebration at Maxim's in New York in 1978.*

Paganini. Of course, spontaneity by itself is not necessarily a virtue. A person is just as likely to be spontaneously mediocre as spontaneously rare and special.

Spontaneity is also an important precondition for the miraculous. As you pry off the blinders of cynicism, you may find there are miracles occurring tailor-made just for you. You may suppose, for instance, that a man who has spent his entire life immersed in music would be a natural-born dancer. In fact, I have to be gagged and dragged onto the dance floor, I feel very self-conscious, and I'm afraid my balance wouldn't inspire confidence in a penguin. Quite frankly I'll make any excuse to avoid the torture. But for one brief day that changed.

Two women from a body-awareness training program came to teach me some exercises that would help me move my body with more ease. I left the room for a moment to change into work-out clothes. I don't understand what happened to me, but when I returned to the living room, I felt I wasn't the same person. I was definitely in some kind of altered state. After bowing deeply to the two women, I amazingly started to dance in a most extraordinary and formal manner, performing a rather complex set of movements as though I had practiced them for months. I must have been following some inner music. It felt like the dance was Southeast Asian, perhaps from Bali or Thailand, and it somehow seemed authentic to the last detail. I had a feeling of intense knowing. It was one of those many events I have never been able to explain. For me to have performed that dance was something of a miracle. The two women for whom I performed seemed mesmerized. They said nothing for what felt like an eternity, then got up from the sofa and, bowing deeply, said, "Thank you," with very reverential looks on their faces, and left the apartment. Everything concerning this occurrence still remains a mystery, but spontaneity was the key to it. I felt as though I was being "danced" like the times I felt when the piano was "playing" me.

I once had a student with the most precise command of whatever she played. Notes rolled off her fingers like perfect ball bearings off the line at a Toyota plant. There was an Olympic quality to her playing. But as active and agile as she undeniably was, she was also somehow sadly disengaged. I cajoled, I coaxed, I discussed, I joked, and finally I assessed. "You need to be more a part of the music you play. It sounds like you're more of an onlooker." When she looked at me with grim despair, I offered, "It's not enough to play it, it needs to be felt; and the audience will feel what you feel and won't feel what you don't feel." We were both clearly relieved when our session was over that day. As she was putting on her coat, I asked her what route she usually took home. The route she described was the most efficient one from her home to my studio. It happened that she had taken the same route in both directions for the three months we had worked together. I suddenly had a thought. I said, "I want you to find a new route when you go home today. Don't map it out now—just take one block, one building, one tree, one cloud at a time. Just feel yourself drawn along; eventually you'll get home." Her poor eyes were now glazed over with confusion.

The next week, I asked the same young lady to play a Beethoven sonata she had been working on. I hoped I wasn't jumping to conclusions, but it seemed that her change of walking routine might already have had some results because her performance showed a marked improvement. Being a pianist was the means; being an artist was the goal. You never know which of your remarks might make a difference. I could sense the start of a new freedom replacing an old habit—a difficult accomplishment indeed. She was learning the magic of spontaneity.

Every summer while I was touring Europe, Maria and I were invited to visit Pablo Picasso and his wife, Jacqueline. Visiting them was like being plunged into the world of his imagination—and what an imagination! Like all great artists, Picasso remained a child at heart. (At one point, Chopin insisted on seeing a pediatrician, saying, "He will help me most . . . as there is something of a child in me.")

Picasso often picked up "junk" as he walked, and some of that junk became his whimsical goats and magnificent baboons. His eye and imagination were constantly triggered and delighted by random things: pieces of metal, a palm frond blown down in a mistral, abandoned bicycle parts, the exquisite patterns of the spine of a filet of sole he had just consumed at dinner. He didn't say, "I'm going out shopping for the materials I need for the baboons I'll make famous six months from now." If you have ever seen photographs of Picasso's studio, you would find altars to spontaneity and labyrinths of his "shopping sprees." His studio seethed with ordered chaos—the artist's credo. Picasso never stopped creating, and he never stopped being spontaneous. He never stopped to create masterpieces—a masterpiece would simply happen.

Did Alexander Calder set out to create a circus, or did a circus emerge out of the telephone booth of Calder's dreams? And what do you suppose Martha Graham's game plan was when she started up with Noguchi's rickrack gowns? Looking back, isn't it inconceivable that the two could have shared a common goal? Could she have had any wild notion of how that structured fabric would affect the history of twentieth-century dance? She did not. Do you think Noguchi consciously began his work to influence dance? He did not have a game plan. Spontaneity started the flow, and the creative act followed.

For me, creativity and the paranormal also come from somewhat the same place. Think how much more information and inspiration these other realities could give us if only we learned how to tune out some of the daily clutter and static that our mental "radio" picks up. Some of us can do that—our focus and passion are so strong. But others are swept up in the current of the latest trend, and the door is locked for spontaneity to enter. The key ingredient for living, for creativity, and for the ability to experience the paranormal is absent. People with an establishment mind-set tend to retreat to the boundaries of their comfort zone, a death knell for progress. "Don't confuse me with the facts," they seem to be saying. When presented with a piece of reality that is behaving in a new and different way (e.g., psychokinesis), most scientists will retreat to saying, "You can't break the Second Law of Thermodynamics."

Where is the curiosity, where is the joy of discovering something new that breaks through the old ways of thinking? Beethoven became Beethoven by breaking one important musical law—he used the "forbidden" consecutive fifths, which, in fact, became a major factor in adding to the originality of his works. Cézanne blasted away old rules of perspective, Picasso fragmented form into new possibilities, Seurat created paintings by using millions of dots—did he realize that with pointillism he was inadvertently moving into a scientific visual mode by using the same elements that are the basis of photography?

23

PARANORMAL
HIGH JINKS

OVER THE YEARS, Maria and I spent some fascinating evenings with Judy Skutch, who with her husband, Bob, a successful businessman, were staunch supporters of research in parapsychology. At their Central Park West home, Judy held a sort of open-ended, never-ending psychic salon. Anybody who was serious in the field of extrasensory perception—scientist, researcher, psychic—felt free to drop by. One night, Maria, Judy, Micheline Lerner (the wife of Alan J. Lerner, the well-known lyricist and librettist), and I were chatting after dinner when I suggested that we have some fun and do a "table."

"Table turning" is a phenomenon that has been around for centuries, and it is capable of producing some extraordinary results. Very often it has indeed turned the tables on people—especially the skeptics. In the presence of a psychic, ordinary tables, cards, reading palms, and so on are merely tools for gathering information by extraordinary means.

The four of us sat at a large card table with everyone's hands resting lightly atop it. I generally seem to be able to activate tables quite quickly, and this one came to life within a couple of minutes. When we started to ask questions, the response was immediate. The table rocked back and forth on one leg, tapping out yes and no answers—one tap for yes, two taps for no—or designating the letters of the alphabet—one tap for A, two taps for B, and so on. I asked if there were any messages for anyone present, and the table began its deliberate response. Maria removed one of her hands from the tabletop so she could take the letters down in a notebook. The message, "Tell Noel to hide the tapes," puzzled everybody. We did have a friend named Noel Behn, whose best-selling book, *The Kremlin Letters*, had brought him much notoriety, but we hadn't seen or spoken to him in months, and I didn't have a clue what this was all about.

We telephoned Noel, and his answering service gave us a Boston number where he could be reached. We told him about the table's message, wondering if it had any relevance. "Well, I'll be damned!!" was his response. He was writing a book and living in Boston for the past two months in an old rented house while doing research and interviewing the perpetrators of the infamous 1981 Brinks robbery, during which two guards were killed. The gang was now doing serious jail time, and Noel felt as though he were in lockup with them as he gruelingly probed their lives. "Well," he went on, "it was the strangest thing. With all the damn rain we've been getting, my front door had swollen with dampness. I can no longer properly lock or even close it. Last night as I went out to dinner, it was pouring rain again, and I was already two blocks away when the thought hit me—the only thing of value I have in the house are those hundreds of hours of taped interviews with the prisoners. I better go back and *hide the tapes*, and I did. Hey, what were you doing, Byron, spying on me?"

It would have been interesting to know exactly at what time this thought hit Noel, but it wouldn't surprise me if it was the exact moment our table was relaying the message to us.

Noel was not as spooked by this episode as one might imagine because it wasn't his first paranormal encounter. His old friend Larry Blyden, who'd been married to the wonderful Broadway dancer Carol Haney, had shared some very strong experiences after Carol's death. Their country house had regularly been filled with the smell of baking brownies because they were Carol's favorite. For months after she died, the smell continued to recur. He told Noel that when he packed up the station wagon for the last time after selling the house, it smelled like a bakery. The delicious odor of brownies permeated the car. "Enough is enough!" he cried. "Oh, for God's sake, Carol, leave me alone!" The smell instantly vanished, never to return.

In the midseventies, I was asked to make a documentary film on the life of Chopin by an independent film company in France and the second channel of French television. We filmed in many places: Chopin's birthplace, Żelazowa Wola; Warsaw; Majorca; Paris; and, of course, the beautiful Château de Thoiry, where I had discovered the two Chopin waltzes. Our last location was Nohant, the lovely country house of George Sand, where Chopin spent summers composing and enjoying the company of such friends as Delacroix and Heine. We started filming one of the interviews sitting in the garden under the shade of a huge old tree. It was quiet, and dappled sunlight and warm breezes played over us as we talked. The director, Adrian Maben, asked that I tell the story of the Chopin mask that had wept (we had brought the mask with us to France to be photographed for the titles of the film). I demurred, not wanting to tell the story. For me it was something too intimate to be spoken of on television. I felt I would betray my closest confidant—in, of all places, the home that Chopin cherished as his refuge. I yielded to Adrian's request only after he assured me that if I didn't like it, it wouldn't be used.

Holding the treasured mask on my lap, I recounted the story, and when I was finished everyone seemed very happy. The soundman waved an "okay," and the director grinned, very pleased with the shot and the mood.

The next afternoon, Maria and I drove back to Paris and later that week went to the studio to watch the rushes of the Nohant shoot. Something inexplicable happened. On the screen came my interview about the weeping mask. The scene looked beautiful. But on the sound track, practically all of my dialogue was obliterated by a cacophony of crowing roosters. The barn had been absolutely quiet during the interview, and no unwanted sounds had registered on any of the recording equipment. How that happened, we will never know. The only thing I know for certain is that Adrian was furious and I was relieved. Chopin must have agreed with me!

The Orangerie in the beautiful Parc de Bagatelle in Paris plays host to an annual Chopin festival at which I performed in 1999. My very dear and very musical friends from Chicago, Chuck and Meredith Fry, were visiting Paris and joined Maria in attending the first of my two all-Chopin concerts. After the first concert, I realized that I had had a "first"—I had forgotten to play one of the pieces listed on the program, an impromptu of Chopin's. Greeting Maria and our friends afterward and before anyone could say a word, I blurted out, "Can you believe it? I forgot to play the impromptu."

"What do you mean?" Chuck asked.

"I left out the impromptu," I replied.

"No, you didn't. Of course you played the impromptu," Maria answered.

"What?!" I was incredulous. It was impossible! It took a lot of convincing to assure me that I had, indeed, played it. I had absolutely no recollection of performing that piece—not one note of it. Where was I? It is a mystery I will most likely never solve. The French radio had recorded the recital, and when I listened, the impromptu definitely was there. I certainly did play it—and I don't think I have ever played it better!

About three weeks later we returned to New York and a most extraordinary thing happened—although "extraordinary" is not a strong enough adjective to describe it.

I went to my closet to take out a suit. As I was removing it from a plastic and canvas garment bag I noticed a large tear toward the bottom of the bag that was well over a foot long. Well, I thought, this is no longer of use, so I asked Maria to come look at it and she agreed that another bag was needed. That afternoon, she bought a new cloth garment bag and was about to transfer my suits into it when she stopped dead in her tracks and called out, "Byron, come here!" As I came to her side, she pointed to the original garment bag and said, "Look." As I leaned in closer, I couldn't believe my eyes—the tear was no longer there! We were both stunned, and after discussing it, realized that it had obviously somehow repaired itself.

Just after writing notes on this story of the wardrobe, I picked up a fascinating book written by Brian Greene called *The Elegant Universe*. I turned it over and on the back cover read, ". . . a universe that consists of eleven dimensions, *where the fabric of space tears and repairs itself*."

Our wonderful son, Stefan, was in his teens when he fell victim to depression that was so hard to deal with that he was hospitalized for a brief round of intensive therapy and medication. A few weeks after his admission, the hospital staff called to request a "family session." At the hospital, Maria and I walked into a large room with a circle of chairs surrounding three others. The doctor indicated that we were to sit in the center seats. A moment later, Stefan joined us. After strong hugs, we took our assigned seats facing the assembled "white coats," all sitting with pads, pens, and charts poised.

The head psychiatrist offered a few pleasantries before launching into his inquisition.

"Ah, Mr. and Mrs. Janis, we understand from your son that . . . objects fly around the rooms in your home?"

Stefan, Maria, and I looked at one another, straining to suppress giggles.

"Well, yes, as a matter of fact, Doctor, they do," I replied.

My son, Stefan, and I are at a UJA-Federation of New York gala in 1988 after we performed a song we wrote for the fortieth anniversary of the founding of Israel.

I wish I could describe adequately the looks on the faces of those nurses and doctors. They all started writing feverishly in their notebooks. I could just imagine the head doctor writing the orders: "Get the parents. Reserve room 687 for them!"

"Well, perhaps it would clarify things if we were more specific," mused the doctor. "Stefan here has told us about somebody's death mask beginning to weep. No doubt, Stefan saw something that logically gave him that impression—which might be quite understandable—we wonder, though, if you know of any incident which might have given rise to that unusual take. We find sometimes that by probing beneath these impressions, we are able to quite rationally disperse the illusion and thus begin the process of retraining the brain to alleviate the cause of mental agitation."

It certainly put Maria and me in somewhat of a bind. We wanted above all else to help Stefan, but we obviously could not disown experiences we took to heart without also betraying our son. For a moment, we opted for nodding and looks of sympathy.

"For starters, Mr. Janis, do you actually own anything that might be construed as a death mask?" the doctor inquired.

Maria looked at me; Stefan looked at me; I looked at the good doctor and said softly, "Well, yes, we have Chopin's death mask."

"I take it," he went on, "this is an art object created by a creative artist to show something of how the artistic temperament is, say, imprisoned inside his physical self, while suffering his own angst within."

"Actually, no, Doctor, it is the death mask made from the face of Chopin after his death. I'm a devoted admirer of Chopin and have closely followed his life for many years."

"You see!" beamed the supervisor. "This is precisely why we invited you here today. To fill in the lacunae around Stefan's experiences and to bring them into rational light."

"Having come this far, then," continued his associate, "might it not simply have been a simple matter of condensation on the mask on a particularly humid day, which gave the outward appearance of weeping? Mind you, I'm not asking whether this was definitely the case, but whether it's possible that condensation was the cause of what Stefan believes he saw."

At this point, Maria quite rationally observed, "Well, if it were condensation, wouldn't there also have been condensation on the windows, on other bits of porcelain, glass? But you see, doctors, there was nothing of the kind. It was a crystal blue day."

This was not the turn of events the assembled medical experts had anticipated. But we had achieved one great breakthrough: Stefan smiled. It was the first genuine, hearty smile we'd witnessed in quite a while. His parents had vindicated him, and the medical authority figures who had been talking him deeper into depression and disorientation were now the ones who were disoriented. Stefan noticeably relaxed, and his breathing became deeper. He no longer seemed like someone waiting to be interviewed at a foreign immigration office because his visa had expired.

We valiantly attempted to explain ourselves and our experiences with parapsychology and psychokinesis, about how it manifests itself and about its myriad unknown elements—a noble effort obviously wasted on our distinguished audience. They were all probably worrying if we could be dangerous! At the very least they must have been collectively thinking, "No wonder this poor young man is having difficulties!" Stefan, Maria, and I have laughed about our "family session" ever since.

When seemingly irrational events happen, as I have mentioned before, a person can either try to open his or her mind a bit more to include the possibility of something he or she doesn't yet understand or, more commonly, try to pretend it didn't happen, usually with the aid of a stiff drink or two, and try to forget the whole thing.

I keep wondering if any of the stories we told that august scientific group got through to any of them. Hopefully at least one of them became "irrational" enough to need that drink. Regardless, Stefan got back on his feet, and Maria and I went on tour to South America. And all of us, believers and nonbelievers alike, continue to cope with both the ordinary and the extraordinary events that occur every day.

Dr. Pfeffer, my GI doctor, scheduled me for a routine colonoscopy. When I arrived at New York University Hospital, I was put onto a gurney by a nurse who gave me a bit of valium to help me relax. As I was waiting to be taken downstairs, the nurse asked, "Are you Byron Janis?"

"Yes," I replied.

"Hmm," she said. "I see you have bad bouts of coughing and spitting blood."

"What?" I answered in disbelief. "That's *never* happened to me. You must have mixed up your patients."

Her tone became firm, and she repeated, "Aren't you Byron Janis?"

"Yes, I am Byron Janis, but I don't have those symptoms."

She was now getting annoyed. "Mr. Janis, I have your chart right in front of me, and that is exactly what it says. There's no point in discussing this any further. Your doctor will take this up with you." As I was being taken downstairs for the procedure, I began to think how this could have happened. She was so adamant about it.

The doctor greeted me, and I immediately told him what the nurse upstairs had told me. He looked at my chart carefully and shortly exclaimed, "I don't know what she's talking about. There's absolutely no such thing written on your chart." I started to think coughing and spitting blood sounded like tuberculosis, which Chopin had suffered from. Had she imagined what she saw? Had it really been on the chart and dematerialized before it got to the doctor? Did it trade places with another patient's chart? Who knows—perhaps dear Chip-Chip decided he wanted to have a little fun!

Cosmic humor comes in many forms. Maria is a painter, and she had rented a studio space in the lower level of our apartment building that was adjacent to our landlord's office, which employed about ten secretaries. It was far from an ideal studio space. Despite its high rent, it was small and not that well lit, but at least she could store paintings and work a little there. Our close friend Uri Geller, whom we had met several months before, stopped by and asked if he could see some of Maria's latest paintings. We went down to her "cell," and as we were moving the canvases front to back, she exclaimed to Uri, "Boy, this landlord of ours is so tight! He charges me an arm and a leg for this tiny space!" She complained further, "You know, he's a real shit—really, he's a total greedy shit." As Maria repeated the S word, suddenly a falling object caught our eye. Something appeared at the ceiling, flashed, and dropped to the linoleum floor of the space where we were standing. We all jumped and looked down to see an old cast-iron key that was about three inches long. An antique, perhaps? Our building was built in 1911, so who knows? Totally puzzled, Maria pocketed the key and we finished looking at the paintings and went back upstairs.

The next morning, at about eleven thirty, Maria got a phone call from the landlord's office downstairs. The secretary seemed rather desperate and said, "Mrs. Janis, we are in big trouble down here. Nobody can find the bathroom key. Have you by chance seen it?"

Well, then it clicked. The key that had materialized the night before was indeed the key to the old bathroom in the basement. It had appeared when Maria said the S word, and we started laughing. Cosmic humor? You bet!

As you may have surmised, there are many different types of para-normal gifts. One fascinating example centers around a gentleman named Ted Serios, a Chicago bellhop whose special ability was being able to mentally produce an image on Polaroid film. The camera, with the lens cap *on*, would be pointed at Ted and a picture taken. When the picture was developed a few minutes later, the image would be of some-thing he was thinking at the very moment the picture was taken. This phenomenon was documented in a major story in *Life* magazine, which showed one of Serios's mentally transferred images of Civil War soldiers in uniform. This gift has come to be known as Thought Photography and has been documented as occurring as early as the 1850s.

Many people wonder if animals possess extrasensory perception. They do indeed, and we experienced it firsthand.

Cats have brought immense joy into our lives. Our first was a beautiful little Burmese we named Elektra, and she was really a "frequent flyer," traveling with us from South America, all over Europe, and across the United States. The sound of jet engines put her immediately to sleep, and she was welcome at every hotel we stayed at except the St. Anthony in San Antonio, Texas, where we ended up standing on the street with our luggage and Elektra after midnight, flagging a taxi to take us to another, more accommodating hotel.

After a concert in Lancaster, Pennsylvania—with Elektra along, of course—we decided to come home by car instead of train. I said, "Let's not take the Pennsylvania Turnpike, it's such a boring drive. Let's take the parallel smaller road that I think will be much more scenic." Maria agreed, and off we went with Elektra, our world trave-ler, in the backseat.

Once we got going, we took Elektra out of her travel case and let her roam free inside the car, a treat she always loved. Suddenly, she began to howl and race around in a crazed fashion. I was driving, so Maria tried to hold her and scratch her tummy, which normally would have put her into a trance state. But nothing worked. We stopped and got food. She wouldn't touch it and continued her shrill caterwauling. We were going crazy when suddenly she fell silent. She stopped howling and tearing around the car, went back to her travel case, curled up, and went to sleep. We were oh so relieved but oh so puzzled!

After we got home and began to unpack, we turned on the television. The lead news story was about the capture of a sniper who had been positioned on an embankment along the Pennsylvania Turnpike and who had been shooting at passing cars, killing four and wounding fifteen. We learned that as this was happening, we were traveling less than half a mile from that exact spot on a small side road paralleling the turnpike. I happened to look at my watch during Elektra's strange episode and again later when she suddenly became calm and quiet. The times of the start of the sniper's attack and his apprehension coincided exactly with the beginning and end of Elektra's wild behavior. It was very sobering to think "what if" and awesome to realize that Elektra had so obviously picked up on the proximity of the danger. Her favorite food was chicken, and we indulged her with it for a week.

Our Abyssinian cat Ptolemy's extrasensory perception was superb as well. Out of our many phone calls, he was always very adept at discerning which ones were with the vet. Each time I spoke with the vet, he would leap off the desk where he had been sitting and disappear somewhere in the apartment and be incommunicado for hours.

For the past several years we have had three cats, and at least one of them always seems to be musical and competes with me for keyboard time. Playing piano recordings seems to make our Burmese Mir want to perform—Prokofiev seems to be his favorite.

24

SAND DRAWING

I WILL LET MARIA TELL THE STORY of one of her own experiences with the paranormal.

"AT&T does not have the market cornered with its catchy phrase, 'We're all connected.' We are all connected, and it actually permits some beautiful and amazing things to happen in our lives, and many of them fall under the category of 'paranormal.' We still don't quite know what to do with them. It's almost like trying to understand not only another language but one that also uses a different alphabet.

"Some years ago, I went without Byron, who had to work in New York, to spend the weekend on Long Beach Island, New Jersey, with our very, very dear friends Dr. Lawrence LeShan and his wife, Eda. Larry is a psychologist who came into the world of parapsychology as a total nonbeliever. He has since become one of the ground-breaking researchers in this field and has written many books on the subject, including one with one of Yale's preeminent professors, physicist Henry Margeneau. Eda was a parent educator specializing in child development and a playwright as well.

"I wanted to get away, as I needed my ocean 'fix,' and it was good timing as I needed some alone time to think. Being constantly busy and on the road traveling lets one become somewhat inattentive to important inner issues. From time to time, I think all of us can probably use, as mission control in Houston calls it, 'a midcourse correction.'

"A question I have always pondered is how to love—better, deeper, and fuller. The answers to one's own report card can be troubling. At that time I was wrestling with my own answers, which seemed to be pointing to a serious deficiency on my part in simply how to love. I was in one of those existential moods: who am I, and am I capable of knowing the meaning of love?

"I went for an early-morning walk on an empty, mist-shrouded beach to think. My emotions were searching for answers, and for some reason I felt compelled to grab a long stick that had been washed up by the waves. I started to draw in the damp sand at the water's edge a rather unusual image. It was kind of abstract but had a combination of geometric forms—a circle in the center of four curved, vertical lines, forming a kind of diamond-shaped object.

"As the tumult in my head was battling with the question of the meaning of love, I could say that all of me was fighting with the answer.

"I finished the drawing, surveyed my handiwork, and then watched the incoming tide gently erase it. In the mood I was in at the moment, I took it to be a searing symbol that added to my "crisis."

"I trudged back to the house for breakfast, no wiser than when I left.

"A good brisk swim and a barbecue helped to brighten the rest of the day, and the time for us to leave came too soon. I was sitting in the backseat of the car when Eda turned around and handed me a little box wrapped with gold-colored elastic chord. She said, 'Larry and I bought this for you. We love you a lot.' I opened it and nestled on the cotton was a gold charm. It was an antique lavaliere. I choked.

I couldn't believe my eyes. There in front of me was the *exact* object I had drawn in the sand ten hours earlier—down to the last detail! Synchronicity? Perhaps precognition?

"What I do know for certain is that it was given to me with so much love and affection. This was a tangible connection, a bond, to two people I loved so very much and who loved me. My questions that morning on the beach about love all seemed to evaporate.

"There is a second part to this story, and it is an example of how these paranormal things seem to operate, how they interface with our 'regular world.'

"Later that week Byron and I had a little dinner party, and among the guests were Walter and Betsy Cronkite and our friend Uri Geller. Between courses, I excused myself and called Uri to follow me into our little office at the other end of the apartment. I wanted to tell him about my remarkable telepathic connection with the LeShans, what had transpired, and what it meant to me. We were standing in the office on either side of a little tray table as I recounted the story. As I was saying, 'This was given to me with so much love and affection—so much love and affection,' I saw a flash a couple of feet above my head, and something dropped onto the table between Uri and myself. I jumped and exclaimed, 'Oh my God!' and Uri half shouted, 'What's that?'

"I grabbed the object and to my shock saw it was the charm I had been telling him about a few seconds before. I bellowed for Byron to come from the dining room. He ran in, abandoning our now very puzzled guests, and I asked him to bring me a small white box from the top drawer of my bureau. (I'm glad my blood pressure wasn't taken then!)

"He came back in with the box, and I opened it. This is where I had placed the charm and its chain for safekeeping. You guessed it—the box was empty except for a small pearl clasp. It had contained only that and the LeShans' gift.

"I regained a semblance of composure, put the charm back into its box, and returned to the dining room to explain to our guests that something had fallen and I had to fix it. I didn't think it would be possible to explain what had just occurred.

"However, Byron took Walter aside and told him what had just happened. He was a good friend and the person who, four years earlier, broke the story of Byron's amazing discovery of the Chopin waltzes on the *CBS Evening News*. Walter, ever the good journalist and wary about the truth of a story, listened intently while puzzling over his own encounter with the paranormal earlier that evening when a square pat of butter that had mysteriously appeared on his suit lapel while he sat at our dinner table (there was no bread or butter anywhere near him).

"Walter just shook his head, and he and Betsy went home with a very big unanswered question on their minds. I have no answer to that question except to point to the connecting power of love between people.

"As for the pat of butter on Walter's suit—what a silly way, in my mind, to make someone aware of the power of the paranormal.

"But who was I to say?"

25

CAPE COD MYSTERIES

AGAIN, I WILL LET MARIA tell the tale of our Cape Cod adventure, since she played the leading role.

"Byron and I were weekending with Larry and Eda LeShan at their Cape Cod home nestled on the woodsy shore of Lake Wequaquet. I remember it was a bright summer day with a slight warm breeze. Cicadas hummed in the dense green bushes and trees. On Saturday afternoon an invitation to a barbecue lunch took us a mile or so away to the home of some friends. It was one of those rambling New England shingled houses with a large screened-in porch and a beautiful view of the lake. Byron hates the sun, so while most of the other guests were running madly about trying to play volleyball in the lush green meadow, he was inside practicing on their small spinet piano.

"We all felt intensely good, relaxed, and happy. For a woman then in her forties who still felt like she was in her teens, I suddenly, spontaneously, wanted to do something I hadn't thought of doing in thirty years—turn cartwheels. Just out of sheer exuberance. I started running, got a little speed, and hurled myself over and over on the soft grass. No one was paying the slightest attention, nor was anyone even near me as they were all busy playing volleyball. When I triumphantly stood up from my two elegant cartwheels, I noticed that something was missing. I clasped my head and realized my scarf was missing. It had vanished. It was my favorite large blue silk scarf, which I always tied firmly under my chin to keep my hair 'in shape' for the evening. It had been on my head when I started my acrobatics, but now it was gone. I looked around on the grass and found nothing but a few innocent white butterflies. I ran the hundred feet or so to the porch, calling, 'Byron, guess what just happened? I don't believe it! Damn, that's my favorite scarf.' I had that queasy feeling in my stomach you get when you return to your parking space and find your car has been towed.

"I grumbled a bit more to Byron and started back out onto the lawn, but something stopped me in my tracks. 'Byron, look!' I yelled. In the air about fifteen feet above the ground, fluttering gracefully and floating down to the grass, was my scarf. A good ten minutes had elapsed between its disappearance and reappearance. Where had it been? Byron and I always ask ourselves that when objects dematerialize then return right in front of our noses. This has happened to us on many occasions. It is one of science's many unsolved mysteries. More was to take place on that beautiful afternoon, but that's Byron's story, and he'll take it from here."

After lunch, some of the guests asked me to play. I declined at first because their little spinet was just about played out. But I finally decided I would try a Bach prelude. Maria came up and stood by the piano listening when suddenly I noticed something slowly emerging from the tiny space that exists between two ivory keys in the upper register of the piano. It started getting in the way of my right hand during certain passages. I asked our son, Stefan, to come over and stand near the keyboard. I wanted him to block the others from seeing this weird thing that was happening. The object was rising higher and higher—finally I had to stop playing and pull the remaining bit out. "It" turned out to be a very old ivory key, yellowed with age. It was narrower than a piano key, and it was grainy and chipped on one edge. It was unquestionably from a harpsichord. The thought popped into my head: could this have come from Bach's era? An idea not, perhaps, so far-fetched as it might sound.

Einstein concluded in his later years that the past, present, and future all exist simultaneously. He believed in no true division between past and future, only a single existence, a concept shared by leading physicists of today. In his book *Everything Forever*, Gevin Giorbran relates that this understanding came to Einstein when his lifelong friend Michael Besso died. In a letter to Besso's family, the scientist said that although Besso had preceded him in death, it was of no consequence, "For us physicists believe the separation of past, present, future is only an illusion, although a convincing one."

Similarly, the great modern British physicist Stephen Hawking, working with Jim Hartle, emeritus professor of physics at the University of California, Santa Barbara, states, "The universe would be completely self-contained—not affected by anything outside itself. It would neither be created nor destroyed—it would just be."

Hawking's statement reminded Maria and me of the ways objects seemed to suddenly appear out of nowhere. There is nothing on the table, and suddenly, in not even a blink of an eye, a framed photograph, a ceramic dish, or whatever would be sitting there. It would just "be." As if that isn't startling enough, an object can make its entrance in slow motion, usually first appearing near the ceiling and making a "slow drop" (as Maria calls it) with never any damage to itself. Sometimes it relates to a conversation we'd been having or sometimes it seems just random. Lastly, there is the Ferrari-like entrance when the object comes racing into your room almost too fast to see; it can happen in any room anywhere.

I could say that Maria and I have gotten used to such things appearing, but the truth is, we never have. They amaze, delight, and jar us into the realization that reality doesn't always only work as we think it should. It isn't fixed, rigid, or run by unbendable rules. Which is why I calmly slipped the yellowed key into my pocket and asked my hosts whether they'd ever owned a harpsichord. They looked surprised. "No," they answered. "Why do you ask?"

"Oh," I said. "Just curious." I let it drop, but then came the rocks.

The next morning back at the LeShans' house, Maria and I were out walking in the woods and discussing how reality can really get tossed around. We were stopped by a rustling sound in the leaves high above us and then a kind of crashing sound, of something falling to the ground very nearby. Then we spotted them: a shower of rocks hitting the ground. They were not close enough to have hit us, but they were certainly close enough for us to hear and to see. We were already standing at the highest elevation of the surrounding land-scape, so there was nothing above to fall down upon us. Moreover, these stones were clearly plummeting in a vertical direction, not like someone was throwing them. We followed the sound with our eyes and feet and went to the edge of the bushes and saw where many of the accumulated rocks of various sizes had fallen. Neither Maria nor I is a geologist, but there were no other similar stones in that whole area—not in color, size, or shape. We could only look at each other—what was there to say? Since there was also nothing else to do, I simply picked up one of the rocks and dropped it in my jacket pocket as a souvenir.

Later that week, back in New York, our friend Uri Geller dropped by to say hello. He'd just been in San Francisco doing research with a team of scientists and physicists at the Stanford Research Institute (SRI). I told Uri the story of the falling rocks and took my souvenir out of the desk drawer to show him. He got that stunned, wide-eyed look when something mystifying happens. "Byron, look!" he said. He reached into his jeans pocket and pulled out a piece of rock the size of a walnut. "This materialized in my pants pocket last week at SRI. I noticed it was sud-denly there because my pants tightened, and it kind of hurt." We held the two stones close to each other and saw that they had the same look, the same color. Uri and I then turned the stones around and we both noticed there was a chunk missing from mine. Rotating Uri's small piece, we soon found, to our shock, a place in my stone into which it "clicked." It was a perfect fit, like a jigsaw piece. We were all dumbfounded. How could it be? But there it was.

These kinds of occurrences make me think about the importance of connections. For me, it is all evidence that Einstein's space–time continuum is not an impermeable barrier. Perhaps someday, when we find out more about these connections, we will no longer feel separated from those who are not physically present.

26

COMPLETING
THE CIRCLE

THE EXTRAORDINARILY GIFTED British medium Ena Twigg was also a spiritualist minister and, in fact, was the first one to be featured on a regular religious program on the BBC in England. Her stature as a medium also garnered her an invitation to speak at the Southwark Cathedral, the first woman ever permitted to do so. She had been invited by the Right Reverend Mervyn Stockwood, Lord Bishop of Southwark, who made a rather interesting and important comment in his foreword to Ena Twigg and Ruth Hagy Brod's 1972 book, *Ena Twigg: Medium*:

> If we were to take psychic studies seriously, we would learn
> to appreciate that our experience in this world is not the

consummation; instead, we live now as *sub specie aeternitatis*.
There are other worlds and dimensions, and this should be
taught in our schools as part of our general education.

Miss Twigg was well known in Europe, the United States, and
throughout the world, and her clients included people in government,
royalty, and people in the business world. Her fascinating life story
provides evidence of the afterlife and reincarnation. One of her more
noted contacts with the other side generated huge publicity. She had
a "communication" with the well-known Episcopalian American
bishop James D. Pike, who, according to newspaper headlines worldwide, at the time was lost with his wife in the Israeli desert. Bishop
Pike was a controversial figure and held some theological views that
were considered close to heresy by the church. He was a great advo-
cate for social issues and reform, and one of his favorite targets
was the infomous senator Joseph McCarthy, who believed that com-
munists were lurking everywhere. At the time of his disappearance,
a seemingly discarnate voice in Miss Twigg's living room suddenly
commanded her to turn on her tape recorder. The spirit voice was
identified as belonging to the missing Bishop Pike, who, unknown
to anyone on earth at the time, had then been dead for twenty-four
hours. (The details of this story were extensively researched and verified and reported in *Ena Twigg: Medium*.)

In 1974, when I had an opportunity to meet with Ena Twigg for
a psychic reading when I was in London. She was particularly known
for her ability to contact those who had passed on. It's strange, but
in spite of my expectations I was surprised when she told me my
father was "around" me very often. I would have expected it to be
my mother. She said he was most proud of me for the elements in my
life outside of music. Ever since my experience as a youth in Dallas
regarding the injustice I saw shown toward the black community,
I had lived up to my principles in matters of racial prejudice when I
canceled my concert in Mobile, Alabama, after the peaceful Selma
March with Martin Luther King Jr. was turned into a bloodbath by
the police. I was so deeply disturbed by it that I vowed to take up

the cudgels of fighting racism in any way I could, so I also refused to perform before a segregated audience in South Africa and refused to accept the South African government's attempt to get around that by offering me a radio concert instead. My father had never expressed any of his feelings to me on these matters, and when I told my mother what was conveyed to me, she completely corroborated Miss Twigg's reading. It made me so very happy.

After my reading was finished, we had some tea and chatted about Miss Twigg's recent trip to the United States. She told me she had been invited to Chicago by Bob Kennedy to be a guest on his morning news and interview television program, *Kennedy and Company*. She had not been to the United States in quite a while and said she would accept the invitation with one restriction: because of a heart condition, she would not give a demonstration by going into her usual trance state, which typically preceded a psychic reading. The producers agreed, and off she went to Chicago.

She described what happened: "As I was sitting onstage doing the interview with Mr. Kennedy, I inadvertently slipped into a trance and apparently said the following: 'There is someone in this room who would have died had it not been for the intervention of a psychic healer.' Kennedy nearly fell off his chair. 'What?! I don't believe this! That person you are speaking of is standing right over there, running one of my cameras. He's my wife's brother, Frankie, and he's now fully recovered from a life-threatening condition.'"

I looked at Ena Twigg in amazement. That psychic healer happened to have been my wife, Maria. About six months earlier, I had a concert with the Chicago Symphony at Ravinia, their summer home. Before we left, our friends Larry and Eda LeShan asked Maria, who had been training with him as a healer, if she would visit the brother of a very close friend who was in the hospital in Chicago. He was about twenty-three and suffered from a grave intestinal disorder for which surgery and other treatments had not offered relief. He was given a very bad prognosis for recovery.

We arrived at our hotel, and before long, Maria said, "I promised Larry and Eda I would go see Frankie, so let me do that now and

I'll be back." She returned some two hours later. I asked her how it had gone and she said, "I really don't know—I did my thing. Boy, a hospital environment is really a challenging place to try to meditate. Frankie and I talked a little—he looked pretty darn sick. Then I sat on the end of his bed to try to focus and get into a meditative state. Bells were ringing all the time, intercom voices calling. An attendant came in with a steel bucket and a mop and started swabbing away at the floor around the bed with some foul disinfectant. Anyway, I went through the centering procedure I'd been taught at our nice quiet retreat training centers in the Connecticut woods—Larry had warned us: 'If you expect perfect conditions, you'll never do anything.' Was he right! Well, I did the best I could and ended up with the Lord's Prayer because I felt so totally helpless. After about twenty-five minutes, I gave Frankie a hug and left. I guess he didn't mind having a visitor, anyway."

A few weeks later, we were told that, to his doctors' astonishment, Frankie had shown significant improvement and had been sent home; he went on to eventually have a complete recovery. As I told Miss Twigg about Maria's visit with Frankie, she looked absolutely elated and asked if I would give her permission to tell this story to the *Psychic News*. She said, "This is so amazing—this completes the circle!"

To follow up, Frankie was fine for about five years. He then needed another surgical procedure and has been in terrific health, raising a family and working hard, ever since.

27

A PICASSO DREAM

MARIA'S REMARKABLE FIRST meeting with Pablo Picasso took place in 1957 on the terrace of the famous Hotel du Cap in Antibes. It was all thanks to her mother's friendship with David Douglas Duncan, the internationally renowned prize-winning photojournalist and an intimate friend of the Picassos. He arranged for Maria's parents, Gary and Rocky Cooper, to invite Picasso and his wife, Jacqueline, down to their hotel for a late afternoon drink. It was an impromptu meeting that was to open a wonderful, rich new chapter in the lives of all present.

But I should allow Maria to tell her own story.

"Those two larger-than-life men, Pablo and Coop, seemed instantly enthralled with each other. My father may have been his usual relaxed self, but my mother was a nervous wreck, even losing her impeccable sense of taste by putting on diamond earrings at five in the afternoon.

"I was excited but calm until my wonderful mother, God bless her, said, 'Oh, Maria, why don't you show Picasso your sketchbook.' I could have killed her, but now I had no choice. David managed to capture on film the moment of complete horror and embarrassment on my face as I watched one of the greatest painters of the twentieth century turn the pages of my lowly sketchbook. When Picasso commented, 'Oh, she can paint,' I was so flustered I couldn't even squeak out a thank-you.

"We next saw Picasso and Jacqueline at La Californie, their beautiful belle époque villa in the hills above Cannes. We walked up the four stone steps with my father carrying a bag loaded with gifts slung over his shoulder. It was literally a 'loaded bag' as it was filled with a six-shooter, a case's worth of loose bullets wrapped in socks and stuffed inside shoes, and the famous white Stetson that he wore in the film *Saratoga Trunk*. Once we arrived and everyone had greeted one another, the 'loaded bag' was eagerly 'unloaded.' With the glee of a teenager, Picasso snatched up his new pistol and led us all out into his garden, the one copiously 'planted' with his large, fantastic iron sculptures. I shall never forget the scene that followed.

"The two men began by arranging their targets—several empty paint cans—atop a not-too-distant stone wall. My father shouted, 'Fire away!' and the fun commenced. First Picasso, then Coop blazed away. Unfortunately, the great painter's shots were landing nowhere near the targets, nor even the wall. Some were even ricocheting dangerously close to where we were standing. As we ran for cover, Jacqueline scooped up children and dogs, and we all cowered behind one of those conveniently placed sculptures. My father, in true gentlemanly fashion, deliberately missed many of his own shots. Despite our brush with death, everyone had fun. As for 'Dead-Eye' Picasso—well, fortunately for us, his aim with a brush was far better.'"

•   •   •

Maria and I always looked forward to my concert tours in the south of France—Nice, Menton, Monte Carlo, Cannes. But we looked forward most of all to our visits with Picasso and Jacqueline. I met him in 1967, and his first remark to me was very flattering: "You look like the day you were born." We spent as much time as we could in the blazing creative atmosphere that enveloped Notre-Dame-de-Vie, his home in Mougins, a village overlooking Cannes. "Perhaps home/studio would be a more appropriate description," as Jacqueline once said. "He always manages to gradually take over every room in our house—there never is enough room for him," she added with a voice edged with frustration.

Our visits with the Picassos included animated discussions as well as jovial chatter. We'd sit at the dining table, which moments before had been commandeered for use as a work area and was covered with

Maria and I are with Picasso at his home, Notre-Dame-de-Vie, in the South of France, in 1967.

pads, colored marking pens, and paints. Picasso would cavalierly push all of that into a corner to make room for some relaxed moments with as much caviar and vodka as we could eat and drink. The great artist had little patience for the many visitors who came by to greet him. Though occasionally he found them amusing and relaxing, visitors took time away from his passion. He was always polite, but when the creative urge overtook him, off he went, never to be seen again.

Picasso had a repertoire of private "tests" for guests and new-comers to see if they could handle the mischievous games he liked to play. On our second visit he presented himself by bursting through a screen door dressed only in his jockey shorts—bare-chested, arms crossed, daring the world to stop him. Jacqueline had just told us he'd been painting all night and that we probably wouldn't have a chance to see him that visit, when—voilà—there he was in a Yul Brynner *King and I* stance, looking completely ageless and ready to work another twenty-four hours. If we'd shown the slightest flicker of shock at his state of undress, we would have failed that test and probably would have been denied entrance to his special charmed circle of close friends.

One day, he challenged me to another test. He asked us to follow him to a room where he kept a huge bronze-colored cowbell on the floor. Standing in front of it, he hoisted the bell as easily as if it were a feather. Turning to me, he said, "*Viens—c'est à toi.*" Or, "Now it's your turn." Generally, I like games, and I especially like a good challenge. But I was feeling unsure about this one. That bell looked like it belonged to an elephant, not a cow. I walked over to the cow-bell, gripped it by its two handles—and couldn't budge it an inch! It didn't even teeter. Picasso chuckled knowingly. I had obviously not been his first victim. What an enormous strength there was in that five-foot-five, eighty-year-old man. We marveled as he would go to a closet to pull out twenty or so huge canvases backed on very heavy stretchers, moving them around like slips of paper. We sensed a certain pride in him that it wasn't just what was on his canvases that we were admiring.

We left the implacable cowbell and returned to our sausage, our vodka, and more conversation. At one point, Maria spoke to Picasso of her frequent frustration at attempts to paint me. Picasso said, "Ah, Maria, when that happens, go and paint a flower and then come back to painting Byron." He was right; it worked. He later showed us some recent pictures he'd been working on—a series of porno-graphic drawings. His face sparkled with the obvious delight he took in showing them off. Another one of his little tests, no doubt.

Jacqueline was the "official" photographer at our gathering and sent us many wonderful photos of our moments together. Some of the mailing envelopes were themselves decorated by Picasso's amus-ingly playful hand. The postman never realized what was passing through his hands.

Picasso would regale us with amusing stories about people who had tried to curry favor with him. He possessed what Maria's father and Ernest Hemingway called a "numero uno" BS detector.

With a glint of his eye, he told us of the time he admired a vest worn by a famous art collector and museum benefactor who came to visit. The fellow promptly stripped off his vest and, handing it to Picasso, exclaimed, "Oh, here—take it, take it—it's yours." As he thrust the article of clothing into Picasso's hands, the painter was of course delighted. But while thanking his benefactor, Picasso noticed a significant amount of money stashed away in one of the vest pock-ets. He naturally started to return it but the man protested, with a flurry of "No, no. Keep it. It's yours, it's yours." He pushed Picasso's hand away. At that point Picasso's BS detector kicked in. Perhaps that vest was not such a spontaneous gift after all. Most likely, the man was one of "those people," someone looking for a return favor down the road. Picasso laughed as he told us that he agreed to accept the money anyway, but as they were all saying their good-byes, he stuffed a little of his newly acquired wealth into the collector's jacket pocket, saying, "Just in case you don't have enough for dinner."

Maria told me one day that a fairly well-known actor friend man-aged to inveigle a meeting with Picasso. En route to Villa La Californie, the actor asked Maria if she thought Picasso might draw him a little *corrida*, or bullfight. "For God's sake. No!" exclaimed Maria. "I would never bring him anyone who would dare ask for something like that!"

But desire overcame manners, and not too long into their meeting the actor asked Picasso, "Maestro, would you please draw for me a little *corrida*?" Poor Maria blanched but was stunned when Picasso promptly sat down with a sketch pad and drew quite a richly colored bullfight scene. Our nameless actor was salivating as Picasso finished the drawing, tore the page out of the pad, and held it up to study it. As the actor's shaking outstretched hands were reaching for the priceless page, Picasso shook his head in disapproval, saying, "*Non, je n'aime pas*," and tore it up into little bits. After dropping the pieces into the wastebasket, he reached down and took out a few crumpled pieces of what looked like a used paper napkin, grabbed a marking pen, and after a few slashing strokes said, "Voilà, here's your picture!" Mr. Famous Actor went looking for a bullfight and got gored in the end.

On the morning of April 8, 1973, I awoke, turned to Maria, and said, "I just had the strangest dream about Picasso."

Maria said, "How absolutely incredible. So did I."

She began recounting her dream: "It looked like we were in Villa Californie. The large rooms were full of stacked canvases in various stages—empty to full—of all the fantasies of Picasso's limitless imagination. Picasso was walking away from us, passing from one large room to the other. As he got to the furthest room, he grasped the door handle, opened the door, and stepped through it—but before closing it, he skipped a few jaunty steps backward, turned, and gave us a hearty salute, with a wave of his hand high over his head and a smile that said, 'So long . . . see you!' All done with a most tremendous joie de vivre. And then—he walked through the door."

I hugged Maria and said, "What an extraordinary dream. Mine was much simpler. The four of us were sitting in that very large wonderful room that we've been in so many times at Notre-Dame-de-Vie. The walls were hung with the usual unframed paintings that he had collected, his own as well as others. Many of his white doves were perched on open balconies and windowsills. And there was that table we always sat at with a bottle of vodka, a jar of caviar, and some chorizo, and we were all laughing at the funny stories he was

This photo of Picasso in Villa La Californie captures the image Maria saw in her dream. Her charcoal drawing of Moscow is on the chair at the left.

telling. A great feeling of joy seemed to prevail." Maria and I were thunderstruck that we both had dreamt of our good friend at the same time.

As we often did, we turned on the radio at noon that day to listen to the news and heard the shocking bulletin: Pablo Picasso had died at his home in France that morning at 11 a.m. French time. His wife, Jacqueline, was at his bedside. "Maria, that's just about the time we were having our simultaneous dreams about him!" How beautiful that this greatest of artists came to us both in our dreams to say good-bye. What better confirmation is needed that death doesn't stop communication.

In 1980, a number of years after Picasso's death, Jacqueline came to visit us in New York. It was very moving to be with her at the Museum of Modern Art as she gazed upon Picasso's famous *Guernica*, his outpouring of rage against the Spanish Civil War. She had never seen the painting before. Standing there in the empty gallery, a lonely figure silhouetted against this huge extraordinary work of art, she said nothing, but her face was filled with anguish. Was she reacting to the painting or did seeing it make her feel she was in a now meaningless world? Picasso had been her life. She had lived for him and through him, and the emptiness was too much for her. Not long after, she took her own life.

28

MEETING
CHAGALL

T HE LUMINOUS LIGHT that is the gift of the Mediterranean Sea
to the South of France, along with its unique landscape, both
fierce and gentle, has long proved an irresistible combination to many
painters. Four of the greatest—Picasso, Matisse, Chagall, Renoir—all
chose to make their homes in this painter's paradise. Chagall settled in
the Riviera village of Saint-Paul de Vence, only a stone's throw away
from Picasso's Notre-Dame-de-Vie. After being with Picasso and his
wife, Jacqueline, visiting the Chagalls was like entering a different
world. Music played no part in Picasso's world, but to Chagall it was
everything. "My muse," he called it. Music was his constant companion while he painted.

I told Chagall how much I admired his two beautiful murals in the Metropolitan Opera House at Lincoln Center. "Ah, you mean *The Sources of Music* and *The Triumph of Music*? Terrible. Terrible, the way they placed them," he exclaimed. "You have to go outside into the cold to the—what do you call it—mall, to be able to see them. They should be called 'Murals for the Mall'!" It was hard not to laugh—or to disagree.

In 1964, André Malraux asked Chagall if he would grace the Paris Opera House with a painting inside its dome. (No issue of placement there.) When it was completed, Chagall presented it as a gift to the city of Paris, a city he loved and which had done so much for him. I told him how magnificent I thought that painting was. Everything about it was music. It sang—and with what colors!

Visiting his studio and taking in his paintings in progress, we couldn't help but marvel at how he managed to put so many different visions into one painting and still give the whole such unity of form. And again, the colors! Picasso once said, "When Matisse dies, Chagall will be the only painter who understands what color really is. Nobody since Renoir has the feeling for light that Chagall has." When the time came for us to leave, I mentioned I was going to play at the Casals Festival in Puerto Rico. He said to me, "Oh—Casals? Do you think he would remember me? I haven't seen him in such a long time."

"I don't think there's any doubt about that," I said.

"Well, then, please say hello from me."

When Maria and I left, we looked at each other with a shared thought, "Would Casals remember me?" Come on!

After Marc Chagall died, his widow asked if I would play a recital commemorating the first anniversary of her husband's death. I was so honored, and, of course, I accepted the invitation immediately. It would take place at the Musée National Message Biblique Marc Chagall in Nice, which is dedicated exclusively to his biblical paintings. How special it was to meet the families of many great artists— Matisse, Braque, Jacqueline Picasso, Renoir—as well as many guests who graced the world of art.

That night there was a scene I shall always remember. Jacqueline happened to catch a glimpse of me while I was closing a backstage door. "Byron! Byron!" she shouted. Her voice rang through the packed auditorium as she ran to greet me. After we embraced, she handed me the most wonderful gift. It was a beautiful Picasso lithograph, something I'll always treasure.

Chagall's daughter, Ida, came backstage after the concert and invited me to lunch the following day at the Colombe d'Or. Not only was I looking forward to our meeting but also to dining at that glorious restaurant with its magnificent views and even more magnificent food.

During lunch, Ida asked, "What made you play that particular Mozart sonata that started your program yesterday?"

"I don't know," I replied. "I play various Mozart sonatas, and I guess I just happened to choose the F Major last night."

"Did you know that was my father's favorite piece of music?" she asked, clearly flabbergasted. "I remember he would often whistle it when we would go out for walks together."

I guess my old extrasensory perception was at work again. What a beautiful synchronicity.

29

ANDREW BOREY

As you have seen, Chopin has played a most important role in my life, and I wanted to relate two further episodes of my encounters with him.

One day a dear friend, Alex Szogyi, who was head of the Department of Romance Languages at Hunter College, phoned me and said, "There's someone in my comparative literature class whom I would like you to meet. Can we make a date to come by?"

On the chosen date, Alex appeared at the door with a very well-dressed gentleman of less than medium height but who was very imposing with his West Point–like posture.

"Byron, this is Andrew Borey. Andrew, my dear friend Byron Janis."

After shaking hands, I noticed that Mr. Borey kept gazing at me intensely. I was nonplussed when he suddenly put his arms around me and started to weep, saying, "You are my family!"

I am usually a rather formal person, especially on first meeting someone, but for some reason, this did not feel like a first meeting. And before I had another thought, I found myself overtaken with emotion. It seemed so natural to me to embrace him in return. When Alex told me his family background, I was in total shock (I know I have used these words over and over—shocked, amazed, unbelievable, incredible—but I don't know any other way to describe my feelings when these astonishing events occur).

Andrew Borey turned out to be none other than the great-grandson of one of Chopin's sisters, Ludwika. I needn't tell you what close friends we became, spending many memorable times together.

We spoke of many things ranging from Chopin, music, and World War I, in which he served as a Polish cavalry officer on the front lines defending Poland from the German juggernaut.

Andrew Borey, the great-grandson of Chopin's sister Ludwika, and I at my home in 1989.

He spoke about his mother, who had one of Chopin's pianos in her house in Warsaw. She told Andrew that the renowned French pianist and Chopinist Alfred Cortot called on her one day, asking if he could see Chopin's piano. She described how he got down on both knees and began to kiss every single key and then took his leave. She also told him about her great antipathy for George Sand, whom she felt was largely responsible for Chopin's death.

After a birthday lunch for Andrew, his son, George, turned on the radio, and the entire afternoon's programming was devoted to the music of Chopin for no apparent reason. Or was it for Andrew?

Andrew would often ask me to play for him. He loved the music of his great-uncle, mostly polonaises and mazurkas.

Some years ago, Andrew died, and George, who carries on the family legacy, requested that I play at his father's funeral. I was so honored to have been asked, and I played one of his favorite nocturnes, the very same one I had played for Aurore Sand.

I feel deeply privileged to have known Andrew.

30

ISRAEL

I HAD WANTED TO VISIT ISRAEL and the magical city of Jerusalem for many years. And now I was just one hour away from seeing its many sacred and secular treasures. Tel Aviv University had appointed me head of its Visual and Performing Arts department in the United States and brought me to Israel for the first time in 1989 to conduct master classes at the university.

To my further good fortune, my close friend Uri Geller and his friend Shipi were also planning to spend time in their home base. As native Israelis, they could show me so many things I might otherwise not have known existed. So we managed to coordinate our schedules to be there at the same time.

The very first place I wanted to visit was Jerusalem, and the university had kindly put a car and driver at my disposal. The pouring rain that had greeted me on my arrival hadn't let up. Uri and Shipi met me in the hotel lobby, which was jammed with people due to the storm. When the driver arrived, he began an animated discussion with Uri in Hebrew. Uri translated: "He is strongly advising us not to go. Because of its location, the rain in Jerusalem would be even worse." "Well, I don't care," I replied. "I want to go anyway." I got into the car, and after a few moments of hesitation my friends reluctantly decided to join me.

As we drove, Uri pointed out debris and remnants of the Six Day War—burned-out tanks, some unexploded shells, charred jeeps—it was all quite fascinating in any kind of weather. However, as predicted, the rain kept pouring down as we approached Jerusalem. "It's just over the hill, Byron!" Uri exclaimed. I could hardly wait; my heart was pounding! But it was raining so hard now that the driver could barely see the car in front of him. "Damn, I won't be able to see a thing."

Suddenly, Uri leaned over from the backseat, and in a conspiratorial tone, suggested, "Byron, why don't you do your thing?"

Doing my "thing" hadn't occurred to me, but I thought, well, why not give it a go?

"Okay, I guess there's no harm in trying," I replied. I lowered my head and did a kind of meditation for about thirty seconds on what I wanted to happen, but I was in no way prepared for what did happen. We passed over that last hill, and there was Jerusalem in all her glistening splendor. While we were being drenched with rain, miraculously, the rain clouds directly over the city had suddenly dispersed, leaving in their path a perfect circle of clear blue sky and sun. It was an incredible sight.

"Oh, God—this is not possible," I blurted out, completely awed by the convergence of events.

The driver turned to Uri in disbelief "What's going on? Who is this man? It's not possible!" He went on and on. Uri was enjoying it all, laughing uncontrollably. He had seen me affect weather before, but it never occurred to me that my efforts could prevail over such a strong storm.

Still in a daze, the three of us got out of the car and started walking around in what was now a totally sunny Jerusalem. We spent the morning visiting many of the ancient sites I'd only beheld in my imagination. It was a beautiful moment for me to pray at the Wailing Wall and slip a written message into a niche in the wall following tradition. We then made our way back to the car, just a few hundred yards away, to start our return drive to Tel Aviv.

Just as we closed the car doors—whoosh! The rain again started coming down in buckets to drench the city with full force—but not before Jerusalem, and a moment of meditation, had given me the gift of a lifetime.

On my next trip to Israel, in 1995, I presented my master classes at the Jerusalem Music Center. The night I arrived, I walked to King Herod's tomb from the King David Hotel, where I was staying. At times I seem to be able to affect lights—they go on or off, or both. The lights above the tomb of Herod started doing just that, flickering on and off, as if they had been choreographed for a dance. It was quite a show. I just stood there and watched.

The public was invited to attend my first master class. I found the first four students had differing degrees of talent but were all basically able young musicians. Next came a young lady who played the slow movement of a Beethoven sonata. It was all I could do to control my temper. I thought, "How could they give me such a hopelessly untalented student?" What could I possibly tell her that would make any difference? I decided to ask her nationality. "I'm Russian," she answered. And I said, "You're playing like a German pedant." I was so angry at that moment I was oblivious to her feelings.

I rushed up onstage and spoke to her for about five minutes. "I don't know what to tell you—the feeling is all wrong. As a matter of fact, it has no feeling! I would never know you had a Slavic soul. You know, Beethoven was not a man in 'chains.' He knew just as much about freedom as the Romantic composers. Don't let the word 'classic' frighten you. *All* music has to come from, and be played with, the heart. Even Bach was a Romantic."

I expected her to get up from her piano seat and leave, but no. She looked at me pleadingly and asked, "Could I please play this again for you?" Her request surprised me. My first impulse was to say, "I'm sorry, we have no more time." But, after my tirade, I admired her courage, and I relented. Inside, I couldn't help thinking, "Oh, God, here we go again."

She sat down and began to play. I was stunned. How could this be? It was as if another person were playing. I had never heard this kind of total transformation before. And, apparently—judging from their response— neither had the audience. Shouting "Brava," I went over to her and kissed her on the cheek. "Do you realize how beautifully you played?"

She looked up at me. "I don't know," she said meekly. "I just played what I felt."

"The secret is, you *felt*," I responded. I then turned to the audience. "Wasn't that extraordinary?"

They shouted back, "Miracle, miracle!" It did have the feeling of a miracle. I've often wondered since what could have brought about that extreme change. Sometimes when a teacher happens to find the right words, the locked door opens and we are able to see and feel a new vision that had been obscured from us before. Socrates once took an illiterate slave boy step by step into a demonstration of the Pythagorean theorem. The boy already knew enough to construct the theorem but lacked the ability to see it as a whole. As Plato said, "A great teacher teaches something to a student that the student already knows, but that he doesn't know he knows."

I then went to Tel Aviv University, where I gave a lecture with music and a video presentation on the life of Chopin. Afterward, I was tired and felt that a good massage would be helpful. I called a masseuse at the Tel Aviv Hilton, where I was staying, and she said it wouldn't be possible—she was totally booked. So I decided to go down to the hotel restaurant to have lunch. Shortly, over the loudspeaker came an announcement: "Mr. Byron Janis, if you still want a massage, I've had a cancellation." I called her and agreed to be there in ten minutes. When I entered her studio, I was hit by a powerful déjà vu. I had been in this room before. I had seen this girl before. I knew what she would say before she said it: "Shall I put the radio on for some light music?" Those are the exact words she had spoken to me before. "Do you like ethnic music?" Again, the exact words as before. "Where do you live?" "New York," I answered. "Oh, I have a cousin there." It was startling. I remember having had this exact experience, down to the minutest detail, but it was in a dream over a year before. Being in that room made the dream come racing back to me. It seemed that a year ago I had lived this future event that I was now participating in! I couldn't help thinking of Einstein's theory that the past, present, and future are all here at the same time.

I returned to Jerusalem and decided to attend Christmas Eve mass at the Church of the Nativity. Security was massive and intense as the ongoing Intifada of that time posed a huge threat. Israeli soldiers were everywhere. We therefore were let off the bus some distance from the church. The night was totally black with a slight drizzle. It must have been a ten-minute walk, in the dark, and I was feeling my way by the quiet sound of the voices around me. Finally, I heard music growing louder and louder, and I saw a few lights illuminating something in the distance. I knew I was approaching the church where some say Jesus was born.

Inside, it was so crowded that at least three hundred people were standing. A beautiful service was being conducted by officiants from three different denominations—Armenian Orthodox, Catholic, and Greek Orthodox. After standing for three hours, I stumbled out of the church at 3 a.m. A car and driver raced me to the airport to catch an early flight to New York. Fortunately, on my trip home from the Holy Land, the usual tedious hours of travel just seemed to fly by. Israel had given me plenty to think about.

31

REINCARNATION

REINCARNATION IS ONE OF HUMANKIND's oldest beliefs. It is the belief that the soul, upon the death of the body, comes back to earth in another body or form. Even in this life, however, many of us have life-changing experiences that require a separation from the past and bring about a rebirth of sorts in order to start life anew. But what do *I* believe about reincarnation? I believe this life is a learning experience, and we cannot hope to get it all "right" in just one trip. Below are just a few of the many famous figures in world history who have strongly believed in its doctrine.

I am confident that there truly is such a thing as living again,
and that the living spring from the dead.
—Socrates (*Phaedo*, translated by Benjamin Jowett)

I look upon death to be as necessary to the constitution as
sleep. We shall rise refreshed in the morning.
—Benjamin Franklin

Many times man lives and dies between his two eternities.
—William Butler Yeats ("Under Ben Bulben")

Were an Asiatic to ask me for a definition of Europe, I should
be forced to answer him: It is that part of the world which is
haunted by the incredible delusion that man was created out of
nothing, and that his present birth is his first entrance into life.
—Arthur Schopenhauer

So as through a glass and darkly, the age long strife I see, where
I fought in many guises, many names, but always me.
—General George S. Patton (*Through a Glass Darkly*)

I once spoke to a Catholic priest about his thoughts on reincarnation. He said, "No, we don't believe in reincarnation, but we do believe
in ongoing energy." Isn't that a large part of what reincarnation is?
Aren't they two sides of the same coin?

You may be surprised to learn that more than sixty million
Americans believe in reincarnation despite the reticence of many
in the West to accept it. Eastern civilizations, which occupy about
two-thirds of the planet, see reincarnation as a natural part of life.
Deepak Chopra, author and lecturer on Ayurveda, spirituality, and
mind-body medicine, explains this conceptual divide beautifully in
Life After Death: The Burden of Proof:

Perhaps it is not a question of belief, East versus West.
Reincarnation may be a question of choice. Consciousness is
useful. We shape it according to our desires. Rather than being
the final word, the denial of reincarnation by Christianity could
be simply a collective choice. Having considered all the relevant

factors, a large sector of humanity says, "I don't want to come back to this place," while another says, "I do." All we can say for certain is that nature depends on the mechanism of rebirth.

Contrary to popular belief, early Judaism and Christianity included teachings on reincarnation. Orthodox Jews have always believed in its doctrine and still do to this day. The Kabbalists taught that if a person didn't need to be reborn for his own growth, he could, "out of compassion for the world, return as many times as needed to help it." According to Professor Gershom Scholem, one of the leading scholars in Jewish mysticism, "The righteous transmigrate endlessly for the benefit of the universe, not for their own benefit."

Today, observant Jews recite a daily prayer known as the Bedtime Shema, in which, in part, they forgive transgressions against them, "whether in this transmigration or another transmigration." A footnote in *The Complete ArtScroll Siddur*, considered to be an impeccable scholarly resource, explains this phrase to "refer to the doctrine of *gilgul neshamot*, transmigration of souls, and is one of the most mystical doctrines in Kabbalastic literature. In very simple terms, it refers to the reincarnation of certain souls for a second period of physical life on earth." Scholars still debate what is meant by the terms "certain souls" and "a second period" of physical life, as opposed to everyone, and many physical lives.

In the New Testament, Matthew taught that John the Baptist was Elijah in a previous life and reportedly said this many times. But skeptics take their antireincarnation beliefs from the following passage in Luke (1:17): "And he [John the Baptist] will go on before the Lord, in the spirit and power of Elijah." They claim from this that John is merely a prophet who was in the ministry of Elijah. Bear in mind that the disciples of Jesus expected the world to end very soon, so the issue of coming back was a moot point.

But in Matthew 11:11–15, Jesus says, "This is the one . . . there has not risen anyone greater than John the Baptist. . . . And if you are willing to accept it, he is the Elijah who was to come." The Hebrew Scriptures also say, "Behold I will send you Elijah the prophet, before the coming of the great and dreadful day of the Lord" (Malachi 4:5). It would seem from all of the statements by Jesus and the scriptures that there was little doubt that belief in reincarnation was a reality.

Origen, a prominent theologian, was an ardent defender of pre-existence and reincarnation. Around 250 AD, he wrote that the soul's very source was God and that the soul was traveling back to oneness with God via reincarnation.

Saint Gregory (257–333), in an early Christian text, stated that "it is absolutely necessary that the soul should be healed and purified and, if this does not take place during its life on earth, it must be accomplished in future lives." Early references to reincarnation in the New Testament, however, were deleted in the fourth century by Emperor Constantine when Christianity became the official religion of the Roman Empire. However, in the sixth century when the empire felt it was losing control of the people, Emperor Justinian took matters into his own hands. He wanted Origen's writings and teachings to be condemned and destroyed, but Pope Vigilius refused to sign a papal decree condemning Origen's teachings on reincarnation. As a result of his disobedience, the emperor had the pope arrested and put in jail. In 543 AD, Justinian convoked the Fifth General Council of the Church and told the pope that he must sign into doctrine whatever the council decided. On the way to the council, under guard, the pope escaped to avoid being forced to condemn Origen's writings. Ten years later, Empreror Justinian convened the Second Council of Constantinople, which ruled that reincarnation was a false belief punishable by persecution and death. The church and the Roman emperors were well aware that the concept of being reborn would weaken and undermine their power over their followers since it would give these people too many chances to achieve salvation. What better way than punishment by death to control the masses?

Dr. Ian Stephenson, a Canadian biochemist and professor of psychiatry, founded the Division of Perceptual Studies at the University of Virginia, which investigates the paranormal. While there was a mixed reaction to his findings on reincarnation, his work is considered by many to be of the highest scientific merit. The philosopher Paul Edwards observed that the modus operandi problem is due to an absence of evidence of a physical process by which a personality could survive death and travel to another body. But there are scientific commentators who found that Stephenson rigorously followed the scientific method in conducting his research. Another well-known philosopher, Robert Aldemar, endorsed Stephenson's research and concluded that the evidence he assembled argued strongly in favor of reincarnation to the point of it being irrational to disbelieve that some people reincarnate. Carl Sagan and Arthur Clark, though both intrigued, felt that the studies fell short of providing proof. Clark, however, admitted that Stephenson did produce a number of studies that were "hard to explain." Sagan also found that details of Stephenson's research could not have come by any other means than reincarnation.

One of Stephenson's most extensive studies was with children under the age of five whom he found were more capable of remembering past lives. Many of the children he studied were from India or the Middle East, most likely because belief in reincarnation is traditionally part of their culture. As soon as these children were able to talk, they told their parents about their "other family," giving details such as their previous name, the name of the village they lived in, songs and dances from their previous life, how they died, and the names of their parents and siblings. More than that, some of the children could actually speak and even answer questions in the language in which they formerly spoke (called xenoglossy). Some of these children also had strange birthmarks or physical deformities that seemed to stem from the way they had died in their previous life. In a notable case in which a child remembered being shot and killed, Stephenson was able to look at the autopsy photos of the actual previous person and compare the bullet entrance and exit wounds with the little round birthmarks on the child.

How can one explain a Mozart, who at the age of four or five could write a symphony? How do children of a similar age show totally unexplainable gifts for such things as mathematics, chess, and music? Those children are often—and I believe rightly so—referred to as "old souls."

I often wonder why the field of the paranormal requires so much more evidence than would be required by the scientific community of any other field of discovery. It would seem that the unknown wants to be kept unknown. Sadly, progress—life's biggest reward—becomes the victim.

The French expression "déjà vu" means "previously seen," and it is a feeling that could be related to the subject of reincarnation. I remember having that feeling when I first saw Paris. Walking down the Champs-Élysées, there was no question in my mind that I had been there before. But the feeling is such a powerful moment that there can be no doubt in your mind about its being true. When I made the fire come up the hill in the South of France, there was absolutely no doubt in my mind it would happen. No logic, no reason, nothing scientific could ever begin to explain that feeling. You just know.

32

THE UMBRELLA

SOME COUPLES ARE VERY SPECIAL in one's life, and Frank and
Pam Military were one of those. They came into our lives at a
most critical time, and our twenty-five-year friendship has weathered
the ups and downs of all our lives. As I related earlier, Frank was a vice
president at Warner/Chappell Music. He is a very soft-spoken man
not given to emotional exaggerations, nor does he have any particular religious affiliations. He's a very private person and he had never
before spoken of what I am about to tell you—not even to his wife,
which annoyed her no end.

As we became very close friends, Maria discovered that Pam also
had an interest in the paranormal. I was telling the story about the
Chopin mask at dinner one evening, and Frank got kind of an embarrassed shy smile on his face as he said, "You know, I just remembered

Maria and I are with Sammy Cahn (next to Maria) and Frank Military, vice president of Warner/Chappell Music, my music publishers. Sammy wrote the lyrics to my song The One Word, *one of the last lyrics he ever wrote. The four of us are at a function at the Plaza Hotel in New York City, honoring Frank.*

something that I have never told anyone before—this happened to me many years ago."

This was the story. One night, Buddy Hackett, the noted comedian, singer, and actor of the 1940s and 1950s; Alan Dale, the popular singer and TV personality of the late 1940s and early 1950s; and Frank were leaving Maksik's Town and Country, a club on Flatbush Avenue in Brooklyn, New York. A hot nightspot at the time, the club headlined such performers as Harry Belafonte, Judy Garland, and some of the biggest acts in show business, and that night, Alan Dale had been performing. Frank was managing Alan at the time, and he was also a very dear friend. Buddy and Frank had gone that night to see Alan's act.

When the show was over, the three friends got into Buddy's car and started to drive back to the center of Brooklyn, where they were living. It was a terrible night—thundering and pouring. On the way home, in the driving rain, they saw a solitary figure standing under the canopy of the el train. As the three friends got closer, they saw it was a girl in a trench coat and a hat holding a pretty but totally inadequately sized umbrella. They decided to stop and offer her a lift.

It was raining so hard, they could hardly see out the window. They pulled alongside the girl and opened the window just enough so that the rain wouldn't flood the front seat. "Would you like a lift?" She was very happy to be rescued.

Drenched, she got into the backseat next to Frank, and they asked her where she lived and told her they'd drop her off. She gave an address that was only about five minutes away. They didn't learn much about her, as the short drive left very little time for conversation. She thanked them and looked hurriedly in her purse for a key that she finally found and clasped tightly in her hand. She got out of the car and walked up a path to a small flight of stairs at the base of a brownstone. The men waited until she was safely inside the house. They saw her open the door with the key and go inside, and then they drove away. A couple of minutes later, they realized that she had left her umbrella in the car. They were still nearby, so they decided to drive back to return it.

Alan and Frank went up to the front door and rang the bell, and an older woman came out and said, "What do you want?"

"Could we speak to Diane?" (They had asked the girl what her name was, and she had mumbled, "Diane.") They thought the woman might be her mother. "She forgot her umbrella," Frank said.

"What are you talking about?" the woman responded.

"Well, we just dropped off a girl here; she said her name was Diane. We saw her come into this house, but she forgot her umbrella in our car and we wanted to return it to her."

She looked at them as though they were mad. She could hardly control her rage and shouted, "Yes, Diane is my daughter, and she has been dead for eighteen years. Now get out!"

Before she could slam the door, Alan managed to ask, "Is this your daughter's umbrella?" She looked at it carefully. It was hard to describe the look on her face. It really was her daughter's multicolored umbrella with the name "Diane" stenciled in an unusual pattern around the edge. The woman looked at Frank and Alan as if they were ghosts and quickly closed the door. They walked back to the car very shaken.

As Frank got into the backseat, he looked at where the girl had been sitting. It was soaking wet. They were completely undone. They tried to remember what she looked like—the funny kind of hat she was wearing stood out in their minds. Frank had been sitting next to her and Buddy was driving, but neither of them shook her hand or touched her. Frank got out of his side of the car, and she got out the other side.

Frank told us, "I'm thinking back. I know it was a long time ago, but there was nothing unusual about her that I can remember, or felt, when I was sitting next to her. And yet what happened was hard to believe. We all kept talking about it afterward. It's a shame I didn't write it down at the time. Buddy's dead and Alan's dead, so there's no one but me to talk about it." But as William Crookes, the famous British physicist and chemist, said, "I didn't say that it was possible. I just said that it happened."

Life is a matter of choices. I'm certain many who have had some strange happenings in their lives have never spoken about them. They thought that they would never be believed, or they were frightened and chose not to believe themselves. What a pity. They don't know what they have missed.

33

UNIDENTIFIED FLYING OBJECTS

I AM GOING TO ASK YOU to accompany me now into an area where some of you are going to be uncomfortable and some of you will be skeptical. All I ask is that you give me a fair hearing. I am going to talk now not just about unexplained phenomena but about unexplained beings.

When we look at photos of our own galaxy and see what a tiny pinpoint our planet is, how is it possible to think we could be the sole intelligence among fifty billion galaxies? The truth—and the incontrovertible evidence—is that we are not.

On an Air France flight from New York to Paris in August 1973, Maria and I were captivated by a rapturous sunrise as we flew over the

Some thirty years ago, a letter from the U.S. government stated that this photo definitely fell into the category of an unidentified flying object. Today, an opinion from optical physicist and leading ufologist Bruce Maccabee states, "There will be no conclusive answer to the puzzle of this photo." Not unusually, other experts disagree.

Atlantic approaching England. Maria took out her ever-present camera. But when the negative was developed, something more than a beautiful sunrise appeared in the shot. There was also a peculiarly shaped object, as you can see in the above photo. It appeared, to Maria and me, to be a three-dimensional transparent nose cone. Could the image have captured the object in some state of interdimensional transition?

Maria captured another curious snapshot outside a friend's house in Kent, England. She was photographing some old wooden fences silhouetted against a series of beautiful Van Gogh–yellow mustard fields and, as with the other image, nothing unusual was visible to the naked eye at the time. She'd taken three or more pictures within a few seconds of one another and, interestingly, the object of interest appeared in only one of them. In it you can see the classic disc shape of a suspected UFO.

Every U.S. president since Harry Truman has had to deal with UFOs in one way or another. But Truman was the first to have to deal with UFOs publicly. In September 1947, Truman passed the National Security Act, which made it easier to mask information the government and the CIA possessed about aliens' presence on earth. Memos NSC 10/1 and 10/2 relieved the CIA from the sole role of gathering foreign intelligence and established a buffer between the president and the activities that were going on. This allowed the president to deny knowledge of any covert activities, terrestrial or extraterrestrial.

On December 30, 1947, Project Sign, an official government investigation of the technical and performance capabilities of UFOs, was initiated at Wright Field in Dayton, Ohio. A year or so later, a formal report titled "Estimate of the Situation" was published, which detailed unexplained sightings by reliable witnesses and concluded that certain UFOs were possibly of extraterrestrial origin. In 1949, General Hoyt Vandenburg, U.S. Air Force chief of staff, rejected the findings of this report and went so far as to have it destroyed. Project Sign was redesignated as Project Grudge and later renamed Project Blue Book in the early 1950s.

Grant Cameron, a renowned ufologist who worked with Wilbur Smith, the head of the Canadian government's flying saucer investigations, came across the story of Leo Bourassa, a U.S. Air Force colonel who was head of the Special Facilities Division within the Office of Emergency Planning. Working at Johnson Library, Cameron learned that "[Bourassa] had been heavily involved in the 1965 blackout of New York City. Like the Kecksburg crash, the New York City power outage had a strong tie to UFOs." On December 9, 1965, a large fireball was seen by thousands in at least six states and Canada and reportedly dropped hot metal debris before crashing in rural Pennsylvania, near the small town of Kecksburg. Bourassa had, incidentally, been the intelligence officer who informed President Eisenhower that the CIA's U2 plane had been shot down over the USSR. While I was visiting the

Soviet Union in 1960, I got more than an earful about Gary Powers and his infamous high-flying spy plane. At the time of the Kecksburg crash, Eisenhower put Bourassa in command of Mount Weather, a secret underground facility that was unknown to the public until December 1, 1974, when a TWA jet crashed into the mountain. The president told Bourassa that it was his job to "save our government!"

Both Presidents Carter and Reagan claimed to have seen UFOs. President Carter tried to obtain further information on the subject but was unable to do so. Some say his efforts were thwarted by rogue military and intelligence entities. A government cover-up was said to be fully operational as well. Why? The most common explanation was that fear would set off mass panic in the country. U.S. Air Force intelligence operative Master Sergeant Dan Morris said, "The government was fearful of our knowledge that there are people on other planets. What the people in power don't want us to know is that this free energy [from energy generators developed with UFO technology] is available to everybody. When this knowledge is found out by the people, they will demand that our government release this technology, and it will change the world."

President Reagan gave three official speeches that touched on the UFO phenomenon. In September 1987, in a speech before the entire UN General Assembly, Reagan said, "Perhaps we need some outside, universal threat to make us recognize the common bond that unites all humanity. How quickly our differences worldwide would vanish if we were facing an alien threat from outside this world. And yet I ask you, is not an alien threat already among us?"

There has been much talk about the hostile nature of UFOs—that they want to attack and destroy us. If that is the case, they have certainly taken their time. Their existence has been documented for at least a couple of centuries. Fearmongering can have its own agenda, but whatever its purpose, for many it feeds the belief that UFOs are real. Soviet leader Mikhail Gorbachev apparently confirmed on May 4, 1990, in the magazine *Soviet Youth*, that "the phenomenon of UFOs does exist. It must be treated seriously." Could Reagan's and Gorbachev's mutual interest in UFOs have been a factor in the détente between our two countries? Were they, as Reagan suggested, teaming up for a greater conflict?

I found out more when I made my third trip to the Soviet Union in 1988 as the artistic head of the delegation of the Global Forum of Spiritual and Parliamentary Leaders for Human Survival. I was asked to perform at the residence of Metropolitan Pitirim, the head of the Russian Orthodox Church. The entire Politburo and the leaders of the religious community sat side by side for the concert. This had never happened before and was due to the efforts of the Global Forum initiative. I took the opportunity to speak to one of the Politburo members. I asked him bluntly, "Do you believe in the existence of UFOs?" He soberly answered, "*Da, konyechna*—Yes, of course. We have had experiences with analyzing the debris of some unknown crash sites." I found out later that the Russians had poured endless rubles into paranormal research on topics ranging from psychic phenomena to UFOs.

Apollo 14 astronaut Ed Mitchell, who holds a Ph.D. in aeronautics in addition to being the sixth man to walk on the moon, said, "Yes, there have been ET [extraterrestrial] visitations—there have been crashed craft, bodies recovered. The question is, how could it be kept secret—it hasn't been kept secret, it's been there all along, but it has been the subject of disinformation in order to deflect tension and create confusion so the truth doesn't come out."

The FBI was aware of "flying saucers" in the 1940s. In a now declassified document from July 10, 1947, FBI director J. Edgar Hoover said in a report concerning a recovered disc, "The army grabbed it and wouldn't let us have it for cursory examination." General Douglas MacArthur said during a speech at West Point on October 8, 1955, "The nations of the world will have to unite, for the next war will be an interplanetary war. The nations of the Earth must someday make a common front against attack by people from other planets."

In 1960, Vice Admiral R. H. Hillenkoetter (ret.), former director of the CIA, said, "It is high time for the truth to be brought out in open congressional hearings. Behind the scenes, high-ranking air force officers are soberly concerned about UFOs. But through official secrecy and ridicule, many citizens are led to believe that unknown flying objects are nonsense." He charged that "to hide the facts, the air force has silenced its personnel."

Larry Warren, an American soldier stationed with the Air Force Security Police at the military base of RAF Bentwaters, then being used by the U.S. Air Force, in England, says he was an eyewitness to one of the greatest military-UFO encounters on record. Known as the Rendleshan Forest Case, or the British Roswell incident, it involved a possible UFO landing in the United Kingdom in 1980.

Warren tells of an even more incredible account involving two far more famous individuals. Jackie Gleason, the comedian and early television star, had a lifelong fascination with the subject of UFOs and had a vast UFO book collection. President Nixon was also a great UFO enthusiast and had a large library of books on the subject, though he was highly selective about with whom he would discuss the phenomenon.

Warren relates how Gleason invited him to his home in Florida in 1986. The comedian told him how Nixon, in 1973, ditched his Secret Service escort (according to his Secret Service agent Marty Venker, Nixon had done this on more than one occasion) and took Gleason to Homestead Air Force Base to show him the bodies of aliens. The bodies were mangled as though they'd been pulled from an accident. Gleason assured Warren they were not human. Gleason said he was unable to eat or sleep for some three weeks. What bothered him most was why the government was hiding the truth from the American people. Gleason's wife, Beverly, also speaks of this event in an as-yet unpublished book.

Surely there are weather balloons, meteors, and who knows what else up there that put us off the track or at least provide convenient explanations whenever a UFO is reported. Someday, if we should be given all the facts, I doubt UFOs will continue to be the subject of speculation.

34

THE BELLS

I WOULD LIKE TO TELL YOU one last incredible story, or rather stories, that all seem to have come together in one glorious celebration.

The resonant sound of church bells calls its parish to mark an event, a holiday, a time of day. Whenever I hear church bells wherever I am in the world, I think of Palm Springs and the beautiful but inexplicable series of events that took place there. Our friends Jack and Linda Marlin, a fun and attractive couple, had offered Maria and me the use of their guesthouse and assured as we'd enjoy as much privacy and independence as we required.

My mother had never been to California, and I knew she would love it. Maria graciously accepted the idea, as did Linda and Jack. When I called my mother, who was then in her late eighties, she sounded as excited as an eighteen-year-old, and she and her companion landed at the Palm Springs airport the very next day. At dinner that evening the conversation was lively. Linda and Jack were singing my praises as an artist and as a human being. Mother replied with one of her classic remarks: "I had Byron for the world!" There was that remark again. The drama hadn't abated.

As we were chatting, we were suddenly interrupted by the sound of a piano coming from another room. Linda looked extremely puzzled—there was absolutely no one else in the house. No cat, no dog, no housekeeper—no one. Maria and I nudged each other under the table. Our hosts were visibly spooked but tried to pass it off with nervous laughter.

The following afternoon, Jack and Linda were again perplexed by some unusual events. Linda had gotten into her car to go grocery shopping, but when she put the key in the ignition it wouldn't start. She finally called Jack to come help. That was when they discovered their car keys had changed places. Jack looked at her key chain and said, "But that's my key." Then he looked at his own key chain, and to his shock, Linda's car keys were on it. It wasn't just that they'd picked up each other's keys—the keys had somehow switched places.

"This is impossible," sputtered Jack. "What the hell's going on? Who's playing games?"

"Don't look at me, Jack," I replied. "I wish I knew."

By early evening everyone was a bit stressed out and eager to relax in the Jacuzzi, but no such luck. It suddenly started turning on and off repeatedly and nobody could stop it. At this point, the Marlins were growing a bit grumpy.

"This has never happened before," Linda moaned, staring at Maria and me. "What is it with you two?"

We decided to beat a hasty retreat, crossing the lawn to change for the evening.

That night, we had a lovely, uneventful dinner. During coffee, I decided to go to the piano to work my fingers a bit in preparation for my upcoming concert. It was getting late—Maria was tired and had already gone to bed. It was about a quarter to two when I said good night to Jack and began the short walk to the guesthouse. Suddenly, I heard what sounded like church bells ringing, gradually increasing to a polyphony of sounds. It was the kind of extraordinary music that only bells can produce. It was uncanny. Unable to determine its source, I ran to the guesthouse to wake Maria.

She stumbled outside barefoot, and I said, "Don't say anything. Listen! Do you hear that?"

She whispered, "Bells—those are bells." A wave of relief came over me, but the puzzle was not yet solved.

"But, Maria, at ten to two in the morning?"

"Oh, my God," she said.

Because the bell sounds might diminish, I wanted to get another witness—our host. I ran to the kitchen and spotted Jack as he was locking up for the night.

"Jack, come out here quickly!" I called.

Just as Jack came out, the bells reached a dazzling crescendo. He looked totally bewildered. "My God! Bells!" he cried. The three of us just stood there in the night-dew-dappled grass not knowing what to think.

"There is a church about two miles from here," Jack offered. "But what would they be doing ringing bells as this time of night? You know, Byron, before you came out here, I was a very happy normal man, barbecuing in the garden, playing golf, doing normal things. And with all these happenings, it's just too much! You're messing up my life! What is this?"

"I don't know," I said. "I wish I could answer you." And I wished I could.

We said good night to a very distraught Jack once more. As we were walking back to the guesthouse, Maria murmured, "I can't believe there isn't a logical explanation for this. We'll find out in the morning."

The next morning we found out that nobody else in the house heard those bells—those very loud bells—except Maria, Jack, and me.

Linda was a bit miffed, "Why didn't you wake me? I missed all the fun."

"I didn't have time," Jack apologized. "Suddenly it was over. But we have to try to find out what happened. Let's drive to the church and speak to the priest."

The church housekeeper called the priest to the door to assist us.

"Father," we asked, "was there any particular celebration in the middle of the night? Any ringing of bells?"

"No, nothing at all," he said. "Why?"

"You didn't hear any bells in the middle of the night?" Jack gently inquired.

"No."

"Yours is the only church with bells anywhere nearby," Jack pressed. "Could someone have gotten up into the belfry, or whatever you call it, and started ringing them?"

"Not without waking me, they couldn't!" the priest said. "I surely would have awoken and heard them."

Undaunted, we went to all the neighboring houses on both sides of the church. We asked, "Did you hear anything last night?" The answer in each doorway was always no.

With every paranormal experience, I always triple-check every possibility. I diligently try to discount it, try to uncover anything else that could otherwise explain it. As has happened so many times before, in the matter of the mysterious nighttime bells, I found nothing.

In some cases, people can hear something that others can't. That doesn't mean nothing's happening. It is a paradox that invites even more scrutiny and controversy. This was an event that *defied all explanation*.

At dinner the next night Maria said, "I think you'd like to hear something I've just learned. I decided to call Mother Dolores, my old friend at the Abbey of Regina Laudis, the Benedictine monastery in Bethlehem, Connecticut. I told her this amazing thing that happened to us last night. She said to me, 'Maria, what time did this take place?' I said, 'Well, it was terribly late—ten to two in the morning.' I heard a strong but gentle laughter on the other end of the line. I said, 'Why are you laughing?' She said, 'Maria, didn't you know that the most sacred time of prayer in all religious orders throughout the world is ten to two in the morning?'"

After dinner we walked out onto the lawn. We all fell quiet as we gazed up at the sky and reflected on the joy of the sounds we had just heard. The unique blending of music and the paranormal—music of the bells and the haunting mystery of the paranormal—was a celebration that would never be forgotten.

EPILOGUE

As you have seen, music has opened the door for me to experience realities that I had always felt existed. But as in the story of the bells, what is heard in one reality is not heard in another. It is not unlike those who still believe we have never walked on the moon arguing with an astronaut who has! "Only that day dawns to which we are awake," said the great American poet Henry David Thoreau.

But with the injury to my little finger and my arthritis, I began to ask myself, "What would I do should I no longer be able to perform? Would those different realities still be there for me?" The answer was a resounding *yes*.

Music is my life's oxygen, and I would always be able to find ways of being creative to fulfill what is the *essence* of my nature. I would still be able to step both spiritually and physically into other dimensions. Through all of the circumstances and experiences in my seventy years as a performer, you have seen that I have been able to experience both. I lived them, I explored them, was awed by them, humbled and exhilarated by them. Music for me has always been and always will be a step into that "more." Artists can destabilize the world and shake up the status quo—that comfortable hiding place for those who fear the change that progress brings. I myself am more frightened of the *known*. As with the universe we are, and will always be, a work-in-progress.

Of the many stories I have told you—musical, medical, glamorous, and fantastic—the subject of the paranormal is probably the most foreign to many, although a recent poll has shown that 73 percent of Americans have had at least one paranormal experience in some form or another.

Throughout the years, I have seen how the mind can affect matter and how the potential for experiencing the paranormal resides in everyone. All that is needed is an open mind and a willingness to believe.

I have seen that almost nothing is impossible, but for the dissenters perhaps this quote from Sir William Crookes, the noted chemist and physicist, is food for thought: "I didn't say that it was possible. I just said that it happened." For the scientists who insist that one can get validation only through repetition, I offer you Sir William James's observation: "Only one white crow is necessary to disprove the notion that all crows are black."

With a mind to the future, I am putting the finishing touches on a documentary, *The Byron Janis Story*, produced by the multi Emmy Award–winning Peter Rosen and airing on PBS in the autumn of 2010. I am continuing composing, teaching, and lecturing and am thinking about releasing several recordings of live performances, as well as making a new one, arthritis permitting. Steinway & Sons has been talking with me about the possibility of making a new piano with a keyboard that has narrower keys to help compensate for the limited extension in my hands. Clearly, I have not run out of options yet.

Whether it is a piece of music I have played, a lesson I have given, or a story I have told of something that is hard to believe, there's a quote that comes to mind by the renowned Bengali poet and musician Rabindranath Tagore, which says, "I know what I have given you, but I don't know what you have received."

As to the paranormal, if you are a nonbeliever, I hope I may have at least persuaded you to say, "Maybe."

Acknowledgments

Our deep gratitude goes to our extraordinary personal assistant and friend, Nicole Engelman. Her insightful suggestions, patience, and tireless dedication were of major importance in bringing this book to completion.

To my literary agent, Douglas Grad, in great appreciation for his expert guidance, enthusiastic support, and belief in this project.

To my esteemed editor, Hana Lane, who "understood" as well as believed. My unending thanks for her help and for making this book possible.

My deepest thanks to David Douglas Duncan, whose extraordinary photographs so captured the spirit of this book. You are a master artist and a treasured friend.

To my friend Glenn Young, who read my manuscript and whose creative comments meant so much.

My warm thanks to Barbara Baker Burrows of *Life* magazine for her help and support.

With appreciation and thanks to the superb team at John Wiley & Sons, Inc: editorial assistant Ellen Wright, production editors Kimberly Monroe-Hill and Lisa Burstiner, copy editor Karen Tongish, and proofreader Sibylle Kazeroid.

To anyone I have omitted thanking, my deep apologies.

Recommended Reading

The Age of Entanglement: When Quantum Physics Was Reborn, by Louisa Gilder

The Conscious Universe: The Scientific Truth of Psychic Phenomena, by Dean Radin

Dogs That Know When Their Owners Are Coming Home: And Other Unexplained Powers of Animals, by Rupert Sheldrake

Einstein's Space and Van Gogh's Sky: Physical Reality and Beyond, by Lawrence LeShan and Henry Margenau

Extraordinary Knowing: Science, Skepticism, and the Inexplicable Powers of the Human Mind, by Elizabeth Lloyd Mayer

The Holographic Universe, by Michael Talbot

Margins of Reality: The Role of Consciousness in the Physical World, by Robert G. Jahn and Brenda J. Dunne

The Medium, the Mystic, and the Physicist: Toward a General Theory of the Paranormal, by Lawrence LeShan

Mind-Reach: Scientists Look at Psychic Abilities, by Russell Targ and Harold E. Puthoff

Musicophilia: Tales of Music and the Brain, Revised and Expanded Edition, by Oliver Sacks

A New Science of the Paranormal: The Promise of Psychical Research, by Lawrence LeShan

For further exploration, you can visit the American Society for Psychical Research at www.aspr.com and the Institute of Noetic Sciences at www.noetic.org. For arthritis information, you can visit the Arthritis Foundation's Web site at www.arthritis.org and their magazine, *Arthritis Today*, at www.arthritistoday.org.

Index

Page numbers in *italics* refer to illustrations.